WRITING AS PROCESS: INVENTION AND CONVENTION

WRITING AS PROCESS: INVENTION AND CONVENTION

Helen Rothschild Ewald

Iowa State University

Charles E. Merrill Publishing Company
A Bell & Howell Company
Columbus   Toronto   London   Sydney

Published by
Charles E. Merrill Publishing Co.
A Bell & Howell Company
Columbus, Ohio 43216

This book was set in Goudy Old Style Roman and Perpetua.
Production Editor: Lucinda Ann Peck.
Cover Design: Tony Faiola.
Cover Art: M. C. Escher.
Text Designer: Lucinda Ann Peck.

Library of Congress Catalog Card Number: 82–061105
International Standard Book Number: 0–675–20014–8
Printed in the United States of America
1 2 3 4 5 6 7 8 9 10—87 86 85 84 83

CONTENTS

PREFACE

As part of your college composition course, *Writing as Process* assumes that writing is a process, that invention or discovery occurs throughout this process, and that the writer's readers implicitly participate in the writer's composing. This text sees the writer as analyzer, problem-solver, and critic engaged in bringing ideas and audience together.

Part I of this text explores what both the writer and the reader bring to and take from the composing situation, as well as what the composing process itself entails. It forges a link between reader expectations and writer principles. Part II examines how generating and clarifying topics, locating supporting information, forming arrangements, and making stylistic choices all involve invention and discovery. Part III shows various ways of arranging ideas and evidence while Part IV focuses on revision strategies.

This text offers several distinctive features. Within each chapter are Process Sheets that suggest what the writer can look for while composing. These sheets should serve as rough guides only, and not as signposts showing THE WAY to write. There is no one way to write. Writing strategies are as various as writers themselves and the audiences they address.

Excellent yet accessible student writing examples are also a feature of this text. These examples represent a blend of personal, academic, and business writings on a variety of subjects. In keeping with a process-oriented approach, the examples variously appear as prep work, rough drafts, or finished products.

This text also presents a new and logical way of classifying arrangements into patterns that isolate, that cluster, and that sequence ideas and evidence. And it shows specialized and mixed patterns. Because this classification is more logical than the traditional narrative, descriptive, expository, and argumentative modes, it is more workable for both students and instructors.

For their writings, I am indebted to my student contributors and to my former Indiana University colleague, Michael Harris, whose narrative appears within these pages. I must also thank Michael Flanigan of The

University of Oklahoma, who introduced me to the process-centered approach; Elaine Gardiner of Washburn University, who class-tested the initial manuscript; and Susan Galenbeck, Neil Nakadate, Lee Poague, Nancy Roundy, and Dave Tedlock of Iowa State University who offered encouragement and support. Not to be forgotten is Sally Dyke who typed the initial manuscript. I am sincerely grateful to the reviewers, Robert L. Brown, University of Minnesota; Eddye Gallagher, Tarrant County Community College; Tori Haring-Smith, Brown University; and Susan Helgeson, Ohio State University, who provided such helpful input and to the editors at Merrill, Beverly Kolz, Vicki Knight, and Cindy Peck. Finally, thanks to my husband Bob, my best critic and friend.

Helen Rothschild Ewald

PART I

WRITING AS PROCESS

1

PROCESS AND PRODUCT

Before this fall, I don't really remember thinking about my audience as I wrote my papers. I was more concerned with getting the paper done, and I saw the writing of the paper as a way for just me to learn, not the reader. But this fall I found myself constantly thinking about how my audience would react to a certain word or phrase. Earlier, this would have been one of the last things I worried about.

Another aspect of writing that I had never really considered before was a purpose for writing. Before there was only one purpose—passing the course. But this fall I began to pick out topics that really interested me (like legal aid services), and I actually found myself trying to educate not only myself but also my audience on the subject of each paper.

Kirk Leeds

This self-evaluation suggests that writing, when meaningful, encourages growth not only in the writer but also in the reader.

This chapter introduces you to such writing by focusing on what the writer brings to the composing situation, what the composing process itself entails, and what both the writer and reader gain from composition.

WHAT THE WRITER BRINGS

To understand what a writer brings to the composing situation we must first consider what a writer is. What is a writer's role? What does the writer offer to his readers? The following student writers have different opinions:

1. A writer is a professional who uses language and established forms well to express his or her point of view. The purpose or role of a

writer is to help us see beyond our own limited scope. He or she can do this either by giving us a new perspective on a familiar subject or by establishing a new subject we had never considered before.

2. A writer is a person who can manipulate words. His role includes persuading and entertaining. Another thing he does is to open our minds to new subjects.

Both of these students think the writer knows a lot more than the audience, and both seem to identify themselves with this less-informed group of readers. Other students see the writer in less distant terms, as a "relay" between the subject and the reader:

1. A writer is the link between his thoughts or imagination and his audience. He takes a subject, idea, or viewpoint, and molds it to interest his readers. The writer's role is to put his thoughts and images into universal symbolism that all readers can understand.

2. A writer transmits her thoughts and ideas to the reader. This is what a writer is, a transmitter. The writer's role is to give the reader something of value through her writing. This may be entertainment, a new way of thinking, or new information like a scientific breakthrough.

In both of the preceding definitions, the students assume that the writer comes to the composing situation with something to say. For them, a writer is someone "in the know" who conveys that knowledge to others.

✒ EXERCISE 1.1

Jot down your own answers to the questions: What is a writer? What is a writer's role? Do you agree that a writer is someone "in the know"? Do you consider yourself a writer?◢

Many people believe that writers are *born* with a natural talent for their craft. They believe that writers automatically have something to say. Does this mean then that a person cannot *become* a writer?

Although some writers do start out with something interesting and important to say, others—many others—discover ideas and topics *while* writing. If writers do not always bring "something to say" to the composing situation, then what do they bring?

Writers bring basically three things: (1) a way of viewing the world, (2) a general knowledge of how discourse (communicating through language) works, and (3) an approach to composing. Let's examine these in more detail.

Your World View

Your world view is the set of assumptions that you accept as true. For example, your world view may consist, in part, of the following beliefs:

1. People are fundamentally good by nature.
2. The way for the U.S. to prevent war is to be strong militarily.
3. Marijuana should be legalized.
4. My parents don't understand me.
5. If you try hard enough at something, you will eventually succeed.

Your own set of assumptions can contain both general and specific ideas or premises just as these do.

▼EXERCISE 1.2

List a dozen or so assumptions that help define your world view. How many of these assumptions have you acquired recently? How many have you held for a long time?◢

When you compose, your set of assumptions helps you answer questions such as "Why does this topic seem relevant to me?" and "How well does my main idea reflect my social and/or ethical beliefs?" It also helps answer: "What is the audience in relationship to me? Is it hostile? Objective? Educated?" "Who is the audience in relationship to me? Is it a teacher? A peer? A mixed group of friends and strangers?" "How well does my audience know my subject? Does my audience share my world view?" In short, your set of assumptions not only provides you with initial ideas but also helps you define your relationship to the subject and audience, as well as their relationship to you.

Your Knowledge of Discourse

Another element that you as a writer bring to the composing process is a knowledge of *discourse*, or the orderly expression of thought. When someone is telling you a story or anecdote, you have certain expectations: the story's beginning will somehow set up the main point and establish the characters and the setting: the middle will contain a happening (a complicating action) and clues or statements explaining the importance of the happening; the end will finish the action and round things off. These expectations represent conventions of ordinary discourse and are highlighted in the sample below:

Main point and character set up:	You'll never believe who I saw today! The Shopping Bag Lady!
Action:	When I was a little kid, there was this old, white-haired lady who lugged two shopping bags—one on each arm—house to house. These were full of hand-made stuffed animals which she sold. She was literally bent out of shape. Us kids all thought she was ancient . . . and we were just a little afraid of her.
Evaluative statements about action:	I guess she sold her stuff to make a living. She sure was independent. She'd be making her rounds in the coldest weather and wouldn't take anything off of nobody.
Conclusion:	Well, today I saw her in the Steak Shop, bags and all. Twenty years later! As old as ever.
Rounding off:	I guess she was doing all right. She was ordering herself a meal when I left.

☛ EXERCISE 1.3

Listen to the stories people tell as part of everyday conversation. Record one, either by taking notes or using a tape recorder, and then write it up as a one to two page narrative. Note how this narrative fulfills the expectations of ordinary discourse suggested above by labeling its elements. ◢

Your knowledge of discourse goes beyond an understanding of how "natural narratives" work, however. For example, you know that *how* a person says something affects *what* is being said. If Jay says, "That's a nice hat," he can do so genuinely or sarcastically, happily or sadly. In other words, any grammatical statement can have a number of "rhetorical" meanings. Furthermore, you know that context can often influence meaning. If Jay says in his most sarcastic manner to Mary, "That's a *nice* hat," and she doesn't get upset, you know there's something in the situation that prevents her negative reaction. It may be that she doesn't want it to be a nice hat, because it's part of her Halloween witch costume. In short, each statement has a grammatical, rhetorical, and contextual (or social) meaning.

In composing, you can apply your general knowledge of discourse in answering such questions as "*How* should I present my message?" and "*How* will my particular context color the grammatical and rhetorical meaning of what I'm saying?"

In short, your knowledge of discourse provides, in any form of written communication, the following principles:

1. The speaker/writer shares certain *conventions* of how discourse works with the listener/reader.
2. These conventions serve as general *principles* for the speaker/writer to follow.
3. These conventions also create *expectations* on the part of the listener/reader.
4. The principles can be applied and the expectations met in a variety of ways.
5. This variety is, in part, represented by the fact that any one statement may have a grammatical, rhetorical, and contextual meaning.
6. These levels of meaning may complement or contradict each other.

With these points in mind, let's turn more specifically to your background in written communication.

Your Approach to Composing

Each writer has a composing style that may operate quite independently from the composing process itself. The following comments outline several student composing styles:

1. I write slowly, stopping often to reread and revise as I go. The speed of my writing depends on how much I know about the subject to begin with, but I am never what you would call fast.
2. After choosing a topic, I sit down and write one draft straight through as fast as possible. Sometimes I can't even read my own writing, but that doesn't matter, because I usually end up throwing most of this first stuff away anyway. It just helps to get something down.

3. My main strategy in writing is procrastination. By this I mean I delay as long as possible before I start to write. That doesn't mean I'm not thinking about the assignment. I spend about 75 percent of my time thinking, 20 percent writing, and 5 percent rewriting. I work best under pressure.

4. The first thing I do is make a rough plan of what I want to say. Sometimes this is in outline form, sometimes not. Then I let this sit, do a little reading, play a little basketball, etc. After a few days, I look over the plan and start filling in pieces. I again let it sit. I might go through this hurry-up-and-wait routine a dozen or so times before my draft gels. I don't write too many drafts after my first one, maybe because I spend so much time getting the first one down.

An important aspect of each of these styles is time management. Time itself is crucial to composing because it allows for the incubation of ideas. "I need a lot of 'down' time when writing," said one student, "to allow my thoughts to work from my fingers up to my head, then go through my head, and then trickle back down again."

▸ EXERCISE 1.4

Describe your individual writing style. Do you have one basic style, or does your style change to fit the composing situation?◂

WHAT THE COMPOSING PROCESS INVOLVES

What is the nature of the composing process itself? The following monologue, which recreates a student's reaction to a particular writing assignment, suggests some answers. The student's assignment was to research an aspect of life in the town hosting the university. The student chose "running a small business" as the aspect to research.

Clarifying a topic	"Running a small business." I guess that's general enough. Too general, in fact. How small do I want to get? And what businesses?
Establishing a focus	Maybe I should start really small, like a one person operation.
Generating a topic	Let's see. Do I know of any? I suppose my friend Jeff runs a one person operation of sorts—brewing

beer. But's that's not really a business. . . . His land-lady would qualify though, renting rooms.

Discovering
information

How could I research her business? I could check city records, but I doubt if that would turn up much. I could talk to Jeff about her operation. Better, I could interview her myself.

Discovering
information

What do I already know about her? Only that she's about ninety, runs a rooming house on Walnut Street, and is a real talker. She'll probably be good to interview.

Considering
arrangement

When it came time, I could write up that part of my paper as question-answer or as a story recreating how she acted and what she said.

Establishing
focus

I'm going to have to remember that I'm inter-viewing her *as a small business owner*, though. I'd better write that down so I don't get carried away.

Clarifying a topic:
non-question

. . . So, let's see. One question I won't ask her is "How did you live so long?"

Considering
audience

That's such a trite question, I'll bet she's been asked it more than once. It might also sidetrack us from my topic.

Discovering
information

What questions should I ask then . . . about running a small business, that is?

Considering
audience

. . . Well, on second thought, I guess I could also ask a few personal questions just to establish rapport. And I'd better write myself a note to introduce myself as a friend of Jeff's.

At this point, what does the monologue establish about the writing process?

1. There do seem to be certain identifiable steps associated with writing. These steps include generating and clarifying topics, es-tablishing focus, discovering information, considering audience, and considering arrangement.
2. Even though there are certain identifiable steps, these steps are recurring; that is, they can be repeated in the same or different order. "Focusing," for example, can occur more than once and at

any point in the writing process. In other words, the writer can *revise* the focus at will. *Revision* is the writer's response to the overlapping nature of the writing process.

3. Although the steps in the writing process can be repeated in varying order, there does seem to be some kind of overall "pecking order." Topic generation and clarification, for instance, take place before consideration of focus and arrangement. Questions concerning style, such as "What voice shall I adopt?", are not represented in the monologue. These questions become important later in the writing process.

4. The writing process features both reconsideration and anticipation *throughout*. Reconsideration, or revision, occurs even at early stages. For example, the monologist both anticipates what the arrangement is going to be like and reconsiders what the focus is going to be: "small businesses" becomes "one person businesses."

5. Because writers can shuttle freely backwards and forwards while composing, they can forget or lose ideas and information. The monologist does well to start taking notes. Keeping a file or notebook for ideas and information is a good idea.

The Emerging Fair Copy

While the preceding monologue recreates the composing process as it exists before a draft is even attempted, the following dialogues demonstrate this same process as it occurs during draft construction.

These dialogues are between the writer and a fellow writer or peer, and between the writer and an instructor. An experienced writer may often conduct such a dialogue with him/herself.

WRITER: This is what I've got so far. I should be able to get good details, since I've got two guys sort of in mind. Is my organization ok?

Controlling Generalization: There are basically two types of guys that live on my dorm floor: ones that are easy to get along with and ones that *aren't*.

I.   The types of men that can be tolerated
    A.   Boyish charm
    B.   Polite—know when to stop teasing
    C.   Brother-like
    D.   Proud to have them as a friend

II.   The types of men that can't be tolerated
    A.   In their eyes, God's gift to women

        B.   Can be polite—but with ulterior motives
        C.   Overbearing at times

PEER: Can you think of better category labels? "Aren't" isn't very de-
        scriptive.

Responding directly to the comment, the student renames her categories and then exchanges her work with another student writer:

WRITER: What do you think of my categories? My organization?

> Controlling Generalization: There are basically two types of guys that
> live on my dorm floor: the pussycat and the Don Juan.

   I.   Pussycat
        A.   Boyish charm
        B.   Sweet, but not sickeningly
        C.   Easy to get along with
        D.   Polite
        E.   Brotherlike

  II.   Don Juan
        A.   Thinks he's God's gift to women
        B.   Flirtatious
        C.   Comes on strong
        D.   Flashy smile

PEER: You might organize this by A. looks, B. personality, and C. effect
        on you, in order. You could use examples of men you've met or
        heard about. You should consider having three categories: guys
        you would like to live with, guys that are nice to have around,
        and those that can hit the highway.

Initially ignoring the three-category suggestion, the writer completes
the following draft:

> "Men: you can't live with them, you can't live without them."
> How many times has this been said by some frustrated college coed?
> My experience of living on a coed dorm floor has introduced me to
> many different kinds of guys, from the naive all-American boy to the
> drugger to the Don Juan who thinks he's God's gift to women. I would
> like to concentrate on two diverse characters though, the "good guys"
> versus the "bad guys."
>
>   It's almost eight o'clock, the time he said he would pick her up.
> "Will he be on time?" she thought, putting the finishing touches on
> her makeup. A squirt of perfume, a last look in the mirror, and she
> bops down the stairs, humming her favorite tune. The door bell and
> clock sound simultaneously. Letting out a sigh she slowly walks to the
> door. "Wow, this guy is really punctual!"
>
>   Standing outside was a slender fellow, his wavy hair combed and
> a slight hint of musk aftershave surrounded him. . . .

The next morning she lay in bed and reflected on the night before. She kept comparing it to the time she had with the last guy she had gone out with, a night she remembers but would like to forget.

That night had bad vibrations from the very beginning. She was ready on time, put an album on the stereo, picked up a magazine, and sat to wait for her date. The cuckoo sang out eight times. "Any minute," she thought. Becoming engrossed in an article, she didn't realize the time until the cuckoo notified her of the half hour. A little worried and a little upset, she got up and looked out the window. Nervously she went into the kitchen and fixed herself a drink.

Finally, at 9:05 he arrived, a half-burnt cigarette hanging from his lips and a nonchalant look on his face. His dark hair was mussed and his jacket rumpled and stained. . . .

Although these two characters are unique, this example shows the two sides of the coin of human nature. Fortunately I have encountered mostly the "good guys," but sometimes I still think, "Men: you can't live with them and you can't live without them."

She again submits her work for peer comment:

WRITER: I think I've got good details here. Do you think they're realistic?

PEER: Yes and no. The first example was, but the second one didn't seem so because I could predict what was going to happen from reading the first.

The writer responds at this point by picking up on the earlier three-category suggestion.

WRITER: I will change the format and write the paper as a narrative of someone walking down the dorm hall and describing the different people in various rooms. My main emphasis will be on what I *first* mentioned in the introduction: the naive all-American boy, the drugger, and the Don Juan. These categories just sound more interesting and less predictable.

She drafts:

"Men: you can't live with them and you can't live without them." How many times has this been said by some frustrated college female? My experience of living on a coed dorm floor has introduced me to many diverse characters, namely the drugger, the naive all-American boy, and the Don Juan who thinks he's God's gift to women. Interestingly enough, they also have more in common than being roommates and male. They have some qualities underneath the surface that make them more alike than people would notice.

Room 3434, two doors down from the john, is known as the woodroom because the walls outside the door are paneled. Freshmen are usually assigned there. This year the woodroom is called home by

Steve, a farm boy from Norway, Ia.; Carl, a suburbanite from Chicago; and Tom, who makes his home in Cedar Rapids.

Steve, the most stereotypical of the three, is always seen in the den at 5:30 watching the evening news. His Squealer Feeds hat and bottle of Pepsi. . . .

Tom stands 6'2"; he is a true blond, complete with clear blue eyes, rosy cheeks, freckles, and a fetching dimple: a walking and talking Ken doll. . . .

The best way to describe Carl is laid back. . . .

At the end of the semester, the three men in 3434 had all mellowed out. Steve does drugs, Tom remains naive, and Carl craves sex, but they had gotten used to each other and their habits had become more compatible.

Before submitting the draft as a product, the student writer comments:

WRITER: If I had had more time, I would have changed both the intro and the conclusion. The intro doesn't seem to fit my new emphasis and the conclusion doesn't seem to conclude all that much.

In the next dialogue an instructor responds orally to a written rough draft (text). The student participates by redrafting the text and by commenting on her own efforts.

Scarlett gently pinched her high-set cheeks to add a pink color to her soft, fair skin. Her green eyes sparkle as she admires her reflection in the mirror. Scarlett's dark, black hair is pulled away from her triangular-shaped face. Her eyes, although they sparkle from underneath the long, curved lashes, definitely have a penetrating look of purpose and adventure.

INSTRUCTOR: At this point I see Scarlett as attractive. I expect you to show in more detail other aspects of her character now.

Scarlett, who was away from her home for a long period of time, returned home to find her mother dead, her father insane, and no food or money in the house. With all these odds set against her, she stood defiantly and swore this would not conquer her.

INSTRUCTOR: Okay, I'm getting the impression that Scarlett is defiant. I guess I expect to discover another characteristic next.

Eventually Scarlett ran a lumber business. She married her sister's man to have money to pay taxes on her plantation. Scarlett loved a man, a man she could not have, because he married someone else. But when his wife died Scarlett realized that she did not love him. She loved the challenge, which was to make him marry her. When the challenge was erased, she realized her true feelings, but this was too late.

INSTRUCTOR: I'm a bit fuzzy on the trait or traits you're developing
               here. I'm also fuzzy on what happened. Did she love
               this second man while being married to her sister's
               man? What made it *too late*?

    Scarlett delved into her first marriage out of irate jealousy. She
married her second husband for financial gain.

INSTRUCTOR: Now I *am* confused. Was the marriage to her sister's
               man her second marriage? Help me out.

    Scarlett had many facets to her that make a complex woman.

INSTRUCTOR'S SUMMARY: The bulk of your narrative simply retells
what happened to Scarlett. How she reacts to things that happen certainly
could reveal "Who she is" as a character. Can you focus on her reactions
to the events rather than on the events themselves?

    Scarlett realized her beauty when she looked admiringly at her
reflection in the mirror. She gently pinched her high-set cheeks to
add a delicate pink color to her soft, fair skin. Her green eyes seemed
to dance as she made sure all her midnight black hair was pulled neatly
away from her face. Scarlett was very beautiful indeed, and under that
beauty lay a woman with a strong personality.
    Scarlett's personality was revealed all through the movie "Gone
With the Wind." . . .

STUDENT: As I continue revising this paper, I realize that the different
            personality traits of Scarlett are all derived from one main
            trait, determination. So now I will go back to the beginning
            and revise to include this idea.
                My focus will shift from Scarlett's personality in gen-
            eral to her specific trait of determination.
                Actually, because determination is a trait everyone
            should have, my audience could now also include those
            who have seen the movie or read the book.

    Scarlett's green eyes danced as she tied her midnight hair away
from her face. She gently pinched her high-set cheeks to add a
delicate pink color to her soft, fair skin. Underneath that softness
though was a hard streak of determination. This determination could
be seen in how she reacted to several events talked about in "Gone
With the Wind." . . .

    The drafting continues with the new focus on Scarlett's
determination.
    In the first dialogue, the writer gradually sharpens ideas present from
the outset of her composing. In the second dialogue, the writer actually
discovers her main point while writing.

Whether the writer is primarily developing ideas or discovering them, her in-draft composing features many of the same concerns found earlier in the process:

1. Considering arrangement
   a. Writer one starts with an outline, renames categories, adds a category, but sticks with her classification structure.
   b. Writer two starts out by telling what happened to Scarlett (narrative) and ends by showing how various events prove Scarlett to be "determined" (exemplification).
2. Establishing focus
   a. Writer one switches her focus from men who are easy to get along with and ones who aren't *to* the pussycat and the Don Juan *to* the good guys and the bad guys *to* the naive All-American boy, the Don Juan, and the drugger.
   b. Writer two switches her focus from what happened to Scarlett to what Scarlett's reactions to the events proved.
3. Clarifying a topic
   a. Writer one makes a subtle shift from answering "What are the two basic types of men on my floor whom I can date?" to "What are the similarities that underlie the differences in the types of men on my dorm floor?"
   b. Writer two changes from answering "Who is Scarlett?" to considering "What one trait defines Scarlett's personality?"
4. Discovering information
   a. Writer one begins with two specific dates in mind but ends by taking a stroll down her corridor to observe the men there and to gather information.
   b. Writer two begins with her memory of the recently seen movie and, basically sticking with the same information, comes to emphasize Scarlett's reactions rather than the story's events.
5. Considering audience
   a. Writer one eventually turns to three categories because they're "more interesting and less predictable" for the reader.
   b. Writer two recognizes that her new emphasis on Scarlett's determination allows her to expand her audience from those who have seen neither the movie nor the book to those who may have seen either.

As in the pre-draft stage, the in-draft composing process features a lot of rethinking and rewriting.

▶**EXERCISE 1.5**

Review the three successive versions of the following student's introduction. What main writing process concerns did the writer consider as he
worked through these versions?

1. Mankind now has the capability of annihilating the human
    population. Complete destruction of the human race is a
    frightening thought, and the thought leaves an empty feeling
    inside oneself. The present situation of the world is pointing
    towards the end of mankind.

    Humanity wiped out of existence is a strange and interesting
    concept. The fear of death is a deep pit, and most people tend
    to cover up or forget the fact that one must eventually die,
    because it is an unknown and unpopular subject. By no means
    is the subject always intentionally avoided, but one must come
    face to face with the reality that there is such a buildup of tension
    in the world today, that nuclear holocaust is very possible. It
    appears to the writer that the prophesied end of the world is at
    hand.

2. The present conditions of the world today are pointing towards
    the end of mankind. With the buildup of nuclear weapons, man
    now has the capability of annihilating himself from the face of
    the earth. There are many ways one can see that man is headed
    for a dead end, beginning with prophesy.

3. Conditions in the world today point towards the end of man-
    kind. With the buildup of nuclear weapons, man now has the
    capability of annihilating himself. Past prophesy and present
    conditions all predict man's dead end. ◢

Post-product Revision

The final fair copy or draft represents a solution or answer to the questions
raised during the composing process. However, the draft often contains
certain problems or unanswered questions that still must be processed.

Researchers in problem solving have discovered that a good way to
analyze the solution to a problem is to analyze the process that led to that
solution. Similarly, a good way to evaluate a draft is to examine the process
that produced that draft.

Future chapters in this text will show methods of evaluating the
process behind the product. For our purposes here, it is enough to examine
two means of post-product evaluation: (1) abstracting each paragraph to
check for the main idea and (2) breaking down each paragraph to check
for supporting detail.

Abstracting paragraphs

The student who wrote the following paper felt that he may have "gotten off track" while writing his draft so he made paragraph summaries as a means of abstracting. The student's purpose in writing the paper in the first place was to answer the question: "What are the types of pollution I see everyday?"

Such problems as air pollution, water pollution, chemical uses in agriculture production, and soil erosion make the world a less desirable place. These problems may be caused by the general public that throws litter out car windows polluting our streets and highways. The farmers of the world could be blamed for the erosion of the topsoil. This reduces the amount of crops grown, thus reducing the food supply of those who desperately need it. Industry can also be blamed for contributing to a large share of the air and water pollution problem. This in turn causes health problems to a large number of individuals.

Paragraph one:

> Here I've set up the types of pollution I want to classify: air, water, and soil. I've also named the three major causes of these: public, farmers, and industry. I guess I didn't really get a good controlling generalization in here.

Almost everyone is responsible in one way or another for these problems. If a person drives a car, that person is using up our limited and precious oil reserves, or he can be seen as polluting the atmosphere with fumes. It may not be very apparent that an individual can cause much of a problem, but with billions of people in the world today, a large amount of littering and pollution can be accounted for.

Paragraph two:

> Here I am showing how people cause air pollution. Littering is another type of pollution that I haven't mentioned before. Also, I can't quite figure how oil use works here yet.

On the other extreme, large industries such as John Deere factories located throughout farm states are major contributors to the pollution problem. In some places, such as Los Angeles, the problem of air pollution may become so severe at times that children and people with health problems are advised to stay indoors. But many of these problems are being overcome with government pollution restrictions.

Paragraph three:

> *Here I name a specific industry that causes pollution in general, mostly air, but I don't say that. Then I show the effects that air pollution can have in L.A. and mention a solution.*

The pollution of waters has become a major concern as large numbers of fish have recently been killed. Industrial waste dumped into rivers can account for a large portion of the problem. This can be seen in nuclear power plants which use water to cool reactors, then put this water which may be contaminated with radiation into streams. Recently government regulations have been put on industrial waste disposal. This is not only used to protect fish, but also people who use the water for cooking, drinking, and bathing.

Paragraph four:

> *Here I go into my second type of pollution—water, and use industry and nuclear power plants as causes. I also mention a solution and why it's important.*

At this point, the student stopped making paragraph summaries when he realized the following:

1. The introduction, not having a clear main-idea statement, set up both *types* of pollution and *causes* for pollution as emphases.
2. This double emphasis later appeared in the paragraph summaries (paragraphs two and three dealt with *causes* and paragraph four with *types*).
3. The paragraphs also introduced additional concerns not mentioned as emphases earlier (oil conservation, littering, *effects*, *solutions*).

In writing his draft, the student had lost track of his question: "What are the types of pollution I see everyday?" This lack of focus caused other problems, including the double emphasis and extraneous concerns. Abstracting has helped the student define the problems in his text.

☛ EXERCISE 1.6

Abstract the following paragraph (which appeared later in the initial "pollution draft"). How does it represent the same problems already spotted by the student? How does it pose new problems?

Farmers many years ago cleared the land of trees and other obstacles which would cause a problem in cultivation. Now farmers turn under vegetation which had protected the soil from erosion. This allows wind, water, as well as gravity to move the topsoil from its origin. If the process is allowed to continue for many years a large portion of topsoil may disappear from spots making it unfit for crop production. The construction industry could also be blamed for large amounts of soil erosion. When a new home is built, earth is stripped of vegetation and moved. Construction also takes huge amounts of land out of production every year. This decreases food supply causing more starvation in the world. ◢

Breaking down paragraphs

Abstracting paragraphs (See pages 17–18.) and breaking down paragraphs are similar procedures. The first emphasizes the topic of the paragraph, the second the supporting details.

In examining the support for the statement, "Unions have both their advantages and disadvantages which you should know about before joining one," the following student dissects the proof offered by an early paragraph.

Brief background of advantages.

Transition

Mention one benefit →

① *Mention specific wage scale usage*

② *No Support?*

Unions have been around a long time. The first unions were created during the later stages of the period of merchant capitalism. These early unions tried to increase the bargaining power and protect the interest of the workers. They were also concerned with maintaining and improving wage rates. Today's unions are still concerned with workers and wages. Through union membership workers can receive many benefits, such as unemployment insurance. Today the biggest changes that unions are making ① are in negotiating for higher wages and new con②tracts. Workers have the opportunity to increase their incomes. Workers receive time and a half for overtime and Saturdays, double time for Sunday, and high time for working above preset heights, usually set around 100 feet.

Through this breakdown, the student spotted two problems: the paragraph did not systematically present the advantages and it did not offer specific support for each advantage. The student decided upon the following remedy:

1. Cut the history portion.
2. Classify the advantages of unions into "benefits" and "wages."
3. Add to the benefits mentioned.

4. Cite specific recipients of the "benefits" and "wages."
5. Cut mention of "new contracts" as assumed in benefits and wages discussion.

With this revision plan, the student intended to sharpen the emphasis on union advantages while becoming more informative to his audience. To reach this goal, the student not only deleted from and added to the original support material but also revised its arrangement slightly (point 2).

✔ EXERCISE 1.7

Break down the following paragraph written as part of the preceding union draft. How is the situation here similar to that in the early union paragraph? How different? What specific revision plan would you recommend for this paragraph? What would be the main goal of your plan?

> Unions also have disadvantages. For this reason a nonunion worker may consider that his opportunities outweigh those of union workers. He or she receives many of the same benefits without paying dues. If the union negotiates a new wage contract, the nonunion workers will also receive a pay raise. Nonunion workers don't have to quit working when there is a strike. The biggest argument for non-union labor is the freedom of self-planning. The nonunion worker doesn't have somebody taking money out of his or her paychecks and setting it aside for vacations. Nonunion workers can also choose what type of plan they want for their retirement. ◢

Both the pollution example and the union example show that revision is still possible, is indeed sometimes quite necessary, even after a fair copy or "final" draft has been written.

Returning to the composing steps

In the pollution example, the writer discovers that he has lost track of what he wanted to say. To correct the problem he must return to the composing steps of establishing a focus and generating a main idea. In the union example, the writer sees that he has to discover more information, or, at least, that he has to reveal more information to his audience. Generating information and considering audience are the composing steps involved here.

Significantly, the steps in the composing process identify the goals of the writer. The step *establishing a focus,* for example, identifies *having a focus* as one goal in writing. The step *discovering information* identifies *having specific support* as another goal.

These goals are tied to audience expectations. Readers expect a piece of writing to have a focus and specific support in much the same way as they expect a "natural narrative" to have a beginning, middle, and end.

And, as this text will emphasize, asking questions is a way for the writer to attain these goals and thus to fulfill the readers' expectations.

▶**EXERCISE 1.8**

Answer the following questions in some detail.

1. In your opinion, what is good writing? What is bad writing?
2. What goals do you as a writer have when composing?
3. To what extent are these goals writer-based (deal with what you want to say)? To what extent are these goals reader-based (deal with *how* to communicate what you want to say to your audience)? ◂

WHAT THE WRITER AND THE READER GAIN

A look at the composing process suggests that through writing, the writer both develops and discovers ideas. In so doing, the writer tests or adds to the system of generalizations that forms his or her world view. The writer also enriches, influences, and shares with others. The writer enhances our understanding of a complex environment.

Thus, as readers, we gain from the writer's work both an experience and a response. The experience is provided by the reading process itself. The process of reading a paper (a text), at least the first time through, is basically a linear one. The reader generally moves steadily from the first word of the introduction to the last word of the conclusion. Occasionally, the reader may stop to look up a word or go back to review a point. But the reader's movement through the text is mainly forward.

Perhaps it is because of the basically linear nature of the initial reading that many inexperienced writers believe composing is also linear. If a text can be read straight through from beginning to end, so the reasoning goes, it can be written straight through, too. But, as has been shown, composing is not linear but *recursive*. Composing is recursive in that it requires the writer to double-back, reconsider, and even rewrite while a draft is in progress. What the reader sees is the end result of the writer's efforts; what the reader does not see is all the shuttling back and forth, all the rethinking and revising that produced that finished product.

In a very real sense, the reading process is not linear either. The reader's interpretation of a text is the result of recursive action. Moving forward in a text does not stop the reader from predicting what will be said next or from comparing what is being said to previous personal experience or to the content of past reading material. A reader's response to a text is determined by how the writer's work fulfills the reader's expectations. This does not mean that the reader should be able to predict exactly what the writer is going to say. The writer may surprise the reader. Reading involves discovery, too. But a reader should never have to strain to discover a writer's main idea and supporting details.

Perhaps it would be wise at this point then to distinguish between two types of reader expectations: those that the reader brings to the text and those created in the reader by the text itself.

Like the writer, the reader brings a world view and a knowledge of discourse to the text. The purpose behind audience analysis is, in fact, to outline the reader's existing assumptions.

The writer normally has little control over the expectations a reader brings to a text and has to work with what's there. But the writer does control the expectations created by the text. Here the writer is obliged to fulfill the expectations. If the writer proposes to discuss the advantages and disadvantages of unions, he must do so. If the writer promises to show how Scarlett O'Hara's reaction to events shows determination, she must do so. The reader will judge how well each does the job.

The reader may take from the reading a wide range of responses: surprise, anger, good feelings, increased awareness. In any case, the reader's response should somehow reflect the writer's purpose. Ideally then, what the writer and reader gain from the composing process and the resulting composition is a mutual understanding.

2

READERS, WRITERS, AND IDEAS

The expectations an informed or experienced reader commonly brings to a piece of writing (a text) suggest what you as the writer should look for in your finished product. The informed reader requires that the text's content: (1) be unified around one main idea, (2) offer evidence to illustrate or support that idea, and (3) make sense. In addition, the reader expects the text's presentation of that content be appropriate, accurate, and concise.

You address the reader's content expectations through: (1) the principle of the controlling idea, (2) the principle of specific, representative support, and (3) the principle of coherence. You address the reader's presentation expectations through the concept of style.

THE CONTROLLING IDEA

"What is the main idea I want to get across?" is answered by the controlling generalization. This generalization governs your approach to a topic, your search for information about that topic, and, eventually, your final paper. In your paper, this generalization, sometimes called a *topic sentence* or *thesis,* may be either explicitly stated or implied.

What does an explicit controlling generalization look like? One way of describing it is grammatical: it has a subject and a predicate. For example:

| *Taxi Driver* | + | is the most revolting movie I've ever seen. |

Another way of describing a controlling generalization is semantic: it commonly mentions (1) the topic of the paper and (2) the writer's attitude toward or thinking about that topic. A controlling generalization also frequently sets up (3) some expectation of how the paper will proceed. For instance, such a generalization may read: "If I wouldn't have made one dumb mistake at the rush party, I would have been invited to join Alpha Gamma that night." This generalization (1) states the topic (a mistake), (2) indicates the writer's attitude or thinking (the mistake was dumb) and (3) sets an expected procedure (the stupidity of the mistake will be established through an anecdote involving a specific rush party).

▸**EXERCISE 2.1**

Locate the topic, the attitude, and the expectation or procedure in the following generalizations.

1. If I wouldn't have made one naive miscalculation, I would have earned a supporting role in *Summer and Smoke* at the audition.
2. An effective counselor helps clients by means of both verbal and non-verbal behavior.
3. Bellow's *Henderson the Rain King* and Sterne's *Sentimental Journey* clearly resemble each other in terms of plots and motifs, but radically differ in terms of theme and type of protagonist.
4. Now that federal funding has proven to be an excellent reform for Presidential elections, public funding must be extended to Congressional elections to further eliminate the influence of big money in government. ◢

A controlling generalization can also be implied rather than stated. When implicit, it is indirectly communicated from the writer to the reader through various means: word choice, detail selection, paragraph emphasis, or overall arrangement. For example, let's start with the following statements.

1. John looked at his watch.	7. John saw the train.
2. Marie looked at her watch.	8. Marie saw the train.
3. John took out a cigarette.	9. John got up.
4. Marie drummed her fingers on the table.	10. Marie got up.
5. John looked at Marie.	11. The train arrived.
6. Marie looked at John	12. It left.

Given only these statements, you could have any number of controlling ideas about John and Marie's situation. Let's say, for instance, that you wanted to express the idea: "John and Marie were anxious to get rid of each other." You might write the following paragraph to convey that idea:

> John looked at his watch for the fourth time in as many minutes. As Marie echoed his action, John maneuvered his last Camel from its package, struck a match, and, after watching the flame edge its way down to his forefinger, slowly lit the cigarette. He sighed, snorting smoke, and casually squinted through the haze at Marie, drumming her fingers mechanically on the table top. Then, avoiding her glance, John again looked at his watch; fifteen seconds had passed. John's cigarette was a smoldering stub when the train crept into the station. John had already grabbed Marie's bags and was loading them onto the train as it stopped. Slipping past him, Marie wordlessly disappeared into the coach. Neither John nor Marie could be seen when the train left five minutes later.

In the preceding paragraph, the main idea remains implicit. It is implied by the way the statements are presented. Now let's say that you wanted to express the idea: "John and Marie were not at all anxious to part." You might write the following version:

> Catching sight of his watch as he encircled Marie's hand in his, John sighed. "It's almost 4:00." Marie mechanically glanced at her watch and nodded; her train was due at 5:00. Releasing her hand momentarily, John fumbled for a cigarette but forgot what he was reaching for when Marie started playfully drumming her fingers across the table and up his forearm. John grabbed her hand and saw himself mirrored in her eyes. The train's arrival startled them. It was 5:00. At 5:05 the train departed, leaving John to linger on the platform as he squinted down the abandoned tracks and remembered her face smudged up against the glass.

In this paragraph, the controlling generalization, again unstated, implicitly governs what is said.

▶ EXERCISE 2.2

Alter and combine the twelve statements about John and Marie on page 24 to form a paragraph showing one of the following ideas. Make the idea you choose implicit in your paragraph.

1. John and Marie can't wait to leave on their vacation together.
2. Although John can't wait to get rid of Marie, Marie still doesn't want to see John go (or vice versa).

3. John and Marie have been commuters on the same train for years.
4. Being strangers, John and Marie are trying to catch each other's attention. ◢

Whether explicit or implicit, what commitments do you make in a controlling generalization? First you make a commitment to yourself by deciding to present and develop a certain idea on paper. Second, in this generalization, you also make a commitment to your readers. Your generalization is a contract between you and the audience. If your generalization sets the expectation that you will show how a stupid mistake at a rush party prevented you from being pledged to a certain fraternity and if your paper then does *not* proceed with the expected anecdote about the party or does *not* show your mistake to be stupid, you have broken your contract. Third, you make a commitment to your subject. In essence, you say to your subject, "I am going to cover you in light of this idea, although I recognize that you contain other ideas." Your controlling generalization, like a pole star, orients you, your readers, and your subject to a certain point.

SPECIFIC SUPPORT

"How can I express my idea in more detail?" "How can I back up my idea?" "How can I make sure my audience clearly understands what I am trying to say?" These are questions addressed by specific representative support. This support may come from personal or outside sources. (Chapter 5 will show you how to discover such support.) Contained in the subject, this support is information that backs up your controlling generalization and that gives your audience a clear picture of what you're thinking.

Being Specific

"How specific does this support have to be?" Before answering this question directly, let's take a look at what "being specific" means. Being specific is a relative rather than an absolute state. For example, let's assume that details serving as support can be placed on a continuum ranging from the conceptual (abstract) to the general and on to the specific:

Conceptual	General	Specific
time	after class	3:20 p.m.
entertainment	watching movies	seeing *Jaws*
male	fiancé	Sally's Dave

Initially, this grouping may seem rather straight-forward, but let's now say you are asked to place the following words in such a grouping:

independence; customer; heroin; Big Mac

Next, to test your placements, you try to complete the continuum for each word. For example, if you chose to list "heroin" as "specific," you would then determine what its general and conceptual counterparts might be:

Conceptual	General	Specific
addiction	drug	heroin

Let's now consider the word "customer" and say that you selected it as a "specific" as shown in the following:

Conceptual	General	Specific
free enterprise	consumer	customer

"But," you might say, "I initially selected 'customer' to be 'general' and used the following continuum":

Conceptual	General	Specific
consumerism	customer	Macy's shopper

"Yes, but," your neighbor might protest, "I selected 'customer' as 'conceptual' using this continuum":

Conceptual	General	Specific
customer	Macy' shopper	Mrs. Savage.

The same ambiguity may develop in placing other words on the continuum as well.

These examples begin to illustrate the relativity involved in "being specific." In fact, the specificity of Mrs. Savage could be even further extended: the wheezing Mrs. Savage of 220 W. 6th in Plainfield, Illinois who weighs three hundred pounds but still tries to squeeze into petite sportswear at Chicago's downtown Macy's.

▶ **EXERCISE 2.3**

As an exercise in "being specific," rewrite the following sentences.
EXAMPLES: The old woman was on the corner looking very sad.

The wrinkled widow slumped at Tenth and Vine, crying.

1. Everyone there had a good time.
2. The record has been at the top of the charts here for some time.
3. He is the star of the team, because he does his job well.

4. I work at a company that demands a lot and pays very little.
5. The child received quite a few toys for the holiday.
6. That person has certain qualities that I admire.
7. My car acts goofy in the morning.
8. Showing her independence, the dog slowly sat down on the plants. ◢

Having completed Exercise 2.3, you might be asking, "Do I always have to be so specific?" Of course not. There *are* certain situations when specificity may not be the wisest option. For example, note the vagueness in the following sample horoscope:

> Taurus (April 20–May 20)   A watchful eye and a firm grip on those in your charge will be necessary today. Lack of discipline could turn your household into a chaotic place.

What if, instead, the horoscope writer had been more specific and had written:

> Keeping an eye on your ten-month-old puppy and a firm grip on its leash will be necessary from ten until noon today because failure to restrain your "Spike" could cause him to turn over the coffee table on your two-year-old niece, Nancy.

Obviously, by being more specific, the horoscope writer would have excluded a significant portion of his audience. While most of his audience might indeed have someone "in their charge," not nearly as many have a ten-month-old puppy, Spike, and a two-year-old niece, Nancy.

Another example of useful generalities occurs in this quote from a political speech:

> "My opponent has spent far too much of the taxpayers' money on office expenses in Washington, and if I'm elected, I will lower those costs significantly while I'm also working to lower taxes, too."

What if, instead, the politician had been more specific and had said:

> "Ms. Cooper has spent approximately $10,000 per month of your tax money on staff salaries, mimeographing, and supplies, and if I'm elected, I will reduce those expenses to $9,500 per month by not purchasing any bond paper, while I'm also working to reduce the sales tax on your food by one-half of one percent over the next four years."

In this case, by being more specific, the politician has given her constituency a concrete yardstick by which to measure her accomplishments. For example, if she lowers the monthly expenses to only $9,600 per month, she can be attacked for breach of promise. In addition, the voters might decide that a $500 per month cut and a one-half of one percent reduction are not enough to warrant a change in representation, and our politician might not have been elected in the first place.

Both the horoscope writer and the politician thus have taken into account their audiences when they determined how specific to be. Their actions suggest one answer to the original question "How specific does the specific support have to be?" That answer is "specific enough so the audience clearly gets the picture."

Perhaps the best way to show the connection between clarity of meaning and specific detail is to show the progressive development of a student paper.

1. *First draft:*

> Sometimes friends can be a pain in the neck. Sometimes they seem to plan and plot ways to hurt you. This can be done in a number of ways.
>
> First of all, friends can let you down in some way. This tears down all the trust and faith you had in them. A common example is when they arrange to meet you at a certain place and don't show. Their excuse of forgetting doesn't help; it only hurts.
>
> Furthermore, friends always can get you in trouble with someone or something. If it's not your family, it's your other friends, and if it's not your friends, it's your school work.
>
> Therefore, I believe a person is better off with no friends at all. Why not put all your efforts and attention on yourself? Start living your life for number one—you. Don't bother with all the hassles that friends bring; enjoy developing yourself instead.

Discussion:

What meaning comes across in this draft? Obviously, the writer has been hurt by some friends' actions; this is clear. But it is not clear what the offending actions were or even if they were serious enough to warrant the conclusion, "a person is better off without friends." In a word, the support is fuzzy. In fact, the student's draft is presently so general that it leaves itself open to any number of possible interpretations, including the following two widely different readings:

First possible interpretation:

> Sometimes friends can be a pain in the neck. Sometimes they seem to plan and plot ways to hurt you. This can be done in a number of ways.
>
> First of all, friends can let you down in some way. For example, yesterday my friends said they would meet me at the grocery store, so I would have company when I did my mother's shopping. Their excuse of forgetting didn't help; it only hurt.

Furthermore, friends always can get you in trouble with someone or something. For example, last week they told my advisor I was having so much trouble with my English term paper that I was thinking of having someone else write it for me. Their excuse that they were only trying to help was a real farce.

Therefore, I believe a person is better off with no friends at all. As the saying goes, if these are friends, who needs enemies?

Second possible interpretation:

Sometimes friends can be a pain in the neck. Sometimes they seem to plan and plot ways to hurt you. This can be done in a number of ways.

First of all, friends can let you down in some way. For example, I asked two of my best friends to be in my wedding. They let my Dad pay for the outfits but didn't show up that Saturday for the wedding. Their excuse that they forgot didn't help.

Furthermore, friends always can get you in trouble with someone or something. For example, last week they told my new spouse that I was unfaithful. Their excuse that they were only trying to bring us closer together was a sham.

Therefore, I believe a person is better off with no friends at all than with friends like these.

Summary:

In the first interpretation, it seems obvious that the writer truly has good friends and, ironically, doesn't realize that they are trying to help him/her become more independent. In the second interpretation, on the other hand, it is equally apparent that the writer's so-called friends do not have his/her best interests in mind, to say the least. As it turns out, the writer of the original first draft had neither of these interpretations in mind as the second draft reveals:

2. *Second Draft*

I have two friends that can be a pain in the neck. Sometimes they seem to plan and plot ways to hurt me.

First of all, these two often let me down. For example, three weeks ago we had all agreed to meet at a pizza parlor after the Homecoming football game. Well, both of them then got dates to the game, so they sat with their dates, and I sat with some other friends. Afterwards, my two friends never did show up at the pizza parlor. Their excuse of forgetting made me feel hurt.

Furthermore, these two often can get me in trouble. For example, just yesterday they invited me to go with them to the lake. Well, their car ran out of gas on the way back, so we didn't get back until late, and I didn't have time to study for my chemistry test which I consequently flunked.

Therefore, sometimes I think I should concentrate more on developing myself. That way I wouldn't have to worry about passing my courses at least, although I think I would still be hurt by anyone "standing me up."

Discussion:

What meaning comes across in this draft? The writer has been hurt by two friends, first when they didn't show up for a pizza "date" and, second, when their car ran out of gas, "causing" the writer to fail a test. This seems clear, but the selection is still not without ambiguity. The support still needs sharpening. For example, how realistic was it for the writer to expect the friends to show up at the pizza place after circumstances had changed? And how justified was it for the writer to blame the friends for the scholastic failure? How were these two incidents *plots* ? Again, because of its general nature, the student's draft leaves itself open to a number of possible interpretations.

▸ **EXERCISE 2.4**

Write a possible interpretation: of the student's second draft above, increasing the specificity of the two supporting examples. Do you think your interpretation will be the same as another writer's? ◢

In the writing a third draft, the original writer not only increased specificity of the supporting examples but, as we shall see, made a discovery about the incidents as well.

3. **Third draft**

My friends Terry and Sandy can be a pain in the neck.

For example, three weeks ago we had all agreed to meet at Giovanni's for some pizza after the Homecoming game. Well, after that, both of them got dates, so, not wanting to be a "fifth wheel" of sorts, I decided not to sit with them at the game. When we were all walking out, we waved to each other, but somehow I didn't have the nerve to ask them if they were still planning on going to Giovanni's. Their showing up would be a test of their remembering. Well, they didn't show, and although I can understand their forgetting, I still can't help being hurt.

Furthermore, just yesterday Terry and Sandy called and asked me if I wanted to go with them to Lake Lemon to water ski. Well, I know now that I should have refused them because I had a chemistry test the next day, but I thought, "I deserve a break." And because I didn't want to spoil their fun, I didn't even mention the exam. Unfortunately, we ran out of gas on the way home, and my little plan backfired. Flunking that test sure hurt, too.

What I have learned from this is I should really stand up for what's good for me and not be afraid to tell my friends what I'm thinking. Sure, they could have said, "Would you mind meeting for pizza some other time?" or "Maybe you shouldn't go if you have a test," but then I would only have myself to blame if I was hurt.

When tailoring the specificity of your support to your audience, then, you should try to be specific enough so that the number of possible interpretations is reduced to a minimum. This, of course, depends on who your audience is. If the student above, for example, were addressing his paper to Terry or Sandy, the representative examples would not have to be as specific. You as a writer should remember, however, that your audience is usually composed of more than your two best friends who shared the experience about which you are writing.

The writings of the horoscope writer and the politician (see pages 28–29) also suggest that purpose, in addition to audience, plays a role in how specific to be. Both writer and politician are less specific than they could be because the one wants her predictions to apply to all those born under the Taurus sign and the other wants her claims to be free from scrutiny as she seeks to be elected. Other factors influence how specific the support is as well. These include how broad or general the focus is and what kind of material is available as support. In other words, there is no one answer to the question, "How specific is specific enough?"

Being Representative

Besides being relatively specific, the support must actually stand for the idea set forth in your controlling generalization. Consider the following:

J. Simpson is running for Student Senate. He believes he has a good chance to be elected senior senator because his positive stands on such issues as barring cars from campus, eliminating student publications from the senate budget, shortening the semester by one week, and having "guaranteed tuition" seem to coincide with those of his potential constituency. And this is no wonder, for prior to his campaign, Simpson had spent his evenings polling campus students, asking them their opinions on these issues, and, after detecting a trend, had formulated his own stand on the basis of the majority opinion. If 61 percent said "yes" to barring cars from campus, Simpson says "yes" to barring cars from campus in his speeches.

The election returns, however, dash Simpson's expectations. Simpson garners a respectable 34 percent of the vote, but this is not enough to defeat the winner who receives 51 percent. In trying to figure out what happened, Simpson discovers that he didn't bother to ask the students in his poll if they were indeed seniors. So while 61 percent of a random sampling of students, freshmen through seniors, were "favorable" to the issues selected, only about 34 percent of the seniors were "favorable" to these same issues; because they were about to graduate, for example, the seniors didn't feel that "guaranteed tuition" was of primary importance and, in fact, didn't see why the subsequent classes shouldn't experience the same tuition hikes that they had. While Simpson, then, would have made an excellent representative for the student body as a whole, he was an inappropriate representative, in this case, for the seniors.

The preceding example, of course, has a moral. When choosing support of your own, you should be sure to ask, "Does my support really represent my point, fit my constituency?"

Using "representative" information to illustrate an idea is not peculiar to writing. In advertising, for example, ad designers commonly pick one person to represent all the skinny Marys who lost weight on "Lose Fast" pills or all the athletic Johns who wear "Fast-Loose" shoes. In reporting, the NBC Nightly News commentator features the Sanchez family picking Ohio tomatoes as representatives of all migrant workers; in running an underworld network, Mr. Big "cuts up" a free-lancing Jack Stray to "make an example out of him"; in teaching, the biology professor has each of his students dissect a fetal pig to learn about mammalian physiology. Obviously, skinny Mary is not the only person to lose weight, the Sanchez are not the only migrant family, Jack is not the only freelancer, and the fetal pig is not the only pig or the only mammal. But each shares enough characteristics with a certain group, be it weight-watchers, migrants, freelancers, or mammals, to serve as a representative of that respective group.

By specifically focusing on representative information, then, a writer can concisely describe a whole group or illustrate a comprehensive idea or controlling generalization.

▶EXERCISE 2.5

Practice recognizing representative information by participating in one of the following activities:

1. Listen to a televised news broadcast. Jot down what specific examples are given and what these examples are intended to represent.
2. Look at a magazine advertisement. Describe the specific information and the idea represented by this information.

3. Take notes on a college lecture. Try to distinguish between the specific examples offered by the professor and the ideas these represent. ◢

Representative information can range from people to objects, from anecdotes to court testimony, from hypothetical comparisons to statistics. In any case, a careful selection of such information allows you to support accurately your controlling generalization without having to report every single bit of information you may have located on the topic.

COHERENCE

In addition to having a strong controlling idea and specific, representative supporting details, your writing should be coherent. Coherence involves the interrelationships established when you unite your controlling generalization with your specific support to form a piece of writing.

Considering Placement

"Where should I place my controlling generalization in relationship to its support?" is one question you can first consider when bringing the two together. Explicit generalizations can be placed either at the end or the beginning of the support. The arrangement with the generalization at the end is called *inductive* or discovery structure. The arrangement with the generalization at the beginning is called *deductive* or commitment structure.

The following comparison/contrast paper by Phil Morris utilizes both inductive and deductive arrangement, as the controlling generalization occurs toward the middle.

The Bird and the Beast

Charles A. Lindbergh flew his *Spirit of St. Louis* across the Atlantic seven months and ten days after I was born. About four years after the Paris trip, I experienced my first day of memory, which, no doubt, was initiated by the presence of a biplane in the sky over our back yard. Not only was it present, it circled, and its engine went silent. A man's voice shouted down, "Which way to the airport?" Mom, who was hanging clothes on the line, pirouetted to an awe-stricken pose with her left arm semaphoring a direction to the northeast. A hand waved "thank you" from the open cockpit, the engine resumed its clatter, and the plane departed for the airport.

Thus, I began my life in a glamorous era of spectacular air achievements. Many influences were in effect to channel my thoughts in the direction of air adventure. Women wore "Lindy Helmets," and little boys wore helmets with goggles. *National Geographics* pictured leather-jacketed, booted, and helmeted air heroes, with goggles up, standing by their airplanes. Movies portrayed such actors as Errol Flynn, James Cagney, and Pat O'Brien, goggles down, flying their Spads in combat against nameless Germans in Fokkers. And I had, as my most treasured toys, a Tootsie-Toy Ford Trimotor; a tin, twelve-engined Dornier flying boat; a cast-iron *Spirit of St. Louis*; and—a cast-iron motorcycle? Somewhere in my early experiences, this "brother" of the unmuffled-engine sect sputtered into the limelight of my consciousness. The first motorcycle I saw up close was probably Beanie Conwell's Harley. What a pleasant smelling and interesting assemblage of gadgetry! What a spectacle to watch Beanie kick the engine to life and take off for unimaginable adventure! During my growing-up years, the sights, sounds, and smells of both the airplane and the motorcycle were strong sensory inputs that somehow merged in my value structure. *Though the two machines were indisputably different, I saw a number of similarities that in later years led to the purchase of my first motorcycle, a surrogate airplane.*

It was obvious to any eye that the airplane and the motorcycle were different. The airplane was a large, fragile, fabric covered, bird-like affair having two wings (usually) to support it in flight and with a propeller on its nose to pull it aloft. It had two side-by-side wire wheels and a tail-skid for moving about on the ground when leaving or returning to the "roost." Otherwise, the wheels and the skid were clumsy-looking appendages that were impediments to flight. The man who flew the plane sat with a major portion of his body "inside" the aircraft . . . and controlled the direction and attitude of his ship by means of feet on a rudder bar and a hand on a "joy stick." In contrast with the airplane, the motorcycle was a comparatively small, beastly-looking, bicycle-like contraption. It had a back-stand to keep it upright when not in use, and two wire wheels, in tandem, that were very necessary for support, propulsion, turning, and braking. The rider sat in a saddle astride the "beast" . . . and held onto horn-like handle bars, which also afforded a convenient means of steering.

My childhood concepts of the similarities between the airplane and the motorcycle were for the most part emotionally oriented, though there were some physical likenesses. . . . Both the airplane and the motorcycle had similar-looking, exposed engines that filled the air and stirred young hearts with powerful sounds from blazing exhaust sticks. Both machines emitted a "sweet" aroma of hot oil and gasoline when silent. In addition to the engine, most of the plane's operating equipment was exposed to the wind and weather. The motorcycle had *all* of its equipment exposed. The same could be said for the "operators"; both men enjoyed a collar-flapping fresh air union with their machines as they banked and turned "in flight" over or through the countryside.

Today, the "differences" gap has widened considerably. The airplane has grown up to become a sleek aluminum cocoon in which the casually dressed pilot, sans helmet and goggles, engages in electronic wizardry in preference to using seat-of-the-pants flying skills. The motorcycle is much sleeker too, but it still retains all the nostalgic advantages it once shared with the airplane. The thrills associated with early-day flying still live on in the motorcycle. I relish the flash-back memories that come to me as I fly through the countryside on my motorcycle, a grim-faced Cagney in pursuit of the Red Baron. I wonder what thoughts or memories, if any, fill the minds of the youngsters I meet along the way on their Hondas and Harleys. They missed "ground school." I wonder if they know that they're really flying.

Phil Morris

What does Phil gain by placing his controlling generalization towards the middle? For one thing, through his intriguing opening anecdote, he succeeds in making me as a reader want to read further. He also establishes the *personal* importance of both his objects of comparison before he begins with his analysis. In so doing, he invites me to identify with what he is saying. And while I don't share his interest in airplanes and motorcycles, I do identify with a certain nostalgia for childhood experiences and I become interested in what he has to say. I'm not sure that I would have felt the same willingness to read further if Phil had begun: "Airplanes and motorcycles have similarities and differences."

Making Sense

"Do the interrelationships I establish between my controlling generalization and its support make sense?" is another important consideration for coherence. The importance of making sense can be established by the annotated selections Figures 2.1 and 2.2. The annotations for the paper in Figure 2.1 reveal that the writer has genuinely confused the reader by not establishing clear connections between sentences and between paragraphs. In the paper in Figure 2.2, the writer has not only confused but also antagonized the reader.

The writer can minimize reader confusion by faithfully fulfilling the expectations set up by the controlling generalization. In the Watergate selection, such expectations are set in the generalization: "The Watergate scandal happened for a number of political reasons." The expectation is

Good. The paper is going to reveal these reasons. ←

Wait. The connection between the book and the "number of reasons" has to be more clearly established. ←

What does the review of past administrations have to do with the issue? ↙

The Watergate scandal happened for a number of political reasons. The book *The Final Days of Richard Nixon* gave an up to date review of his administration as well as past administrations.

Is this a political reason? The first sentence sets the expectation that you will be enumerating a number of political reasons. ←

Is the psychiatrist's office part of Watergate? Are you expanding your focus? ↖

What is meant by "tactfully" here? Burglary doesn't seem very tactful. ←

President Nixon organized a plan. That plan was to send a specialized team into Democratic headquarters and burglarize a well-known psychiatrist's office in hopes of finding information or strategy leading to the upcoming election; however, word leaked to Democratic leaders that there had been a plot to gather information that may be harmful or may be used tactfully against the Democrats in securing votes.

Wait. Has your paper focused on the "consequences" of Nixon's actions? I thought we were dealing with causes (reasons) and not with effects (consequences). ←

The book *The Final Days* elaborates in more detail the consequences the Nixon administration suffered for eliciting those acts.

FIGURE 2.1 *Annotated Paper*

that reasons for the scandal will be enumerated. This expectation is not fulfilled, as the writer provides a very limited plot summary of *The Final Days* and concludes by emphasizing political consequences (the effects) of Watergate rather than the reasons (the causes).

The Wiley Coyote selection in Figure 2.2, like the Watergate piece, does not really pursue the controlling generalization throughout the paper, because it does not proceed with examples of "skill and ability" as expected. The Coyote selection presents an additional problem in that its tone is not well established. Consequently, the reader becomes increasingly unsure as to whether the writer's idea is to show actual or pseudo (false) "skills and abilities."

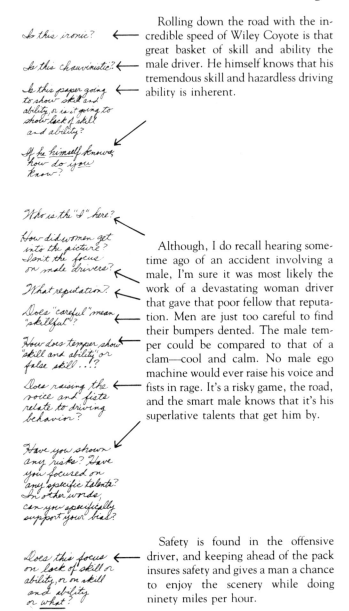

Is this ironic? ← Rolling down the road with the incredible speed of Wiley Coyote is that great basket of skill and ability the *Is this chauvinistic?* ← male driver. He himself knows that his tremendous skill and hazardless driving *Is this paper going* ← ability is inherent.
to show skill and
ability, or is it going to
show lack of skill
and ability?

If he himself knows,
how do you
know?

Who is the "I" here?

How did women get
into the picture?
Isn't the focus
on male drivers? ← Although, I do recall hearing sometime ago of an accident involving a male, I'm sure it was most likely the *What reputation?* ← work of a devastating woman driver that gave that poor fellow that reputa- *Does "careful" mean* ← tion. Men are just too careful to find *"skillful"?* their bumpers dented. The male tem- *How does temper show* ← per could be compared to that of a *"skill and ability" or* clam—cool and calm. No male ego *false skill…!?* machine would ever raise his voice and *Does raising the* ← fists in rage. It's a risky game, the road, *voice and fists* and the smart male knows that it's his *relate to driving* superlative talents that get him by. *behavior?*

Have you shown
any risks? Have
you focused on
any specific talents?
In other words,
can you specifically
support your bias?

Does this focus ← Safety is found in the offensive *on lack of skill or* driver, and keeping ahead of the pack *ability, or on skill* insures safety and gives a man a chance *and ability* to enjoy the scenery while doing *or what?* ninety miles per hour.

FIGURE 2.2 *Annotated Paper*

▶**EXERCISE 2.6**

Revise one of the annotated selections in Figures 2.1 and 2.2, working primarily to improve the coherence and sense of the piece. ◂

STYLE

The principles of the controlling idea, of specific representative support, and of coherence guide you in fulfilling the reader's expectations regarding content. The concept of style, on the other hand, helps you address the reader's concerns regarding how that content is presented.

From the writer's standpoint, style in writing is like style in dress. Both involve the question "How do I look?" Both feature a variety of options ranging from informal to formal, from blue jeans to tuxedos. Style communicates a message to onlookers. That message may be "I'm cool" or "I'm sophisticated" or "I'm just an ordinary person" or "I haven't got my trip together yet."

From the reader's standpoint, style in writing forms a context for the writer's message. The reader is less concerned with "How does it look?" than with "Does it work?" Therefore, "Does this language belong?", "Does it mean what it says?", and "Does it get to the point?" become key questions for the reader.

In general, a writer's style works best when it is appropriate, accurate, and concise.

Appropriateness

To understand stylistic appropriateness requires review of a few linguistic principles.

Everyone has an individual way of speaking or *idiolect*. No two people have identical idiolects. Groups of people, however, do share enough characteristics in their individual language use to be classified as members of a certain *dialect* group. There may be many such dialect groups within one language.

Within this system of dialects are "situational dialects." That is, speakers can speak more than one dialect of their own language according to their situation and their purpose for speaking. For example, you speak one way when you talk with your friends; you speak another when you address your boss. Such situational dialects are called style.

Similarly, everyone has an individual way of writing. No two people write exactly alike. Groups of people, however, do share enough characteristics in their individual ways of writing to be classified as members of a distinct group. College-educated writers, for instance, form such a group. College-educated writers are expected to know and to be able to use standard English. (College grammar handbooks define the conventions of standard English.)

Within this system are "situational styles,"often equated with levels of usage. In fact, you may already have had experience adjusting your style

June 20

Hi Buzz!

The Fourth sounds fine. Just so we don't end up with five bean salads and no watermelon like last time. And remember your bat and glove!

Incidently, I saw in <u>Business News</u> that Allied has an Ad. Ass. job open. Do you know anything about this? I realize that you're not into personnel, but I thought you might give me a few clues as to what qualifications they're looking for. Obviously, I think my qualifications will speak for themselves, but a little extra whipped cream never hurt. And I assume that because you wrote me such a fine letter for Beaman, you will do the same for me here, but if you feel a recommendation "from the inside" would do more harm than good, let me know. I won't mention you until you give me the go ahead.

My best to Lon, and we'll see you for the fireworks.

Yours,

J.

FIGURE 2.3   *Personal Letter*

so that it was appropriate to a particular composing context. Consider the letters in Figures 2.3 and 2.4, for example. In the first letter, J.B. uses unclarified references such as "the Fourth sounds fine," or "like last time," or "letter for Beaman," because Buzz, as his friend, will automatically know what the reference means. J.B. takes no such liberties in the Steadman letter and is even careful to note where the Steadman opening was advertised and where he, J.B., can be reached by phone. Correspondingly, J.B.'s word choice is informal in the first letter, formal in the second.

926 Olive
San Juan, CA 95600
June 15, 19xx

R. M. Steadman
Personnel Director
Allied Incorporated
Leesford Heights, CA 94966

Dear Ms. Steadman:

I am applying for the opening of Administrative Assistant in your Advertising Division as listed in May's Business News.

Since 1976 I have been working as an Co-assistant for Beaman Corporation where my duties include supervising the Heads of Marketing and Distribution, coordinating public relations releases, and directing the Term-fax project. Prior to 1976 I served as the Head of Marketing for Excise Products (1974–76) and as Sales Coordinator for Nice Industries (1972–74).

Several of my more noteworthy distinctions include: Linc-Corporate Merit Award (1978), District Manager's Award (1976), and Jesper's Honorarium for Inventive Marketing (1974).

The enclosed vita details my school and work experience; letters of recommendation are available upon request.

I would like to arrange an interview at your convenience. My phone number is 774-3577. I look forward to hearing from you.

Sincerely,

J. B. Cotter

J. B. Cotter

FIGURE 2.4   *Business Letter*

▸EXERCISE 2.7

Choose a situation and write a separate letter concerning it to two different audiences. For example, you have run out of money before the end of the semester, and you must request help from your parents and a college financial aids officer. Note how your different audiences affect both what you say and how you say it. ◢

As J.B.'s letters demonstrate, an important factor influencing a writer's situational style is the audience. Another factor may be the writer's choice of *persona,* of an idiolect other than his or her own. A writer does not always choose to write with a persona, but does so only when it fits his or her purpose.

A persona is a "voice." This voice may range in formality from "I shall now proceed to prepare the midday sustenance" to "I'm gonna fix lunch." When establishing a persona, the writer must be careful to be consistent in the type and level of usage. Certainly the reader would be jarred if the "voice" said, "I'm gonna fix lunch" and in the next breath said, "Perhaps you would appreciate a morsel of mint with your Bouillabaisse?" Establishing a distinct voice requires consistency in word choice.

Consider, for example, the interview with Alf Landon included in Chapter 7. In this interview, Jan Hermann actually uses two voices for telling her story: that of an excitable and naive reporter for the introduction and conclusion, and that of a calm and experienced interviewer for the question-answer section. Jan creates her excitable voice or persona by including such phrases as "A minute . . . sixty seconds . . . oh God!" and ". . . my deodorant would have never made it!" Significantly, this voice has been tempered somewhat by the experience of the interview, because she can *inconspicuously* place a tiny fingerprint on the glass of Landon's door. Before the interview, had such a move been attempted, I can only picture it resulting in "Oh NO! . . . a Gigantic Smudge!"

The second voice, that of a experienced reporter, comes through in such well-prepared and factual questions as "What influence did you have in the enactment of the Kansas oil proration law?" The fact that Jan uses two voices in presenting her interview does not detract from the unity of her piece. Quite the contrary. Most of us have had experiences where we might have been intellectually prepared for an event, as Jan was with her questions, but where we were still emotionally unprepared or nervous. In capturing both feelings through her voices, Jan thus recreates the "whole" experience. In using both voices, Jan fulfills her purpose.

▶EXERCISE 2.8

To practice recognizing different styles, speculate about both the identity of the speaker and the nature of the intended audience in each of the following statements. You will be drawing from your knowledge of how certain groups of people speak in certain situations as you complete this exercise.

1. Mr. President, Senator Greeley, Distinguished Visitors and Guests.
2. Alright guys, knock it off.
3. For maximum implementation, the retrenchment strategy should be effected forthwith before the market collapses.
4. And this here is one of my very favoritist things. See? See?
5. Shocking . . . quite shocking!
6. Ambience? Good Lord, I'd rather face an ambulance than another ambience.
7. He's had to bear the blunt of her criticism for time amoral.
8. Brothers and sisters, we are gathered here today to right a wrong.
9. Everytime I come home, it's the same story! I'm getting sick of it, I tell you. Sick. Sick. Sick! This is it, I tell you. This is the last straw! You've really done it this time!
10. Cain't yous see! He's a creep, dat's all. So's end wit him, de creep. It ain't gonna break your heart. ◢

You address the reader's concern that you "dress for the occasion" then, by asking such questions as: "Does my level of usage match my chosen audience? My overall situation? Does my choice of language fit my purpose?"

Accuracy

In addition to appropriateness, accuracy influences your effectiveness as a writer. You address the reader's expectations regarding stylistic accuracy when you distinguish between denotations and connotations in word choice and consider emphasis in phrasing.

Denotation and connotations

Denotation involves the direct meaning of words; *connotations,* the emotional overtones associated with them. Denotatively, *home* may mean 306 Ash Street; connotatively, *home* may mean security. Both denotative and connotative values play a part in wording accuracy.

You influence reader response with every word you choose. Consider the following sentences:

1. A field of flowers surrounded the shack.
2. A field of flowers surrounded the cottage.

Shacks and cottages are different structures. However, the words *shack* and *cottage* not only have separate denotative values, but different connotative values as well. A shack is generally perceived more negatively than a cottage.

The reader thus responds to the two sentences differently. The reader sees different buildings. The reader also picks up from the first sentence an implied contrast between the shack (undersirable, ugly) and the flowers (desirable, beautiful); the reader gets no such contrast from the second sentence.

The reader, in turn, expects the implied contrast between shack and flowers to have some importance, just as he or she expects the harmony between cottage and flowers to serve some function.

Sometimes, inaccuracies in diction can occur that cause miscommunication between writer and reader. Consider the following sentences that contain a particular type of denotative error or faulty diction: the *malapropism*.

　　　　　　　council proscribed
　　1. The counsel prescribed Socrates for corrupting youth.
　　　　　　　　　　　　　　　　　　　　respectively
　　2. The witch and warlock, female and male, respectfully, performed
　　　　　conjurative
　　　　various conjugal rights.

Such errors are not necessarily the same as spelling errors. "Counsel," "prescribed," "respectfully," and "conjugal" are all proper words given the appropriate context.

▸EXERCISE 2.9

Spot and correct the diction errors in the following sentences.

　　1. The party happened spontaneously when football fans met at Rosie's Disco at their own discrepancy.
　　2. The jury was under the allusion that Mr. Briggs was a creditable witness; consequently, it discovered that its implication was incorrect.
　　3. Although he gladly excepted the principle's invitation, John later had an attack of conscious for his passed actions.
　　4. Siting the general's fortuitous behavior in the previous battle, the committee expressed its gratuitious feelings by awarding a meritorious service metal.

5. Because the building had histrionic significance, the commission recommended renovation legislation which unfortunately incurred an absorbent financial burden to some tax payers.

6. Her comments inferred that she had been deeply effected by his marriage proposal. ◢

While the errors in Exercise 2.9 involve inaccurate meanings, connotative errors involve inappropriate overtones, as in the following sentences:

1. Jean wore a *gaudy* silver fox fur to the Queen's coronation. (*Gaudy* implies not only lavish but also tasteless ornamentation; unless the fur itself is outlandishly trimmed, a fox fur does not seem inappropriate apparel at a coronation.)

2. The child *reverted* to thumb-sucking as soon as its mother left the room. (While *revert* does mean "to go back," it also implies "to return to the distant or ancestral past," which seems inappropriate to this context.)

Such connotative errors often occur when a writer uses a *Thesaurus* without also using a dictionary.

▶EXERCISE 2.10

Practice spotting and correcting the connotative misjudgments in the following sentences:

1. Pastor Jones respected Miss Penny's glib manner and her perceptive self-opinion.

2. The barbaric village had common privies.

3. Kari had the ignominious distinction of having to submit two paper propositions before finally getting one accepted.

4. Although cryptic, the speech clearly propagandized various methods of birth control.

5. Showing dotage for his newborn son, the young father bought a slew of toys on sale for cheap.

6. In evenly-matched play, the chess master finally vanquished his victim after seven titilating hours. ◢

You can reduce such inaccuracies in diction with careful dictionary use.

Emphasis in phrasing

Emphasis in phrasing also influences meaning. Emphasis in phrasing involves coordination, subordination, and placement.

When ideas are *coordinate*, they are of equal importance. Correspondingly, when two parts of a sentence are joined by coordinating conjunctions (and, but, or, for, nor, yet, so), each part has equal weight. For example, in the sentence "Carla maintains an A average, and she plays varsity basketball," both maintaining "A's" and playing basketball enjoy equal importance.

When one idea is *subordinate* to another, the two are not equal in importance. Correspondingly, when two parts of a sentence are joined by subordinating conjunctions (because, although, if, while, when . . .), the part introduced by the subordinator carries less weight than does the other part. For instance, in the sentence, "Although Carla maintains an A average, she plays varsity basketball," playing basketball acquires, and perhaps strangely so, more importance than maintaining excellent grades.

The effects of coordination and subordination can be modified by phrase placement. For example, in the sentence "Carla plays varsity basketball, although she maintains an 'A' average," maintaining "A's" takes on more importance than it did in the immediately previous sentence. Because it occupies the final position in the sentence, it's the last thing the reader sees and therefore acquires more stress. Maintaining good grades here still does not have the importance of playing basketball, but it is approaching coordinate emphasis.

▶EXERCISE 2.11

Note how changes in emphasis affect the meaning of the following sentences:

1. Karen appreciated her mother's advice, and John refused to listen to his parents.
2. Karen appreciated her mother's advice, even though John refused to listen to his parents.
3. Even though John refused to listen to his parents, Karen appreciated her mother's advice.
4. Karen appreciated her mother's advice, but John refused to listen to his parents.
5. John refused to listen to his parents, but Karen appreciated her mother's advice. ◢

⟩EXERCISE 2.12

Practice writing several versions of one sentence, using coordination, subordination, and phrase placement to create shifts in emphasis and meaning. ◢

Learning to use emphasis in phrasing effectively increases the accuracy of your presentation and helps you address your reader's concern that you mean what you say.

Conciseness

In addition to appropriateness and accuracy, conciseness helps bring your message to your reader. You address the reader's expectations regarding concise style when you shun wordiness and maintain consistent paragraph emphasis.

Wordiness

Strengthening Vocabulary.   Overall wordiness in writing prevents the reader from quickly understanding the writer's meaning. Sometimes wordiness can stem from an inadequate vocabulary, as the following editing suggests:

1. The politician's ~~by his~~ vote ~~exercised the power to bring about~~ *effected* the campaign reform.

2. The doctor ~~blew air into~~ *insufflated* the patient's lungs.

3. Jim had an attitude ~~that was free and easy but at the same time was arrogant.~~ *cavalier*

4. The King travelled ~~under an assumed name to disguise his identity.~~ *incognito.*

5. The writer's ~~writing~~ style was characterized by ~~the unnecessary or superflous use of words.~~ *redundancy.*

Having a versatile vocabulary does not mean that your paper will contain sentences like this: "The grig garroted the garrulous misogynist subsequent to the latter's pyretic harangue." Such langauge does not contribute to a writer's readability or style.

▶**EXERCISE 2.13**

Rework the vocabulary of the following sentences for economy:

1. When the rapidity of the motion of the roller coaster increased, the persons traveling on the roller coaster let out loud and noisy screams.
2. As the travelers arrived at the depot station, they had to keep their eyes partially closed, because the sun shone off of the chrome of the train engine with a strong and steady light.
3. The general plant life of the secluded mountain glen was verdant green and quite unique.
4. While eating his johnnycake made of corn, the man drilling for oil in the unproven territory was accidently crushed by the framework that supported his drilling machinery.
5. An invisible aura moved around his head as the seance meeting took an unexpected and surprising turn. ◢

Mastering new words is always difficult. For instance, when I was in seventh grade, I checked Charles Dickens' *Oliver Twist* out of the library. I was intrigued by the title. I soon discovered that I had to look up about every other word, but I refused to give up. Reading that novel was perhaps one of the most painful tasks I've undertaken, but when I finished, I had considerably reduced my fear of new words and had certainly increased my vocabulary.

To increase your vocabulary, you should not only look up unfamiliar words but also use them in a sentence or in a conversation. A good desk dictionary is a must.

Wordiness can not only come from a weak vocabulary. It also can stem from certain habits in phrasing or a lack of editing, as the following edited example shows:

. . . The main value ~~that~~ a Rabbit Diesel ~~has to offer~~ *offers* is the incredible mileage. According to *Road and Track* ~~magazine, a reputable authority,~~ the Volkswagen, equipped with ~~an~~ optional five-speed transmission, ~~achieved~~ *averaged* ~~an overall~~ forty-three miles-per-gallon ~~mileage rating.~~ With a ~~recorded~~ high of sixty ~~m.p.g.~~ and a ~~recorded~~ low of forty ~~m.p.g., this Rabbit Diesel has excellent advantages.~~

One trade off, however, for superior mileage is ~~the lack of neck-breaking speed of~~ *slow* acceleration~~,~~ ~~The Volkswagen Diesel is slow. It has a 0-60 m.p.h. time of~~ *from 0 to 60 in* 22.9 seconds. This time can be ~~cut down~~ *assisted* considerably *by* with ~~the addition of~~ turbo-charging~~,~~ ~~It's~~ *and using* a process of rerouting the discharged exhaust ~~and using it~~ for combustion ~~purposes~~. However, ~~this process~~ *turbo-charging* is not yet available on the Rabbit~~Diesel~~. Aesthetically, the V.W. is ~~a~~ practical ~~means of transportation~~. *interior accommodates four adults.* The car's ~~exterior is styled for four adult-sized people. Consequently, the~~ *exterior* ~~shape of the body~~ is boxy, rather like a stagecoach.

In this edited selection, the use of linking verbs, prepositional phrases, the "it is" transformation, and redundant wording all contributes to the wordiness.

Eliminating Passive Voice.   Wordiness can also be caused by using passive instead of active voice. In the two sentences "John hit the ball" and "The ball was hit by John," the content is the same but the emphasis is different. The second sentence is in passive voice.

Passive voice is constructed with a form of the verb "to be" plus "by." Passive voice is grammatically correct, yet many experienced writers avoid it, primarily because it is uneconomical.

Let's examine the following excerpt for passives.

> This particular worry is not based on fact or reason but merely on psychological fear. As a matter of fact less than 1% of all accidents result in fire or submersion. Most people may find it hard to believe, but seat belts actually help you survive this type of accident. . . . Another big argument used against the wearing of seat belts is that if you are thrown from the car in an accident you are much safer than if you remain in the car. This is a false assumption. Although there are incidents where the victim might have lived if he had been thrown clear of the car, hundreds of people end up in a worse position and die. A study by Cornell showed that 12.8% of the occupants in accidents who were ejected through open doors of the car were killed, while only 2.6% of those who were wearing seat belts were killed. This proves that the risk of death is five times greater if a person is thrown from the car and that you are far better off in the car.

This passage regularly features passive constructions: is based, are thrown, were ejected, and were killed, as examples. Forms of the verb "to be" occur elsewhere in the passage as well: argument . . . is that, *are* much safer, this *is* a false. . . , there *are* incidents, that *were* wearing, death *is* five times, you *are* far better. . . . In fact, the writer has made "to be" the verb of choice over fifty percent of the time.

How could the excerpt above be revised?

> . . . The argument which contends seat belts trap a driver in cases of fire or submersion is misleading. Such cases represent less than 1% of all accidents. And in such cases, seat belts may actually help rather than hinder. . . . Furthermore, the argument which claims seat belts prevent a driver from being safely thrown from the wreckage ignores statistics too. 12.8% of ejected occupants die; only 2.6% of those remaining in the car die.

Granted, the above revision eliminates more than the passive voice. It eliminates many of the prepositional phrases, for example. Yet the revision shows the economy possible with active voice.

Passive voice, however, may be advantageously used where it preserves the established emphasis of a paragraph:

> The rat wriggled from behind the refrigerator and scratched across the linoleum toward the pantry. It slipped between the corner cupboard and the wash basket, the folded towels teetering slightly in the rat's wake. Sniffing nervously, the rat surveyed the five-foot gap between it and the pantry door. Twitching its ears, it eased up on its haunches to get a better look. Suddenly, the rat *was snagged by* the cat.

Consistent paragraph emphasis

At its simplest, having consistent paragraph emphasis involves maintaining one grammatical subject and one verb tense per paragraph. In the preceding paragraph, *rat* remains the actual or understood subject of every sentence and each verb is in simple past tense.

Consider, however, the following:

> ORIGINAL: The laboratory specimen was analyzed by the doctor. It was found to contain pre-cancerous cells. The patient was advised by the doctor to undergo other tests. These tests were to determine if the pre-cancerous cells here indicated the probability of the patient having cancer elsewhere in his body.
>
> REVISION: After finding pre-cancerous cells in the specimen, the doctor advised the patient to undergo other tests to determine the probability of existent cancerous growth.

The original version has three subject emphases: the lab specimen, the patient, the tests. The revision has one: the doctor.

The following example clearly shows the economy gained by having a single subject emphasis per paragraph.

ORIGINAL: The pitcher received the sign from the catcher. The catcher had signalled the pitcher to pitch a curve ball. The hitter, meanwhile, scratched at the dirt at home plate and hunched in the batter's box. The pitcher, for his part, glared at the hitter. The hitter also glared at the pitcher. The pitcher then lurched into his windup and launched the ball. The catcher waited for the pitch with open mitt.

REVISION: After receiving the catcher's sign for a "curve," the pitcher glared at the hitter who glared back, scratching at the dirt and hunching in the batter's box. The pitcher, then, lurched into his windup and launched the ball towards the catcher's open mitt.

The original version wastes words by moving from pitcher to catcher to hitter; the revision economizes by having only one emphasis, the pitcher.

▸ EXERCISE 2.14

To practice revising for emphasis, try reworking the following paragraph. After you have selected one particular emphasis and worked it through, try a second.

The man in the gray business suit approached the sidewalk shelter. He nodded to the woman who was already sitting there. She nodded back. He then tapped his umbrella on the sidewalk. She tapped her fingernails on her purse. It was almost as if they were playing a game. The man stuffed his hands in his pockets. The woman slipped her hands into her gloves. You wondered what they were going to do next. The man looked at his watch, and, you guessed it, the woman looked at the church clock. I almost began to laugh. The man blew his nose into his handkerchief. This blowing made a loud honking noise. The woman looked up quickly. We were all ready for her to take out a kleenex. Then the bus came. I guess they were both just impatient to catch the bus. ◢

In the next excerpt, the writer edits a paragraph for tense use, in this case a more consistent use of imperatives.

Skylab is falling*!* ~~and you can~~ watch all of the outerspace action

from your own backyard! Just grab a pair of binoculars and join in the

dying spacecraft,

fun of watching/glittering stars,and revolving planets. ~~You need not~~ *Don't think* *you have to be*

~~be a professional or~~ a scientist, although knowledge of astronomy

Remember,

would be helpful./As a beginner, the star "buff" has ~~many styles and~~

professional astronomer.

techniques in common with the/~~scientist.~~ ~~In contrast,~~ both the

"doctor"

~~scientist who has a college degree in astronomy~~ and the dilettante

~~who seeks astronomy only as a hobby~~ are "comparable" in terms of

three aspects.

The primary advantage the edited version will have is a more consistent use of imperatives (watch, grab, don't, remember). Another advantage is the parallel use of "couplets"; you, scientist; beginning star "buff," professional astronomer; doctor, dillettante.

The degree of conciseness demanded by the reader varies with the rhetorical context. In a narrative such as a mystery story, the reader may not want the writer to be very concise, at least in the story's telling. The reader may enjoy the suspense involved in the writer's not coming to the point immediately. In an expository piece such as a business letter, the reader expects the writer to be always *on point.* Conciseness in wording and phrasing then helps the writer meet this expectation.

▸ **EXERCISE 2.15**

For initial practice in meeting reader expectations concerning content and style, write a one to two page communication in response to one of the following composing situations:

1. As a preliminary to writing a full-fledged report for one of your classes, you have been asked to write a brief proposal in which you establish the topic of your report, state its purpose, provide initial background information on the subject, anticipate the report's scope, and predict its significance.

2. One month ago you were hired as a part-time sales clerk, and only now do you feel you are catching on to the various procedures

involved in your job. While the full-time employees are given a two-week orientation course before starting on the sales floor, the part-timers are expected to pick up what they're supposed to do from the full-timers. However, sometimes part-timers are paired with part-timers, or part-timers are paired with various full-timers who assume the "other full-timer filled you in." You guess an orientation course for part-timers would be economically impractical, and you also realize the difficulties in scheduling a large number of employees. However, you think the part-timer's situation could be alleviated by having a concise list of procedures printed up and placed at every cash register for reference.

Write a message to your supervisor setting forth your idea. Be sure to include why your idea is needed and what your proposed reference list would contain. You may use the memo format as shown in Figures 9.5 and 9.6 if you wish. ◢

PART II

INVENTING THROUGHOUT THE PROCESS

3

DISCOVERING, CHOOSING, AND CLARIFYING TOPICS

"I just can't seem to get started." Lesley paced the lounge area. "If only Mr. Bruce had let us choose our own topics. But . . . no. And now I don't know what I'm going to do!"

"You think you've got problems," Rich winced as he poured himself a fourth cup of coffee. "I don't even have a topic! Ms. Ruisi thinks we ought to be *free* to choose our own. Free to be entirely lost is what that means."

"Why don't both of you just start writing down possible ideas?" Carlton sighed. "At least you'd have something to show for your time."

As the above conversation suggests, whether a writer is assigned a topic or must generate one, getting started often poses a problem in itself. Carlton's way of handling the problem is interesting to me because it suggests, and correctly so, I think, that writing is in part a *physical* activity. In other words, the very act of actually putting something down on paper may be just what is needed to "prime the pump." Of course, getting started is only the beginning, although some writers would make it an end in itself.

You won't find a list of topics in this chapter. What you will find are questions that should help you to discover, choose, and clarify a topic. If you already have an assigned topic, you will find the section on topic clarification of most interest to you.

The questions in this chapter involve the three concerns of self, audience, and subject: "How can past experiences help me discover a topic?" "What do others know that might lead me to a topic?" and "What general subject areas might offer a topic?" are a few such questions.

DISCOVERING A TOPIC

The discovery of a topic takes place within a context. That context may be abstract, such as a writer's internal need to write; it may be concrete, such as a specific writing assignment. In any case, the composing context will include the elements of purpose (aim) and audience. Both purpose and audience can range from the general to the specific. For example, you may want to write something to persuade people very much like yourself that all is not right with the world. More specifically, you may want to write an exposé to persuade fellow students that your university suffers from mismanagement. The more specific your purpose and audience, the more decisive their influence on topic discovery. For instance, to persuade people very much like yourself that all is not right with the world, you could discover topics covering a wide range of subject options, from the Afghan refugees in Pakistan to the firing of a police chief in your home-town. But, to persuade college freshmen on your floor that your university suffers from mismanagement, you must be more limited in your potential subject range. Even within the narrower range, however, numerous topic options can be discovered. Mismanagement in the Registrar's Office, the incompetence of certain residence assistants, violations in the athletic recruiting program, misappropriation of financial aid could all be topics appropriate to your purpose. Each could be appropriate to your audience as well. For example, while college freshmen might not be interested in general mismanagement in the Registrar's Office, they may be concerned about specific mismanagement that results in their being unable to take a required course.

Important preliminary questions for discovering a topic are "What is the context involved?" and "Do I have a tentative purpose and an initial audience?"

It must be stressed that if your purpose and audience have not been assigned, you might find yourself adjusting your initial assessment of what each entails. Such adjustments are common in the writing process. But because purpose and audience influence topic discovery, it is a good idea to have at least a preliminary notion of what and who they will be.

Articulating Purpose

Chapter 2 establishes the importance of having a main idea. Having that idea involves having a purpose. Your purpose may be to inform, to explain, to persuade, or to interact with your audience in some other way. In setting up your own purpose, you can simply complete the sentence, "In this paper I want to _____." This sentence rarely appears in the actual finished paper. It does, nevertheless, give direction to your initial inquiries and to the various phases in the composing process. It also implicitly includes an audience. If your purpose is to inform, you are assuming someone needs to be informed; if to persuade, someone needs to be persuaded. Perhaps a sentence like "In this paper I want to persuade (action) someone (audience) of something (subject)" better reflects the concept of purpose.

Sizing Up Audience

As a writer, you may be assigned an audience or you may select one. In either case, the actual size of the audience is important.

Let's say that you have chosen one person, Amrish Mathur, as your audience. You have a clue to Amrish's interest from this excerpt of his writing.

> I read an extremely funny piece of political satire in the February 1980 issue of "National Lampoon" magazine. An advertisement about a fictitious motion picture was placed in the middle of the magazine. "Towering Inflation" was the name of the film that was misdirected by three administrations and starred Jimmy Carter, Gerald Ford, and Richard Nixon. The title theme for the movie was called "Whistling in the Dark" and composed by the Council on Wage and Price Stability. Co-starring in the film were such well-known people as Leonid Brezhnev, James Schlesinger, G. William Miller, and the Ayatollah Khomeini. I laughed so hard as I read the advertisement that I thought I would die.

From this single sample of his writing, could you discover a topic that might appeal to Amrish? Would you guess him to be interested in satire, economics, politics, and humor? Does the fact that he reads *National Lampoon* imply that he thinks it important to get nonstandard perspectives on current events?

As you may have already concluded, when you have an audience limited in size, you also have a limited range of possible topics. But trying to discover a topic that will reach a very large audience is also limiting in its own way.

Let's say that you have the broadest possible audience: everyone who can read English at the first-grade level or above. Could you discover a topic appropriate for an audience that ranges from that sticky-fingered six-year-old to the wizened Nobel Prize winning physicist?

Usually audiences, whether given or generated, represent a well-defined middle ground. As such, these audiences have world views and rhetorical expectations that are accessible to the writer.

▶ EXERCISE 3.1

Before we consider topic discovery, answer the following questions:

1. What is the context of my writing activity?
2. What is my tentative purpose?
3. Who is my initial audience? How will this audience limit my discovery of topics? ◢

Asking such questions can help you discover a topic and make you less dependent on inspiration. Inspiration is a wonderful thing, but you cannot always rely on it to meet deadlines. What happens if your deadline is March 1 and you become inspired May 2? After considering this question, you will probably find yourself ready for suggestions on how to encourage invention.

Inventing from Self

Free writing

Because you bring to the composing process a personal world view, you might begin your topic search by asking, "What do I have in my mind right now worth writing about?" And one way to tap your mind is through free writing.

Free writing means writing down whatever comes to mind for a given period of time, say five minutes, without stopping. The following example by Tim Votaw shows how such an exercise can lead to a topic idea. The printed portions indicate the original free writing, and the script notations show where the writer, a day later, went back to jot down some ideas generated by the writing.

Sitting here trying to write and not a thing comes to mind. Blank. Music not right, bad coffee, boring place, lonely heart. No outstanding ideas—no ideas at all. Free writing goes nowhere. Cold. Hot. Hunger.

Topic: What dreams I have?

Thirst. Dreams of love and marriage. Time to settle down. Bringing home the bacon or soy protein. How to

Topic: Commitment to work?

get closer to God, through prayer. Why don't I? Lazy? I want God but don't want the work. Too lazy to save my

Topic : Types of necessity ?

Topic : Ways we are conditioned ?

Topic : Inflation of wants and of prices ?

life. . . . Preoccupation with booze and sex and physical desires won't get me anywhere. Who needs them? A new car, new stereo. Clothes, bikes, candy, flowers, jewelry, junk, junk, junk. Who really needs all that junk? Nobody. We are conditioned to want, to desire, to need a bunch of stuff we don't need, at constantly increasing prices.

Tim Votaw

▸EXERCISE 3.2

Jot down topic ideas that *you* get from reading Tim's free writing. Now free write for three minutes. Then look for possible topics in your writing.◂

Free association

A similar method in searching for topic ideas within yourself involves selecting one word at random and then quickly listing other words that you associate with the initial word or with generated words. The final step involves listing possible topics that the words suggest. Student Linda Eagleton offers this example:

THE WORDS:	bed-pillow—feathers—chicken—G'pa's farm —holidays—Easter—The Messiah Concert —Bethany College—Debbie—high school— drill team—summer camp at K.U.
THE PROCESS:	I chose the word "bed" then moved on to pillow, feather, chicken, which should seem fairly clear. My Grandfather raised chickens on his farm. We used to spend almost all of our holidays there. The last holiday was Easter. We went to the Messiah Concert at Bethany College where my cousin Debbie goes to school. Debbie and I went to high school together. We were both officers of the drill team. One year the drill team officers went to summer camp at K.U.
POSSIBLE TOPICS:	elements of the rural lifestyle; benefits of extracurricular activities. . . .

This free association method suggests another question you can ask when using yourself as a source for topics: "What in my past experience is worth writing about?" There are many ways to tap your past experience, such as thumbing through photo albums, or day dreaming about "the day I met Lester Clooney," or reviewing a personal journal.

Keeping a journal

Keeping a journal, a habit many experienced writers develop, is not exactly the same as keeping a diary. Journal keeping involves recording your sensual perceptions of the world around you—what you see, hear, smell, taste, feel. Just as a diary, it may also include your emotional responses to that world, your explanations of it, and your beliefs concerning it. But a journal is more analytical, more objective. In it, you typically record the answers to such questions as "What did I see?" "What led to my reactions?" "How did the experience today compare to one last week?" "Why should my point of view of what happened be accepted?" Below are some sample journal entires.

1. Ever worked in a ladies' clothes store—guarded the dressing rooms with your life? Excuse me, may I try these on? Sure—how many—only three at a time—leave your package please. Oh Miss, could you tell me what you think of these jeans. Good luck, Lady, how did you get them zipped up! Think they're too tight— too tight—ha—is the pope Polish? Be a diplomat. Well . . . they might be if they shrink which they probably will—go up a size larger. I'll get it for you. . . . Excuse me, Miss, What do you think of this shirt—What! Have you no shame—put your bra on; it's a sheer blouse. Be a diplomat. Well, Ma'am—they are usually worn with a coordinated cowl neck underneath. Let me run get you one. . . . Pardon me Miss, does this go? Orange plaid western shirt and burgandy plaid knickers, blue knee socks—Oh, not the socks. Be still my burning eyes. I'll tell you what that shirt would really look good with—see this Levi vest and jean set? Oh my, what size did that lady in the tight pants need? What? 5:00. Quitting time. All right! Here's your jeans, lady. Bye! Boy do I have a headache.

   Lori Wilmers

2. Being involved in the investigation of numerous homicides over the past several years for the Police Department, you find yourself being able to rationalize the fate of a majority of the victims. Investigation, research, studies, and interviews with suspects and witnesses usually reveal that the victim was in some way re-sponsible for his own fate.

   By responsible, I mean playing hero or threatening the perpetrator. Yes, threatening the perpetrator with remarks like,

"The cops are going to get you," "I'm gonna tell," or "I'll see you go to jail for this!" Any of these actions or remarks can cause the person committing the crime to go into a homicidal frenzy and kill his victim or victims. It does not justify murder, but it is a contributing factor. So, as the investigative wheels in a homicide start rolling, you find yourself being the spoke in the wheel that second guesses the victim.

As a second guesser, you attain an attitude. Over a period of time you can put compassion in a closet before you go to work; and after your day's work is done you can come home and put it on like an old friendly sweater. You develop a coldness, become indifferent towards the victims of homicides, and maintain your sanity.

All this works fine, or you think it does, until you find a three-year-child that has been murdered. There is no rationale, no second guessing. What can a three-year-old possibly do to be a contributing factor? You find it difficult to maintain the coldness and indifference that has worked so many times before. You forget to put compassion in the closet that day and find yourself working with controlled anger and frustration.

Richard E. Fahy

3. With the decay of morality and social institutions, man has dug himself into a deep pit, because he has ignored religion and God. The loss of popular respect for religion is the dry rot of social institutions. The idea of God as the creator and Father of all mankind is to the moral world what gravitation is to the natural; it holds all together and causes them to revolve around a common center. Take this away, and men drop apart; there is no such thing as collective humanity, but only separate molecules, with no more cohesion than so many grains of sand.

Matt Asher

The preceding journal entries suggest numerous general topic areas: Lori's suggests "waiting on customers" or "diplomacy" or "frustration," Richard's suggests "coping as a police officer" or "victim psychology" or "frustration," Matt's suggests "the decay of morality" or "the decay of social institutions." Thus, asking "What does my journal contain?" is one method of discovering topics.

☞ EXERCISE 3.3

As an investment in future topics, keep a journal for two weeks. Then note down the possible topics suggested by the entries. (A 6" × 8" spiral

notebook makes a convenient, portable journal.) You might find keeping
a journal a habit worth developing. ◢

Inventing from Others

Talking to others

Just as you have your own world view, so do others. And a natural way to
tap others' experiences in your search for a topic is to converse with them.
The following dialogue, for example, suggests several possible topics.

ELAINE: Say, by the way, are you going to help with the anti-Nuke
            posters tonight?

JOE: I suppose . . . if I have time.

ELAINE: I don't get it. Last week you were more than willing to *make
            time* to help with the human rights issue. What's the deal?

JOE: Well, I guess, I haven't made up my mind about nuclear
            power yet. The waste disposal, that's a problem for sure, but
            so is OPEC. Air pollution, too.

ELAINE: Next thing you'll be doing is siding with Mark, saying that
            Americans deserve to run out of power, period.

JOE: Could be. At any rate, part of it might be I'm tired of being
            anti. Anti-consumerism. Anti-interventionist. Anti-nuclear
            power. I could go for a change of pace.

ELAINE: (smiling): How about being pro-E.R.A.?

In addition to bringing up big issues such as nuclear power as possible topic
areas, this conversation also suggests less defined areas that might eventually provide topic ideas: protesting, being negative, being yourself.

Brainstorming

Brainstorming, the unrestrained suggesting of ideas by members of a group,
can also generate topics. Consider the question-answer brainstorming session below:

Question	Answer
What are some ideas we could discuss?	Politics, sports, history.
With history, what time period?	Contemporary.
History of what?	Cultural trends.
What trends, for example?	Racial equality, T.M., fashions.

| T.M.? | Transcendental meditation. |
| How is that a cultural trend? | Well, things that promote getting in touch with yourself seem pretty popular. It's a place to start from: T.M., a cultural trend. |

▶EXERCISE 3.4

For practice, try the following activities to aid topic discovery:

1. Converse and listen. Later jot down the topic ideas you see in your everyday conversation.
2. With a group, brainstorm to generate a topic. Or free associate with such a group to discover topic ideas. Record these ideas for later reference.◀

Inventing from Subject Areas

Questioning experiences and beliefs

In addition to asking "What do I know?" and "What do others know?" in your search for a topic, you can also ask: "What subject areas offer possible topic ideas?" *Personal experience* has already been mentioned as a possible source for ideas. Some other general areas are suggested in the questions: "Do I have, or do others have, a *personal prejudice* worth evaluating?" "What about commonly held *beliefs*? Is there any such belief worth examining?" Likewise, "What about *public figures*? Do any bear examination?" These general questions often lead to more specific questions. Following are a few student-suggested questions from common topic areas:

1. What in my military experiences can I write about? (Area: operating from personal experience)
2. Why do I always get angry when I read Art Buchwald's column in the paper? OR Why don't I trust people who won't look me in the eye? (Area: examining personal prejudice)
3. How does Jimmy Carter compare with John Kennedy? OR How can I assess the achievement of Alfred Hitchcock? (Area: dealing with public figures)

4. Is it true that "the toys are old but the children are new?" (Area: examining commonly held beliefs)

5. As a lobbyist in Washington, what would I say to convince others of the importance of farm parity? (Area: adopting a persona or "voice")

The last question introduces another area for possible topics: hypothetical situations. Consider, for example, the following questions:

1. How would I spend my extra time if I didn't have to sleep?
2. What if there were such a thing as "time travel"?
3. What if modern medicine eliminated death?
4. What if I could read other people's minds?
5. What if two figures from two different periods in my discipline had a dialogue?

▶EXERCISE 3.5

Compose specific questions dealing with the following topic areas. Do any of your questions suggest a topic worthy of your attention as a writer? If so, jot it down.

1. List one question that you could ask yourself regarding either *personal* experience or *personal* prejudices.

2. List one question that you could ask yourself regarding either *public* figures or *public* beliefs.

3. List one question that you could ask yourself involving a *hypothetical* situation. ◢

Subject-splitting

Another way of inventing from subjects involves subject-splitting, which is particularly valuable to a writer already committed to a particular area. For example, take the general subject area of consumer protection.

Such a subject area can be split according to past concerns, present issues, and future implications. "Why did consumer protection become necessary?" addresses the subject historically. This question can be answered by brainstorming in the following manner:

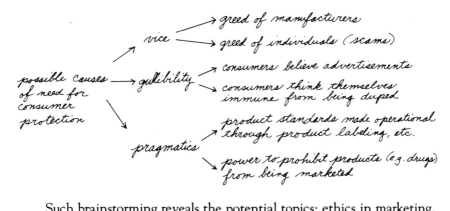

Such brainstorming reveals the potential topics: ethics in marketing, common scams (it *can* happen to you), blackballing potentially beneficial drugs, among others.

Considering present issues, the question "Where has consumer protection been in the news recently?" may prompt the following response:

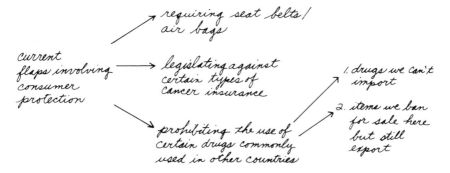

In the "current flaps" example, one subject division suggests two particularly fruitful topics (drugs we can't import; banned items we export).

Future implications of consumer protection may be represented as follows:

products liability—"Will consumer legislation define the parameters for damage claims?" "What do current trends indicate?"

future importance of consumer protection

constitutionality—"Will consumer protection rob us of certain individual rights through government interference?"

future invention—"What types of things will consumers need protection from? Will this protection extend to institutional products, such as military nerve gas?"

Subjects can be split according to various classifications. Past, present, and future is only one. Problem/solution would be another. Promised performance and actual performance could be a third. Such classifications lead to further divisions which eventually suggest a variety of possible topics.

➤ EXERCISE 3.6

Practice subject-splitting on several of the following topics:

1. Labor unrest
2. Conservatism
3. T.V. programming

4. Psychological hangups
5. Medical advances
6. Architectural design ◢

Inventing from Reading

An abundant source for topic ideas is reading. Reading, whether in books, magazines, or newspapers, allows you to see how other writers have answered the questions, "What shall I write about?" and "What is worth sharing with my readers?"

The following short story written by student Larry Cowger, and the exercise following it, will suggest how reading can generate topic ideas.

EIGHTEEN

Old news blew across the floor from the far end of the hut where the door stood held open by a tarnished one-five-five canister. The wind did little to cool the tin shed and the thick heat reminded him of the inside of his car, locked up in the parking lot of the Vo-Tech school on an August afternoon. He lay motionless on the bunk and the thought of the car stirred in him a hint of anger which pleased him. His emotion seemed lost and strange so long had it been since he had last felt anything. But thinking of that car, he wanted to strike out. Thoughts crowded into his head. A tear slid off his face into his ear. He was home again.

He was cruising the access road, the motor sounding a deep-throated bass as the speakers in the doors belted out the guitar licks he knew note for note. He tapped out the rhythm on the car top with his hand and looked at himself in the rearview mirror with a satisfied smile. This was his world, the car, and he had built it all from scratch. As he admired the sun gleaming off the hood, off the eight coats of hand rubbed lacquer he had labored over with such care, he smiled again. This was a gem, a real gem, and the run-down neighborhood his Dad called home made it sparkle and shine all the more. This was his ticket out. Three more weeks and he would get in that car and drive away from that burg, eighteen and free. He would be in California and be a marine and be away from that stupid bastard of a father. His father didn't own a car and had fought him every step of the way when he bought the heap of a '57 Chevy which he had turned into something clean. Clean and mean. He chuckled to himself.

The old man was a slob. He was tired of cleaning up after his ass. Beer cans and crushed out Pall Mall reds constantly littered the living room where the T.V. and yet another beer were his father's ever-present companions. Ever since Mom passed away, it had just gone to hell and he was getting out. He didn't drink or smoke or stink like the old man. He didn't have a beer gut or sleep until noon either. Jesus, he was sick of that useless son-of-a-bitch. He'd made life unbearable for Mom, and now that she was gone, he'd tried to do the same for him. Mom always said it was Korea that made him the way he was, but he never bought any of that shit. That was just Mom making excuses for him. None of that seemed to matter now, because he was getting out and the old man could piss up a rope as far as he was concerned.

Those weeks had passed like days. He had spent every one of them getting ready for the big move. Recruits weren't supposed to have cars, but he had plans to keep his in a garage somewhere in San Diego until boot camp was over. Then he could spend his two weeks of leave driving to his next duty station. Duty, now that was something he understood. He had promised Mom that he would finish High School and he had. He'd worked weeknights and long days during the summers pumping gas and waiting. He had promised to stay with the old man until after graduation and he had done that too. When the old bastard had refused to sign for him to join the service, he didn't ask again. He had just waited. Now the waiting was over and the car was packed and filled up. His clothes, few but clean, were neatly packed in his Mother's worn traveling bag along with her picture. He had his tools, his car, and he was ready to put some miles between himself and that place.

That Saturday morning was all coming back to him now, how he had leaped from his bed and flown down the stairs, his feet scarcely touching a one. He had been awakened by the sound of his car's motor. That sound he knew so well sounded strangely muffled. When he threw open the garage doors, he stood frozen, unable to believe what he was seeing. Oh, it was a neat job alright. The chrome ends of the dual exhausts were bound tightly with silver-gray duct tape (not the cheap plastic stuff but the good heat resistant kind). These were fastened securely to two pieces of brand-new rubber hose which ran the length of the car and disappeared into the fogged windows on either side. Both windows had been sealed neatly with the same silver-grey tape. Through the back window he could see his father slumped behind the wheel. A half pint lay on the dash.

His thoughts of that long bus ride to San Diego were interrupted by the piercing scream of the siren and shouts of "In Coming" from outside the hut. As he heard the first rockets explode and the sound of men scurrying like rats into the bunkers, he slowly lifted himself from the pillow. Reaching under the mattress for the ammo pouch which contained his burnt spoon and the well-worn needle, he had a thought which made him smile. Lumbering towards the back of the hut to the head where he could get some water, he shook his head. As he sat on the hard lid of the toilet with his belt biting into his arm, he thought for the first time in his life, he didn't really mind that his name was Gary Jr.

Larry Cowger

► EXERCISE 3.7

Answer the following questions about Larry's story.

1. Where do you think Larry got the idea for his story? Personal experience? Another's experience? Did he get his idea from the subject of father-son relationships or of what war can do? From reading? From a combination of various sources?

2. What is the main idea Larry wants to share with us in his story? Have you ever read a story with the same idea? Have you ever heard or thought of a similar idea yourself?

3. Turn to Michael Harris' "Five Tableaux of My Father." (See pages 226–30.). Are there any similarities between the Harris account and the Cowger story? If so, what are they? What about differences?

4. List two possible topics that the comparison between the Harris and Cowger pieces suggests to you.

5. List any other topics you may have discovered by reading either piece separately. ◢

Inventing from premises

The previous exercise postulates that comparing one idea with another can lead to still other ideas. Exploring the relationships between two distinct premises can be viewed as *idea-sparring*. During the examination, the premises act very much like boxers, sparring before a match, demonstrating their skills before you. The title bout begins when you, as the contender, enter the ring. In fact, examining the relationships between two distinct ideas often does suggest further ideas or premises. The ideas may be related by comparison; that is, they may involve similarities or differences in kind or degree. Or the ideas may be related by cause and effect or contradiction, for example.

Consider the following premises by writers Caroline Seebohm and Linda Flower:

1. Lateral thinking (sidestepping a problem) often proves better than vertical thinking (grappling with the problem head on) in solving problems.[1]
2. Problem analysis involves six steps: defining the conflict, placing the problem in a larger context, making the definition operational, exploring the parts of the problem, generating alternative solutions, coming to a well-supported conclusion.[2]

In examining the relationships between these premises, you may conclude:

1. They are similar in that they deal with problem solving.
2. They are different in that one explicitly recommends lateral thinking while the other implicitly recommends a type of vertical thinking—approaching the problem analytically, step by step. In other words, they differ in the kind of approach they suggest and in the degree to which the approach is explicitly recommended.
3. There are no causal relationships between the statements themselves, although both statements seem to arise from the same thing: the difficulties problem solving presents. Each tries to offer a better way of solving problems.
4. Initially the statements seem at odds. But a closer look shows that Seebohm probably isn't contradicting Flower. Seebohm could be saying, if the vertical approach doesn't work, try the lateral approach.

After examining these relationships, you may find yourself asking certain questions:

1. Both authors are talking about problem solving, but are they talking about solving the same types of problems?
2. The authors recommend different methods. Are these methods equally appropriate to any given situation? Are there more than these two methods available?

3. Each author addresses the "problem" of problem solving. What makes problem solving so difficult?

4. Flower recommends one approach, Seebohm another. What if neither works? Are there problems that defy solution? Such questions, in turn, might suggest a few topics:

    a. Types of problems. (For example, will a scientist's search for a cancer cure and a coach's search for a game-winning play involve different types of problems?)

    b. Ways of solving problems. (Are there different ways to solve the same problem? Is one way preferable to another in any given context?)

    c. Roadblocks to problem solving.

    d. Insoluble problems.

☞ EXERCISE 3.8

Examine the following premises. What relationships exist between the two? What ideas or topic areas do these suggest?

1. Playing sports is a good way for young people to learn the teamwork necessary in life.

2. Football is a form of ritualized aggression in which fans vicariously participate. ◢

Idea synthesizing

In *idea-sparring*, the premises remain intact. In *idea-synthesizing*, on the other hand, one idea or thesis meets another idea or antithesis, and results in a combination-idea or synthesis. Consider the following premises:

1. Verbal taboos exist only because of middle-class sexual hangups.

2. The function of obscenity in language is to denigrate women.

Both premises deal with language, specifically with language that is prohibited by convention or considered obscene. Both acknowledge that such language exists in a social context.

The first premise regards such language as basically neutral; that is, this premise contends that obscenity is "in the ear of the hearer" and that those hearers are somehow at fault for any negative effects the language may have. The statement focuses on the listener and not the speaker.

The second premise focuses more on the speaker. It assumes that obscenity has a function; that is, it assumes that the speaker uses obscenity for a purpose. And that purpose, according to premise two, is to attack the status of women.

It may be true that part of the reason obscenity has the power to denigrate women is that listeners impose their sexual hangups on the language being used. If so, a possible causal relationship exists between the two statements.

In any case, at this point our discussion has not yet gone beyond idea-sparring. Continuing on to idea-synthesizing involves accounting for both premises with a new or "larger" premise. What idea, then, could incorporate both statements?

FIRST CONSIDER: Much of the potential power of obscenity rests in its sexual base.

Such a premise focuses on neither listener nor speaker, but identifies the central element of sexual bias in either case. It therefore covers both bases.

CONSIDER ALSO: The effect of obscenity depends on the speaker and listener sharing the same language taboos.

Here the premise transcends the issues of speaker-intent and listener-interpretation by showing that each depends on the same thing: shared social convention.

Forming a new premise through idea-combining requires thinking and practice. It involves finding an emphasis that will account for the message in each premise.

▸EXERCISE 3.9

Examine the following premises and devise a new premise that synthesizes the two.

1. People start thinking in black-and-white terms during times of social crisis and tend to see but two alternatives in any given situation.
2. All of us have an inborn sense of how we should and should not behave. ◢

Idea-shooting

Another method of inventing from premises is *idea-shooting*. Idea-shooting can begin with a single premise. Take, for example, Herbert Spenser's idea that:

> The consciousness of being perfectly dressed may bestow a peace such as religion cannot give.

The next step is to question the premise. One method of questioning could involve the relationships important to idea-sparring:

1. How does this statement *compare* to a statement such as "Clothes make the man?"
2. How does the peace of perfect apparel *compare* to religious peace?
3. What *causes* dressing perfectly to attain such value?
4. What *causes* religious peace to fail us in certain situations?

Another method of questioning the premise could involve the journalistic elements of who, what, where, when, how, and why.

1. *Who* needs to be perfectly dressed?
2. *What* is perfect dress?
3. *Where* is perfect dress important? Assuring? *Where* is it unimportant?
4. *When* does being perfectly dressed give more security than can religion?
5. *How* does one achieve perfection in dress? *How* does one know what perfect apparel is?
6. *Why* does being perfectly dressed acquire so much importance?

Such questioning shoots you into various topic areas that are related to but not identical to that of the original premise.

▸EXERCISE 3.10

For practice, examine and then question the following premise: The women's liberation movement cannot succeed if it is anti-male. What topics does your questioning suggest?◂

The premises initiating such invention can come from your own set of assumptions, from the beliefs of acquaintances, from your reading, from movies or television, or from a myriad of other sources. In the words of science-fiction writer Ray Bradbury: "Ideas lie everywhere, like apples fallen and melting in the grass for lack of wayfaring strangers with an eye and a tongue for beauty whether absurd, horrific, or genteel."

The Process Sheet on page 76 reviews the questions helpful in discovering topics. Can you think of any further questions to add to the sheet?

► EXERCISE 3.11

Use the Process Sheet on page 76 to help you generate possible paper topics for the following assignments:

1.   Your context is a freshman writing class. You may choose from one of the following *tentative* purposes: to entertain, to explain, or to persuade. You may change your purpose if necessary during the composing process. Your audience consists of members of your peer group. You may identify your *peers* as fellow classmates, as co-workers, or as those with similar political or religious beliefs, or as those in the same socioeconomic class. You may change your peer group identificiation if necessary during the composing process.

   You may include in your list of "possibles" any of those topics which are appropriate that you have already discovered in the course of doing the exercises in this chapter.

2.   Your context is a summer job. Your purpose is to improve the morale of your fellow employees through some sort of project. Your audience is your boss and possibly sponsors for your project. Your project to improve morale may be extracurricular in nature (like organizing a picnic or forming a team). A "special expectation" is that your proposal be submitted as a single-spaced, one-page memo. (See Exercises 9.5 and 9.6 for memo form.)

   You may specify the place of employment and the cause for low morale as you wish. ◄

CHOOSING A TOPIC

Have you ever entered a store and, because you liked either everything you saw or nothing, you left empty-handed? To a certain extent, you are in that position when you have discovered several topic ideas and must choose from among them. You may like all or none and remain without

DISCOVERING A TOPIC

What is the context for my topic search? What is my tentative purpose? Who is my initial audience?

What do I have in my head right now worth writing about? Does free writing offer any clues? Free association? The journal?

What information do others have in their heads worth writing about? Will conversation tap others' ideas? Group discussion? Question-answer session?

What subject areas offer possible ideas? Personal experience? Prejudices? Commonly held beliefs? Public figures?

What hypothetical situations suggest topics that are worthy of my attention as a writer?

What topics does subject-splitting suggest?

What topic ideas can I find in my reading?

What topics emerge from idea-sparring? Idea-synthesizing? Idea-shooting?

Does my list of tentative topics complement my initial purpose and audience?

PROCESS SHEET

76

a topic to write on. This section suggests questions to help you out of this stalemate.

Choosing for Self

A basic place to start is to choose a topic that interests you or is important to you personally. "What interests me?" and "What determines that interest?" are questions with broad philosophical and psychological implications. But let's discuss a few limited answers to them in terms of composition.

For example, Matt in his journal entry (See page 63.) talks about social decay. He evidently has thought and read about this topic because he is ready to offer a possible solution to the problem: accepting God as a cohesive force. That a blend of social and moral concerns is of general interest to Matt is demonstrated in another of his entries:

> Most of us need to improve on it, and some of us in our hurried lives have none at all. Technology has caused a lack of it and our helter-skelter life styles have seen it fade away. I am speaking of patience. There is no such thing as preaching patience into people unless the sermon is so long that *patience* is required to listen to it. No man can learn patience by going into the hurly-burly world and taking life just as it blows. Patience is riding out the gale. If man would slow down a bit to smell the roses, he may be able to enjoy himself and his world and the people in it to a greater extent.
>
> *Matt Asher*

Given a choice, then, Matt would probably write on a topic that reflected his intellectual interest in social or moral issues.

Some topics may hold more importance than interest for us. For example, both Lori Wilmers and Richard Fahy write about frustration in their journals. (See pages 62–63.) While neither is probably interested in being frustrated, the topic becomes important because they must face frustration every day as part of their jobs.

In the following case, the student chooses a topic because of a physical problem he must live with every day:

> It altered the destiny of an empire; Rome was its victim. . . . It is present in all social and economic levels; the White House and the flophouse have witnessed its destruction. The problem is easy to name, the abuse of ethyl alcohol, but the solution is complex. . . .

As you may have guessed, the student has chosen to write about alcoholism. The student is an alcoholic. The topic may be painful for him, but he has chosen it because of its importance. "What is important to me?" may be a separate question you can ask yourself in determining your choice of topic.

➤EXERCISE 3.12

Examine some of the assumptions that inform your world view. What do these assumptions suggest about your interests? About what you consider important?◢

Choosing for Audience

Choosing a topic involves asking, "What subjects will interest or be important to my audience?" Another question worth asking is, "How broad, or how narrow, is my audience?" An audience can be broad or narrow in several respects, including the actual number of members, and the range of what is of interest or importance to them. The answers to the preceding questions depend, of course, on who your audience is.

Let's say that you have as your audience your class members. Most in this group might have an interest in certain "common" topics such as sports or leisure activities in general, media offerings in film or on T.V., popular music, or fads and fashions. Similarly, most might find importance in such common areas as interpersonal relationships, racial issues, personal development, careers, politics, drugs, and so on. These common topic areas represent fields where battles are often fought. But there are also less frequented fields, and these can involve "specialized" topics ranging from stock-market portfolios to day care center licenses, from brainwashing to money laundering, from house construction to hairline recession, from bumper stickers to pornography.

It is not always the topic itself that generates interest or importance. It is the possibilities for *identification* which the topic offers.

Audience identification

What is *identification*? An example of a type of identification can be seen in this excerpt written by student Paul Engler:

> I am a soldier in the United States Army fighting a war for freedom. The smell of death is upon me as I dive into a nearby foxhole for protection from flying shrapnel. Dressed in battle garb, soiled and stained with dirt, I gaze across the battlefield. Up on the hill, there is an enemy position. I yell back at my squad to charge up the hill as I jump out of my foxhole. "Kill! Kill! Kill!"
>
> In the distance, I faintly hear a voice calling my name. My best buddy says, "Sarge, it's your Mom. You have to go home and eat now."
>
> . . . It is difficult to understand children unless we recall our own childhood filled with fantasy.

Paul has recreated the child's perspective by using a description imitating his own childhood experiences.

Like Paul, you are separate from your audience when you write. However, you share with it the same physical world and many of the same types of experiences. It is a combination of this separateness and this sharing that enables *identification* between you and your audience. When, for example, you as the audience first read Paul's excerpt, were you reminded of your childhood fantasies? If so, you *identified* with the passage, with what Paul had to say. And your childhood fantasies need not have been identical to Paul's to trigger that identification.

Another type of identification occurs through idea-synthesizing. (See pages 72–73.) For example, let's say that you begin with the idea that "Growing your own fruits and vegetables can save you lots of money." Let's say, in turn, that a friend believes "If you add up all the costs of gardening—seeds, tools, water, fertilizer, pesticides (if you use them), and time—you'd see that you'd be better off buying your produce at the grocery store."

In discussing the merits of each statement, you and your friend decide to conduct an informal cost analysis. This analysis shows gardening to be less cost effective than you thought, but less expensive than your friend thought.

An examination of the two ideas, coupled with the cost analysis, prompts you to form the premise (synthesis): "The rewards of gardening are not necessarily measured in dollars and cents." *You* can identify with the premise because it contains the idea that gardening is rewarding. *Your friend* can identify with the premise because it allows for the idea that gardening has hidden costs. You both can identify with the premise because it represents a more complete and therefore more enlightened view of growing your own produce.

Not every form of writing requires identification. It merely represents a factor to consider when choosing a topic with an audience in mind.

Choosing for Purpose

When a purpose is strictly conceived or assigned, it can be used as a screening device in choosing possible topics. For instance, if your purpose is "to examine the decimation of wildlife species from an ecologist's perspective," your topic choice is restricted. It is restricted to wildlife species, and only to those species that are, in fact, being decimated. Starlings wouldn't do for your purpose; whales would.

When a purpose is fundamentally abstract, it acts as a different type of screen for possible topics. Just as a certain camera lens filter produces an effect separate from that of any other filter used for a given photo, so too a set purpose produces a perspective different from that of any other on a possible topic. For instance, let's take the possible topic: "Father-son relationships in the son's teenage years." If your purpose were to explain, you might explain the different roles expected of the father by the son during adolescence. If your purpose were to argue, you might argue for a liberalization of child custody laws in view of the father-son relationship during this time. If your purpose were to show how someone can discover something about himself, you might write a short story such as Larry Cowger's. (See pages 68–70.)

Choosing for Specialized Expectations

Occasionally, topic choice involves specialized expectations that override—at least initially—considerations of self, audience, and purpose. Take, for example, the assignment: "Write a comparison/contrast." Here the question "Which of my potential topics best lends itself to comparison/contrast?" becomes a factor in selecting a topic. Similarly, a requirement that the paper be three to five pages in length makes "Which of my potential topics can be best covered in the assigned length?" a question influencing topic choice.

In any case, "Are there any specialized expectations that I should consider when choosing my topic?" seems a prudent question to ask.

The Process Sheet on page 81 reviews questions you can ask yourself when choosing a topic. Can you think of any questions that should be added to the sheet?

▸ EXERCISE 3.13

In Exercise 3.11 you were asked to generate a list of possible topics for a freshman writing class. Use the Process Sheet on page 81 to select one of those topics to write on. ◢

CLARIFYING A TOPIC

After you have searched for and chosen a topic, you are ready to clarify it. The advantages of topic clarification are like those of planning a family vacation. Through planning, the family can determine a destination, make the necessary reservations, and consider the preferences of individual family members. Similarly, through topic clarification, you the writer can

CHOOSING A TOPIC

TOPIC POSSIBILITIES I HAVE GENERATED:

AUDIENCE:

PURPOSE:

What interests me in general? What do I think about? Get excited about? What am I involved in? How do the topics listed above rank in terms of my interests?

What is generally important to me? What concerns me physically, emotionally, intellectually? How do the topics above rank in terms of what I think is important?

How broad or narrow is my audience? What common and/or specialized topics would this audience find of interest or importance? What topics could offer identification to this audience? How do the above topics rank in terms of my audience?

What is my purpose? Does it eliminate any of the above topics? Does it suggest how to view any or all of the above topics? Which topic best complements my purpose?

Which topic receives the highest ranking overall in terms of self, audience, and purpose? Does this topic fulfill any "specialized expectations" involved?

decide the main focus of the topic, reserve the factors to be discussed within that focus, and consider the audience. Trip planning and topic clarifying can also help generate the enthusiasm and commitment needed to complete the "journey."

Factors Within the Topic

Asking questions about the topic, or subject, aids in topic clarification: "What is the primary question my topic raises?" "What are the secondary questions?" "What are the questions my topic does not raise?"

The primary question

First, what is a primary question? In its most basic sense, a primary question is the writer's *topic* and **purpose** stated together as a question. For example, if my topic is *35mm cameras* and my purpose is **to show how these cameras work,** then my primary question is "**How** do *35mm cameras* **work?**"

Secondary questions

Secondary questions include those questions raised by the primary question or by the answer to the primary question. If the primary question is "How does a 35mm camera work?", then "How does its lens work?" and "How does the film work?" become secondary questions. There is no limit to the number of secondary questions that might be asked.

Asking secondary questions both clarifies the possibilities of the topic and opens the door to new topics. For instance, let's say that among your secondary questions is "How does the camera lens bend light?" and this question, in turn, leads you to ask, "How does light bend?" You might, at this point, find "How does light bend?" a more interesting topic than "How does a camera work?" And if you are not in a restricted situation with a prescribed purpose, audience, and topic, you should feel free to explore an intriguing secondary topic.

"Non-questions"

"What questions is my topic *not* asking?" is also a question of topic clarification. At first, this question might seem to be a poor joke (like having to look up the spelling of a word without knowing the first four letters), yet finding out what is not asked does play a role here.

Let's call those questions that seem to relate to the primary question but, in reality, do not, "non-questions." For instance, "How much does a 35 mm camera cost?" might seem to relate to the question "How does a 35mm camera work?", because both questions deal with 35mm cameras. But because how much a camera costs probably has little or nothing to do with how a camera actually works, "How much does a camera cost?" is an inappropriate query, a non-question.

Non-questions, like secondary questions, may trigger a topic idea that suggests a change in topic choice. Non-questions also show a writer where an individual topic will not go. Non-questions set boundaries.

Effect of Audience

"How will my audience affect my topic?" is a question of topic clarification. Answering this question will show you the narrowest and broadest range your topic can cover. In other words, it will show you how exclusive and inclusive you can be with your topic. For example, in writing about "How 35mm cameras work," you could range from a narrow subject range, the highly technical, to a broad range, the "aim and shoot" approach. Your choice of how technical or practical to be depends on how technical or practical your audience is.

Concerns of Length and Format

"How much space will I need to cover this topic?" is also a question of topic clarification. And "how much space do I have to cover this topic?" is the question to ask here in case of an assigned length. The reason behind asking questions of length is a practical one. Let's say that you have chosen as your topic: "The differences between high school sports and college sports." Even if you do not go into extensive detail about all the differences between all the sports played at both the high school and college level, you still have a topic that requires quite a bit of space to develop. At this point, therefore, even before you start thinking about all the differences you could consider, it might be wise to reconsider your topic.

One way to reconsider your topic without changing it altogether is to look at the secondary questions. Perhaps one of these questions will yield an alternate topic that will still serve your purpose and fit your audience. If one of your secondary questions is, "How does a typical high school basketball game differ from a typical college basketball game?", then you have an alternate topic that you can start clarifying for primary and secondary questions.

Gauging the approximate length of a paper before you start writing takes experience. But it is an important element of topic clarification.

The Process Sheet on page 84 shows how a group helped clarify the topic: "Styles in Long Distance Running." The writer's audience is fellow college freshmen in the composition class, and the writer's purpose is to explain.

TOPIC CLARIFICATION

TOPIC: *styles in Long Distance Running*   AUDIENCE: *Peer group: college classmates*

PURPOSE: *To explain what the styles in long distance running are.*

What is the primary question this topic raises? *From the way the purpose is stated,*
we get two:
1. What are the different styles in l.d. running?
2. What makes a "style" in l.d. running? (Maybe)

What are the main secondary questions?
1. Is there any style that works best?
2. Who are the famous l.d. runners and what are their styles?
3. Historically, has there been any change in styles?

What are some issues the topic does not address?

1. Records in l.d. running.
2. Training for l.d. running.
3. Why the U.S. should support the Olympics.

Is there a secondary or non-question that deserves consideration as the primary topic?

The historical aspect might be a good topic.

How will the audience affect the topic? (How broad or inclusive and how narrow or exclusive can the writer be?)

Everyone in the group of students expressed some interest in sports
and would like to see some pretty specific physical descriptions.
Also, were you going to say anything about mental preparation?
Is that part of a style?

How long will the paper on this topic be?

Just guessing, you probably will have about 5 typed pages here if you
have, say, three main styles with examples.

Is there any designated format?

Type. Double-space.

Suggestions:

We think you could make your purpose a bit
clearer. Also, we think that if you picked two famous
l.d. runners and described their styles, it would be more
interesting than just describing the styles themselves. How
about putting them in the Boston Marathon together,
for example? Could you use Frank Shorter and Bill
Rodgers here? (Sandy thinks she knows someone going to the
Minneapolis Marathon next month.)

84

Topic clarification can reveal to you the possibilities of your topic and the options it will not allow, the general range of your topic, and its direction and feasibility.

Before you tackle the clarification of your own topic, let's examine how topic clarification can work, even in a highly structured and stressful situation such as an essay test.

Interlude: the Structured Context

Topic clarification is important even in the highly structured context of an essay exam question. Such questions have a given topic, a built-in audience (usually the instructor), and a ready-made purpose indicated by such words as "define," "explain," "trace," and "evaluate." The essay test also assumes that you are familiar with the subject matter through lectures, notes, reading, and the like. Considering all this, why not just plunge in and start writing? You would seem to have everything you need. Yet, let's take the following test question as a case in point.

> Using comparison/contrast, discuss the role of setting in the films *The Wizard of Oz* (1939) and *The Wiz* (1978). Write legibly. 25 points.

You have the audience: the instructor; the direction: discussion of similarities and differences; and the topic. Now let's assume that you immediately begin writing without further clarification:

> *The Wizard of Oz* and *The Wiz* were produced approximately forty years apart. And, as the saying goes, "you've come a long way, baby." Since 1939, there have been all kinds of advances in movie making. As critic Daniel Klugherz recognized, the early sixties saw a real breakthrough in the documentary film, for example. *Mills of the Gods*, a prize-winning documentary of the Vietnam war produced in 1965, used such artistic devices as montage and mood music in subtly criticizing American foreign policy. This documentary was produced by a woman, Beryl Fox, which proves that women filmmakers can successfully deal with traditionally male subjects. The female characters in the *Wizard* and the *Wiz* have come a long way too. The first Dorothy was a young Kansas farm girl; the second is a Black New York City school teacher. Despite this rather dramatic change in character, however, the two women share the same naive nature. Dorothy in the *Wizard* had reasons for being naive. Significantly, she was pictured as a pig-tailed school girl whose main concern was protecting her dog Toto from a wicked bicycle-riding school marm. But the second Dorothy *is* a school teacher, and one wonders how such a naive person could be trusted with educating even elementary children.
>
> The *Wizard's* Dorothy began her adventure after a tornado whisked her off to the land of Oz. The *Wiz's* Dorothy begins hers as

she runs out after her dog in a snow storm after her aunt has urged her to try high school teaching and to find a husband. The tornado was appropriate to the Kansas setting as the snow storm is to the New York setting.

Now while the preceding essay does demonstrate some knowledge of movies, especially documentaries, and some awareness of the *Wizard* and the *Wiz,* especially its characters, *it does not really answer the test question;* it does not compare and contrast the role of setting in the movies *Wizard* and *Wiz.* You will avoid such misreadings if you take the time to clarify the given topic thoroughly before you start writing.

What, then, are the questions the test question is raising? In the *Wizard* —*Wiz* sample, the primary question includes two concerns: How is the role of the settings of the two films similar as a whole? and How is the role different? Additional or secondary questions may include: How are the roles promoted by certain details in the settings? Do the similar details have any common aspect, such as the use of special effects? Do the contrasting details have any common aspect, such as the relationship to "real" places? What is the significance of the similarities and differences? What is your opinion of each? Does the year in which each movie was made affect the choice of setting? Does it affect the role each setting plays?

Questions not asked include: How do the main characters of each work compare and contrast with each other? and What is the history of the documentary film? Therefore, to write about characters or film history in your answer is a waste of your effort and of your reader's time. In short, topic clarification prevents you from getting sidetracked and helps you meet audience expectations.

☛ EXERCISE 3.14

Use the Process Sheet on page 88 to clarify your own topic, selected during Exercise 3.13. Or, if you have the opportunity, work in a group to clarify each other's topics. Use the completed Process Sheet on page 89 as a guide if you need help. ◢

☛ EXERCISE 3.15

Some writers find that writing up a quick rough draft once they have chosen a topic helps them test the workability of the topic. Such a draft is written before information is formally gathered and arrangement is chosen. Even if you are not usually one to use the quick-draft strategy, write down now a preliminary draft for your chosen topic. Then answer the following questions:

1. Does the quick-draft indicate the need for further topic clarification? For a different topic choice altogether?
2. At this point, what pleases you about the draft? What bothers you? ◢

▶ EXERCISE 3.16

For additional practice, write a quick-draft of the memo in Exercise 3.11. Again answer the questions:

1. Does the draft indicate the need for further topic clarification? For a different topic choice?
2. At this point, what pleases you about the draft? What bothers you? ◢

After you have clarified your topic, you are ready to begin searching for answers to the primary and to some of the secondary questions it raises. Before you begin your search, you may want to form a tentative, or "working," controlling generalization to govern your investigation. Such a tentative or working generalization can immediately be formed from the primary question the topic raises. For instance, let's return to the "Long Distance Running" example. If your primary question is "What characterizes the different styles in long distance running?", then one tentative controlling generalization might be: "Different long distance running styles represent a combination of distinct coaching methods and the individual runner's preferences." This controlling generalization mentions the topic (different styles in long distance running), your attitude (these styles develop from a combination of factors), and reader expectation (certain runners will be shown as examples).

The same primary question could lead to other tentative controlling generalizations as well, such as "The different styles in long distance running involve both physical and mental characteristics." In short, the controlling generalization you begin with may not be the generalization you end with. But having a tentative controlling generalization will give you a starting point and should prevent you from aimlessly circling the options within your topic until you collapse from exhaustion.

TOPIC CLARIFICATION

TOPIC:

AUDIENCE:

PURPOSE:

What is the primary question my topic raises?

What are the secondary questions?

What are some issues my topic does not raise?

Is there a secondary or non-question which deserves consideration as the primary topic?

How will my audience affect the topic? (How broad or inclusive and how narrow or exclusive can I be?)

How long will the paper be?

Is there any designated format?

Remarks:

88

▶EXERCISE 3.17

Formulate a tentative controlling generalization for each of the following primary questions. Remember to check that you have stated the topic, indicated an attitude or idea about the topic, and set some expectation for your audience.

EXAMPLE: What is the main feature of waiting on customers?
            "In my job as a salesclerk, I have found waiting on customers to be a singularly frustrating task."

1. What skills are needed to perform well in police work?
2. What is the significance of T.V. advertising?
3. Should requirements for high school graduation be stiffened?
4. How does a "junk food" diet affect teenage behavior? ◢

The information you discover in your search for details about your topic may verify or confirm your tentative controlling generalization, or it may suggest a new controlling generalization. If your information verifies your tentative generalization, it can then be used as support. If your information suggests some unifying thread that differs from your tentative generalization, it can be used to formulate a new generalization. Such reformulation is a common aspect of the writing process and you should not regard it as a sign of weakness or failure, as a sign that you "couldn't get it right the first time." Quite the contrary. You should see it as evidence of the dynamic quality of the composing process.

NOTES

1. Caroline Seebohm, "How To Change Your Point of View," *Invention & Design*, 3rd. edition, eds. Forrest D. Burt and E. Cleve Want (New York: Random House, 1981), pp. 193–97.

2. Linda Flower, *Problem-Solving Strategies for Writing* (New York: Harcourt Brace Jovanovich, Inc., 1981), pp. 21 ff.

4

DISCOVERING SUPPORTING INFORMATION

Where are you getting your ideas? Why should I believe what you say? Your paper has poor credibility. How do I know this is not your own conjecture?   RHH

Using so many examples in your argument really makes your paper effective and makes people aware of the need to do something— which is your purpose. One suggestion as far as giving examples I have is that you might include what some of the false claims and faked tests were so people can say, "Gosh, I believed that. Those dirty rats tricked me too!"   J.W.

The quotations above are reader responses to two different papers. As can be seen, readers place a premium on the writer including detail. Without support, a paper "has poor credibility." With support, a paper is "effective" and convincing.

This chapter suggests how to search for such supporting material in personal sources, in "social" sources, and in library sources. Any or all of these sources may be appropriate to your chosen topic.

DISCOVERING PERSONAL SOURCES

When searching for specific information, you can begin by asking, "What do I know about my topic?"

Let's say that you have chosen the topic "The Effects of Stress." Your purpose is to define stress to your fellow students in a way that instructs them in coping with it. Your primary question is, "How does stress affect a person's behavior in a crisis?" Your working generalization is, "Stress can produce some unexpected responses in a crisis situation."

Using Your Journal

Then, to answer the question, "What do I know about my topic?", you turn to your journal and find the following entry:

> As a child I remember my parents discussing the funeral of John F. Kennedy. Specifically, they were commenting on the fact that certain servants in the Kennedy household had quit after hearing the family members humorously tell some rather irreverent stories about the assassinated President at his wake. "What's a wake?" I had asked. "A wake," explained my father, "is when relatives stay up all night and talk about the person that has just died." "And they tell jokes too?" "Yes," my father smiled. "I don't understand," I said. "They should be crying." "Well," my father said gently, "I hope you can laugh at my funeral." Although I couldn't imagine it at the time, at my father's funeral the whole family laughed, and laughed a good deal. For example, there was something terribly incongruous and therefore funny about that steel casket draped in an American flag being solemnly pulled down the church aisle ahead of us on a squeaky cart. We stifled our laughter then, but could not contain it when later at the grave site, after taps had sounded and we climbed back into the hearse, it wouldn't start. The hearse, in effect, had died. We roared. "Dad would have loved this," I laughed. "Would have loved it?" my sister grinned. "It's like he planned it."

In locating the preceding journal entry, you have generated some possible supporting information for the generalization: "Stress can produce some unexpected responses in a crisis situation."

Tapping the Experiences of Friends

Your friends and associates are also personal sources worth investigating. Let's say that you are discussing your topic with a friend, and she shares with you the following account:

> My sister, two years old, had just fainted. She had been to the doctor, but he had said she would be all right. Mom took her to the Emergency Room, so we had to stay over at my aunt's. A while later, my cousin came over and said Mom called and said not to let me and my brother go to school. I knew something was wrong then, but nobody looked sad or worried so I figured everything would be all right. When Mom came home, though, she was crying and talking crazy. She was saying that she wanted her baby. I couldn't figure out what she was talking about. Or maybe I did. I tried to read

something—anything—out of her words but that my sister had died.
. . . I never did cry, not like everyone else. Mom told me later that
that had bothered her, me not crying. I guess I've always kept my
deepest thoughts deep.

Dee Ann Green

Dee Ann is also talking about behavior that is somehow unexpected. Her
account thus supports your generalization, "Stress can produce some unexpected responses in a crisis situation."

Having acquaintances ask you questions about a past personal experience, even if they haven't shared in it, may also help you discover information. A clear example of such group participation in an individual's past
experience occurred when I was taking a composition course for college
teachers. One of my colleagues had written a few lines in his notebook
concerning his escape from Hungary during the 1956 Revolution; he had
been about four years old at the time. His topic was "The Psychology of
Being a Refugee," and his purpose was to give the average American
citizen a better understanding of the difficulties facing refugees, so that
these citizens could better welcome the refugees into their communities.
From his sparse notebook entry, he wanted to develop one representative
example for his paper. We volunteered to help by asking him these questions: Were there any soldiers around as you left town? Were there any
tanks? How did you travel? When did you leave, day or night? How was
the weather? How many were with you? Were you afraid? Did you know
you were leaving home for good? Were your parents afraid? Had they
discussed the trip beforehand? Did you end up in a refugee camp? These
questions enabled him to recall half-forgotten details that he then could
use in developing a significant example to support his tentative controlling
generalization: "Being a refugee is above all a state of mind."

In this instance, questioning helped the writer retrieve information
that was already known. Sometimes questioning can also help you determine what information you don't know but need to know to develop a
topic.

Simulations, for example, can show you where your personal source
information may be inadequate and may also suggest where you can go to
obtain the necessary additional information. Consider the following sample simulation:

MARY'S TOPIC: Mary, a student senate member, has been asked the
                         question, "Is it feasible to serve beer in the univer-
                         sity dorms on special occasions?" To discover an an-
                         swer for her constituents, she consults her friends in
                         the senate, but all they know is that it hasn't been
                         allowed before. Mary thus asks her composition

classmates to discover *the types* of information, both pro and con, that would help her answer the question and write up a paper presenting the issue.

THE SIMULATION: The class divides itself into three task forces, one representing the Dean's office, one the city Chamber of Commerce, and one the student resident hall committee. Independently, each task force determines its initial stand and then seeks avenues of support. Although each task force decides to consult a lawyer, the groups are generally divergent in the sources they choose to explore.

THE FOLLOW-UP: The task forces assemble to discuss what they discovered to be "unknown" and therefore researchable areas outside their personal experience.

►EXERCISE 4.1

Using the previous simulation as a working model, design a simulation to discover what is "unknown" about the topic question: "Would it be feasible to eliminate grades as a basis for evaluating a college student's performance?" ◢

DISCOVERING "SOCIAL" SOURCES

Social sources are typically individuals or groups of people who live in your community and who possess some expertise on your topic. These sources are valuable because they can give you information and insights not found in a library but necessary to the development of your ideas. You can tap these sources through interviews or surveys.

Interviews

In planning an interview, you will be concerned with two types of questions: those for the interviewer and those for the interviewee. As an interviewer, you might begin by considering:

1. Who am I going to interview? Who will have significant information to contribute to my understanding of the topic? What background information is available on my interviewee?

2. What questions am I going to ask the interviewee? When planning an interview, you can choose from a variety of question types:

    a. Yes/no questions, such as "Do you own a dog?"

    b. Multiple choice questions, such as "Did you vote Republican, Democrat, or Independent in the last Presidential election?" A variant of this type of question is the scaling question that allows the interviewee to indicate the strength of a given response, such as "Would you strongly agree, agree, disagree, or strongly disagree with the statement: Marriage infringes on the personal liberty of the persons involved?"

    c. Direct questions, such as "Where were you on the evening of July 10?" Direct questions commonly deal with facts.

    d. Open-ended questions, such as "What is your stance on the death penalty?" A probe, such as "Tell me more" or "How so?", is also open-ended. Open-ended questions commonly deal with opinion.

    e. Hypothetical questions, such as "If you had it to do all over again, would you live your life in the same way?" Like the open-ended question, the hypothetical commonly deals with opinion. Hypotheticals usually occur at the end of an interview.[1]

3. How am I going to arrange my questions? Shall I group together all my questions dealing with the "personal aspect"? How shall I include a "concluding cue" in my final question so that the interviewee will know the interview is about over?

Additional questions you may ask yourself deal with your personal role in the interview:

4. What is my approach to the interview going to be? (Argumentative? Objective? Casual? Formal?)

5. What is my relationship to the topic under discussion? (Expert? Naive? Pro? Con?)

6. How am I going to establish rapport with the interviewee so that he or she will freely answer my questions?

7. When and where will the interview take place? How will I sit in relationship to the interviewee? What should I wear?

8. What will be my method of recording information?

Figure 4.1 shows a student's interview prep work that considers many of the previously outlined questions. When the student actually made the phone call, he could write the respondent's answers directly on the prep sheet. To show the process that student Paul Sullivan went through to determine his interview questions, we present his prep work unedited.

An Interview ✓

Questions for myself:

1. What should my topic be?
2. What information do I expect to obtain from this interview?
3. Who would be most qualified and available for the interview?
4. What questions should I ask?
5. How could the content of these questions be structured to maximize the amount and quality of information needed?
6. What type of environment in which to hold the interview would be most helpful in obtaining good answers?
7. How long should the interview last? ✓

Questions for the Interviewee: ✓

What is your name?
How are you involved in the topic?
1. What motivated you to become involved in this area?
2. Have you ever negotiated becoming involved?
3. How long have you been involved in this area?
4. Do you enjoy what you do?
5. Are you satisfied with your current position?

6. Considering your interests, what are your views concerning specific points in the topic?
7. Is there anything that needs to be changed in the present situation?
8. If so, what would you recommend?
9. How could these changes be implemented? Are you currently in the position to promote and launch these changes?

Answers

1. My topic will be the Wichita Police and fire strike of 1978.
2. I want to find out how the strike started and what can be done to remedy it.
3. For the Police, Fireman's side, Chief Floyd Hahn would be highly qualified.
4. I would like to find out what the terms of the ... proposed contracts were and what the problems management made them inacceptable.
   What specifically were the original problems and have or could they be remedied? If so, how?
   I would also like for him to comment on the nature of the settlement and how it was arrived at & future problems

FIGURE 4.1 Prep Sheet for Interview

Q. Have you have a wealth of knowledge of how the system operates from first hand experience. So has anything like this ever happened during your tenure?

A. One case that came close in 1970. No strike. Firemen wanted more than city wanted to give. Not uncommon.

Q. You say it's not uncommon, has this sort of thing happened with other public service departments of the city?

A. Yes. Police strikes weren't just for sympathy. They also have had problems getting their money.

Q. Surely the city commissioners aren't just being stingy. Doesn't your department have sufficient funds to operate?

A. Of course if they aren't stingy but having money to operate & not having enough money to live or are two totally different things. Salaries are pretty tight, difficult for men with families.

Q. So, essentially, but Maria were the cause of the strike. Was there anything else involved?

A.

---

5. These questions will probably be most effective if they were open ended. This would allow the personal opinion to shine through.

6. Since I am here at Waldhurst and he is there in Wichita the interview will probably have to be done over the phone - preferably not on Monday or Friday (beginning or ending of the work week). The best choice of a day would probably be Wednesday and the time should be somewhere around 2:00 (after lunch but not near quitting time).

7. Since it will be a phone interview, it should be as short as possible to avoid the long distance costs.

The Interview

I. Introduce myself & explain why I am interviewing him.
   A. Term paper for Political Science —
      Local Government
   B. Topic - The strike
   C. Issues involved as I see them
      1. Police or sympathy strike
      2. 3 contracts rejected before settle

II. Questions for Fr. Stoble
   Q. How long have you been the Fire Chief?
   A. About 15 yrs.

FIGURE 4.1 Continued

A. Low salaries were a major cause but important the firemen were also concerned about working conditions such as; shift change, cleanup and maintenance duties, and the general environment (low morale).

Q. What provisions were made in the contract to change these conditions?
A. The last contract contained provisions for relaxation of shift exchange rules and maintenance duties were limited to jobs taking less than 30 minutes.

Q. Was this part of the settlement?
A. Yes

Q. Were both sides satisfied with the settlement?
A. The city paid a little more than they wanted to + the firemen didn't get the 10% increase they had originally asked for — more like about 6%. The city only wanted to pay about 4%. Generally, I think the firemen came out on top.

Q. In your estimation, then, did the strike accomplish what the firemen wanted it to?

A. Yes, but I don't condone their actions. What they did was against Kansas state law and it could have caused very serious tragedy. We were just lucky there were no major fires during the strike.

Q. What about next year when contract negotiations start for 1980, couldn't that sort of thing happen again?
A. Of course we hope it won't, but there is always that possibility if neither side agrees. I'm hoping we have deterred that action through prevailing the offenders. Another deterrent could be that this strike has so very ___ on everyone involved. The firemen and their families won't ever forget that.

How do we know that this won't

Q. Then you could safely say that their action won't be a trial?
A. Yes, I think both sides will be a little more lenient from now on.

Any "cues" to the final Q?

FIGURE 4.1   Continued

I would like to the structure the
interview in conversation style. This
could best be done by first writing an
√ introduction to inform the reader
of the general situation and then
integrate the information gathered
from Chief Hobbs into the formal
using direct and indirect quotes.

It should follow this pattern
  I. Introduction
     A. The strike
      1. cause
      2. length
     B. The solutions
  II. The interview
     A. Fire Chief Floyd Hobbs
      1. Professional background
      2. Sentiment toward firemen
√   B. Oppinions
      1. Background of strike
      2. Causes
      3. Contracts
      4. Problems
      5. Solutions

Paul Sullivan

FIGURE 4.1 Continued

Some guidelines for effective interviewing

Whether designing an interview or a survey (essentially an interview with a multiple target), there are a few guidelines you should consider to assure the quality of your questions:

1. Avoid marathon questions that are unnecessarily elaborate or that demand more than one answer. Example: "In your brief tenure as a city school board member, how was it that you voted not to approve the 9% salary increase for teachers when inflation is running at 11%, especially since you campaigned as a teacher's advocate, at least in the two months previous to your election, or perhaps you have discovered factors unknown to you during the campaign but which became evident after you assumed office?" Such questions, because of their complexity, may confuse or annoy the interviewee.

2. Avoid broad questions that use absolute words (all, always, each, every, never, nobody, only, none). Example: "Do you think that everyone should have children?" In this case, if the interviewee answers no, he or she may be interpreted as saying that nobody should ever have children; if yes, he or she may be interpreted as advocating that everybody should have children, even those who would make terrible parents. The problem with broad questions is that they do not easily allow for exceptions.

3. Avoid connotative questions. Example: "Do you think eighteen-year-old kids should be allowed to drink?" Because connotative questions are slanted or loaded in their wording, the interviewee may be unduly influenced by the prejudices of the interviewer.

4. Avoid leading questions. Example: "How many times have you been to Rick's opium parlor?" In this case, the interviewee is assumed to have been to Rick's at least once, which may not be the case. Leading questions often are self-incriminating for the interviewee and smack of the courtroom.

5. Avoid questions with imprecise comparatives (few, most, more, less, about)." Example: "Do you think most people are honest about paying their income taxes?" The interviewee can answer this question "yes" if he or she believes that 51% of taxpayers are honest, or if he or she believes 99% are.

6. Avoid questions with multiple negatives or perplexing wording. Example: "Are you opposed to the stance of the anti-abortion protesters?"

In each of the preceding cases, weak questions may puzzle the interviewee so that his or her answers may be vague, noncommittal, or even unintentionally misleading.

The Process Sheet on page 101 includes many of the previously mentioned concerns regarding interview preparation.

►EXERCISE 4.2

Use the Process Sheet to design an interview for the topic you selected in Exercise 3.13. Then answer the following questions:

1. Would an interview be a particularly appropriate way to gather information on your topic? A basically inappropriate way? A way without clear advantages or disadvantages? Explain.
2. What types of topics best lend themselves to interviews as a means of generating information? Be specific.◢

PREPARING AN INTERVIEW

TOPIC:

AUDIENCE:

PURPOSE:

TENTATIVE CONTROLLING GENERALIZATION:

Interviewee:

Relationship to topic:

Time: Place:

Method:

What types of questions am I going to ask? Yes/no? Multiple choice? Direct? Open-ended? Hypothetical?

What are these questions?

How am I going to order these questions?

Do I group all the questions dealing with the same aspect together?

Where is my "concluding cue"?

What is my relationship with the interviewee going to be?

What is my relationship to the main topic of discussion?

How am I going to establish interviewee rapport? How am I going to respond to his or her answers?

101

DISCOVERING LIBRARY SOURCES

Conducting interviews or surveys are two ways of addressing the question, "What specific information do others have concerning my topic?" Conducting library research is a third. "What information does the library have?" and "How do I gain access to that information?" are two related questions that require knowledge of how a library is organized.

Gaining Access to Sources

Essentially, a library operates on a classification system in which every book, microbook, magazine, microfiche, index and microfilm is categorized and correspondingly numbered. The number assigned to a particular library source is permanent, just as your social security number is permanently assigned to you and only to you. A source shelved under FM 202 .06 KK 2 in your university library will appear under FM 202 .06 KK 2 in the Library of Congress or any other library using this almost universal system of labeling.

Important tools in gaining access to these numbered sources include the card catalog, the *Reader's Guide to Periodical Literature,* and other specialized indexes.

The card catalog

The library card catalog is an alphabetical index of cards in which sources are listed in two, and often three, ways: (1) according to the author, (2) according to the title, and frequently (3) according to one or more subject headings. Besides author, title, and subject cards, the catalog also contains informational cards regarding catalog listings and classifications. Consider the examples in Figures 4.2, 4.3, 4.4, and 4.5.

Body language

Material on this subject will be found in this catalog under:

    Nonverbal communication (Psychology)

FIGURE 4.2 *Informational Card Giving Classification*

Nonverbal communication

Related material on this subject will be found
in this catalog under:

Drum language
Expression
Gesture
Paralinguistics
Personal space

FIGURE 4.3 *Informational Card Listing Cross References*

BF637   NONVERBAL COMMUNICATION.
C45
K54   **Kleinke, Chris L**
        First impressions: the psychology of encountering
    others / Chris L. Kleinke.—Englewood Cliffs, N.J.:
    Prentice-Hall, [1975]
        147 p.; 21 cm.—(A Spectrum book)
        Includes bibliographical references and indexes.
        ISBN 0-13-318436-6.   ISBN 0-13-318428-5 pbk.
10–75
ss   1. Nonverbal communication.   I. Title.
        BF637.C45K54   158'.2   75-2074
                                            MARC
        Library of Congress   75

FIGURE 4.4 *Subject Card*

BF637   First impressions.
C45
K54   **Kleinke, Chris L**
        First impressions: the psychology of encountering
    others / Chris L. Kleinke.—Englewood Cliffs, N.J.:
    Prentice-Hall, [1975]
        147 p.; 21 cm.—(A Spectrum book)
        Includes bibliographical references and indexes.
        ISBN 0-13-318436-6.   ISBN 0-13-318428-5 pbk.
10–75
ss   1. Nonverbal communication.   I. Title.
        BF637.C45K54   158'.2   75-2074
                                            MARC
        Library of Congress   75

FIGURE 4.5 *Title Card*

The process of answering the question "What information does the
card catalog contain about my topic?", however, involves more than an
understanding of what catalog cards actually look like. The following

interior monologue suggests the type of thinking that often accompanies the process of using the card catalog.

> Well, I guess with my tentative controlling generalization I've finally committed myself. I hope I can prove my main idea that "the draft ultimately leads to armed conflict." Not that I'm necessarily against the draft. I'd just like "reasonable" reasons to oppose it if I choose to do so. Let's see. I'd better look up some books on the draft to see if *I'm* being reasonable. I should maybe start in the *subject* catalog under "Draft."
> "Draft," "draft" . . .

```
   Draft and capacity of chimneys.
```

I think I'm in the wrong place. Hmm.

```
UB
340       The draft: a handbook of facts and alter-
D783         natives. Edited by Sol Tax.
```

Sol Tax? That sounds like an alias. But he was writing in the sixties, so an alias might have been necessary. Here's another possible:

```
UB343
085       The draft and its enemies. O'Sullivan,
            John.
```

I guess I know where old John stands on the issue. But it will do me good to read different points of view. At any rate, it looks like the UB 300s are devoted to draft books. There aren't too many listed here though. Maybe if I looked under the "Army," there would be more.
  "Army," "army" . . .

```
   Army, see U.S. Army.
```

  "U.S. Army". . . . Here, "U.S. Army: recruiting, enlistments, etc." It's really the "etc." I'm interested in.

> U.S. Army: recruiting, enlistments, etc.
> Related material on this subject will
> be found in this catalog under:
> U.S. Army—medical examinations
> U.S. Army—vocational guidance

This sounds like they're trying to induct me. Wait!

> H35
> D35   Buehler, Ezra Christian. . . . Compulsory
> V.8   military service.

Good: a new general call number, H 35. And here's a different book, this time in the UB 300s again.

> UB323
> M28   Marmion, Harry A. The case against a
> 1971   volunteer army.
>
>   includes bibliographical references

We ought to get old John and Harry together. Well, now I have some options at least. I could run to the stacks to pick up that Marmion book right away. That bibliography of his indicated by the catalog card might lead me to other sources. Or . . . let's see. . . .

> E601
> A9   Ayers, James T. The diary of James T. Ayers,
>   civil war recruiter.

That gives me an idea. Not that I want to talk about the history of the draft, but I could look under the Vietnam War for more draft information. There were a lot of draft protests then. And maybe the resisters had some proof regarding my tentative generalization.

> DS559.8
> D7   Vietnamese conflict 1961–1975—Draft Resisters
> B37   Baskiv, Laurence M. Chance and circumstance.
> 1978

Chance and circumstance? That sounds like my research method right now. But with the 1978 call number date, the book might have

some recent material. What else? Draft protests. . . . Sure. I could
look under "Protest."

"Protest," "protest" . . .

> JX1963
> F497p   Finn, James. Protest: pacifism and politics;
>   some passionate views on war and nonviolence.
>
>   includes bibliography references

Bingo! I guess I'm ready to scour the stacks—the UB 300s, the H 35s,
the DS 500s, and the JXs—for some material. I particularly want to
locate the Marmion and Finn books for the bibliographies.

The preceding interior monologue suggests several questions that you
should ask when using the card catalog. Among these are "To what
classification heading does my subject belong?" "To what other categories
is my subject related?" "What call numbers belong to books in my topic
area?" "More specifically, what sources, as listed in the card catalog,
contain bibliographies or indexes which may expand my list of possible
references?"

The Reader's Guide

After exploring the card catalog and its offerings, you might also ask,
"What does the *Reader's Guide to Periodical Literature* have to say about
relevant magazine or journal articles?" Essentially, the *Reader's Guide*
works similarly to the card catalog; that is, the guide lists, by topic classification, those articles written on a particular subject area. You could,
therefore, look under familiar headings such as "draft" or "protest" for
possible periodical references.

Here is a sample periodical listing on "Military Service, Compulsory":

Should U.S. revive draft? [interviews] S.A. Nunn Jr.; M.O. Hatfield.
US News 88: 37–8 F 11 '80.

In this listing, "Should U.S. revive draft?" is the title of the article; Nunn
and Hatfield, the authors; *US News,* the magazine; 88, the volume; 37–8,
the pages; F 11 '80, the date. The bracketed information indicates that the
article features interviews on the subject.

Other indexes

"Are there any other indexes pertinent to my topic?" is yet another
question important to your library search. Although collections vary,
libraries generally house a variety of specialized indexes, ranging from the
Art Index to the *Wallesley Index to Victorian Periodicals* and from the *New
York Times Obituary Index* to *Selected References on Environmental Quality as*

It Relates to Health. Also available are various abstracts, including *Abstracts in Anthropology, Crime and Delinquency Abstracts, Abstracts of Folklore Studies,* and *Child Development Abstracts and Bibliography.* Abstracts contain a brief overview of the content of each listed publication. Moreover, the *Vertical File* contains information on a variety of pamphlets. And, the librarian remains one of the best resources any library has to offer.

▾EXERCISE 4.3

Take a topic with its controlling generalization which you have generated or take a topic for which you have been assigned to do research (for your psychology class, for example), and look up possible sources. Write down the information from the card catalog or *Reader's Guide* or other indexes that will help you locate the appropriate sources. Then browse through the stacks, selecting those materials you would like to explore to support the tentative generalization you have generated.◢

EVALUATING AND USING LIBRARY SOURCES

Scanning Potential Sources

Scanning involves quickly reading the material you have located. In scanning potential sources you evaluate both their quantity and quality.

Quantity does not guarantee quality. In fact, if your topic turns up an overwhelming number of sources, you might do well to refine your focus before researching further. Similarly, if your topic scares up a meager number of sources, you might have to reconsider your emphasis, especially if your readers expect library material as supporting detail. Both refining your focus and reconsidering your emphasis involve returning to topic clarification. (See pages 80–89.)

If the quantity of sources on your subject pronounces it "do-able," then you can move on to assess what's there. Two questions basic to initial source assessment are "What does the title indicate about the source?" and "What does the table of contents reveal?"

Take, for example, these book titles: *Cognition, Convention, and Communication* and *Transpersonal Communicating: How to Establish Communication with Yourself and Others.* Both titles have communication as one concern. The first, however, implies, with the word "cognition," a more theoretical or technical perspective. The second, with the reference to "personal" and the "how to" approach, indicates a more pragmatic perspective.

Examination of the respective tables of contents bears out the inferences drawn from the titles. Consider the major subheads of each:

1. *Cognition, Convention, and Communication:* Preliminaries; A Metatheoretical Perspective; Interaction, Cognition, and Situation; Situation and Convention; Meaning and Language; Perspectives on Communicative Action Systems; Concluding Comments: Foundations and Extensions.

2. *Transpersonal Communication:* Introduction: What is Transpersonal Communication?; Intrapersonal Communication Skills; Interpersonal Communication Skills; Transpersonal Skills in Communication; Holistic Perspectives in Education; A Parents' Guide to Transpersonal Communication.

Consider also some sample chapter titles:

1. *Cognition, Convention, and Communication:* Critique of Transformation Models; Situation Trajectories; Reflexivity; Constraints on Meaning; Perlocutionary Systems.

2. *Transpersonal Communication:* The Art of Talking to Yourself; The Magic Carpet Ride in the Classroom; Stop, Look, and Listen; Riding the Cosmic Roller Coaster; Transpersonal Communication at Home.

Consider, finally, the supplementary material noted:

1. *Cognition, Convention, and Communication:* Appendix A: Abstract Machine Theory; Appendix B: Convention; Appendix C: Speech Acts; Appendix D: Meaning.

2. *Transpersonal Communication:* List of Activities (including: Tension Awareness, Developing Intuition, Eye Contact, and The Rescue Game).

▶EXERCISE 4.4

Characterize the audience for each of the preceding books from what you know about their titles and tables of contents. Speculate as to each author's purpose. Identify the types of papers that could benefit from using each source. Be specific in stating why your answers work for each text.◢

Besides scanning the title and table of contents, you can initially assess a potential source by reading its introduction or preface, previewing any major headings and subheadings contained by its chapters, looking at any lists or graphs or illustrations featured in its text, and scanning its chapter summaries or conclusion.

For example, such a survey of *Cognition, Convention, and Communication,* reveals:

1. The author's purpose is to explore an idea suggested by a confrontation of his "underlying interactive model of knowledge" and a "conceptualization of language" which did not fit into his original model; the idea explored represents a "metatheoretical understanding" of the interaction between knowledge and language.
2. The headings show the author is concerned with models and critiques of models involving various perspectives.
3. Despite the emphasis on models, the author makes no attempt to visualize his theories through illustrations or figures.
4. The author expects his study to have both psychological and linguistic implications.

In sum, the author writes at a very abstract and advanced level about the communication process.

A survey of *Transpersonal Communication* shows:

1. The author's purpose is to improve communication skills in schools and families.
2. The headings emphasize awareness, skills, and problem solving.
3. The numerous self surveys, descriptive charts, and sample contracts all highlight the author's pragmatic, self-help approach.
4. The book's conclusion lists suggestions on how to introduce transpersonal communication into the school district.

In short, the author speaks at a relatively concrete and fundamental level about the communication process.

▶ EXERCISE 4.5

Select two books written on the same subject and scan them to assess their character as sources. Write up a brief summary of your assessment. Be specific.◢

Skimming Potential Sources

The difference between scanning and skimming is one of degree rather than kind. In skimming, you pay closer attention to the support the source offers for its ideas. To do so, you look for the controlling generalization of each chapter or major section, read for the major subgeneralizations and even the topic sentences of paragraphs, glance at the summary sentences of sections and of paragraphs, and possibly do some preliminary reading in parts of the text that look particularly interesting or important in terms of *your* controlling generalization. Some writers find it useful to place book markers in places that deserve subsequent special attention.

In any case, your purpose at this point is both to gather ideas and to designate sources for your tentative bibliography.

Forming a Tentative Bibliography

After you have roughly assessed your potential sources, you are ready to form a tentative bibliography consisting of those sources that, at this point, seem particularly relevant to your subject and controlling generalization. For example, if your were doing a theoretical study of types of communication, you would probably include *Cognition, Convention, and Communication* in your tentative bibliography. If, on the other hand, you were doing a paper on applied communication concepts, you would include *Transpersonal Communication* in your tentative bibliography. If you thought both theory and practice were going to be covered in your paper, you would probably include both sources.

It is important to note here that *relevant* does not necessarily mean *supportive*. It is possible for sources to be relevant because they *contradict* your tentative controlling generalization. Remember that idea-synthesizing (pages 72–73) is still an option at this stage. Remember, too, that being aware of opposing viewpoints is helpful in assertaining reader expectations. In addition, consider that a scientist often begins with a tentative controlling generalization or hypothesis and then tries to *disprove* it rather than to prove it. The scientific method dictates that a theory must be modified or even discarded when evidence is discovered that is incompatible with the theory.

In any case, recording tentative bibliographical information on notecards is a good practice because you can readily carry them with you when you're doing additional research and can easily arrange them alphabetically when you prepare your final bibliography.

Although final footnote and bibliography formats vary from discipline to discipline, the forms themselves usually contain similar information. For a book, this information includes the author(s)' name(s), the title (underlined), the place of publication, the publisher's name, and the date of publication. All of this information plus the book's call number should be noted on the tentative bibliography card. See Figure 4.6.

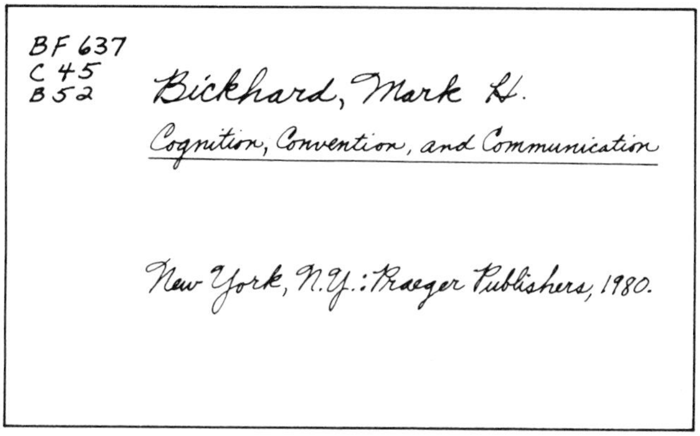

FIGURE 4.6 *Bibliography Card for a Book*

Likewise, for a magazine or journal, the information includes the author(s)' name(s), the article's title (in quotation marks), the magazine's title (underlined), the volume number, the date (month, day, year) of publication, and the page numbers on which the article appears. All of this information plus the source's location should be noted on a bibliography card. See Figure 4.7.

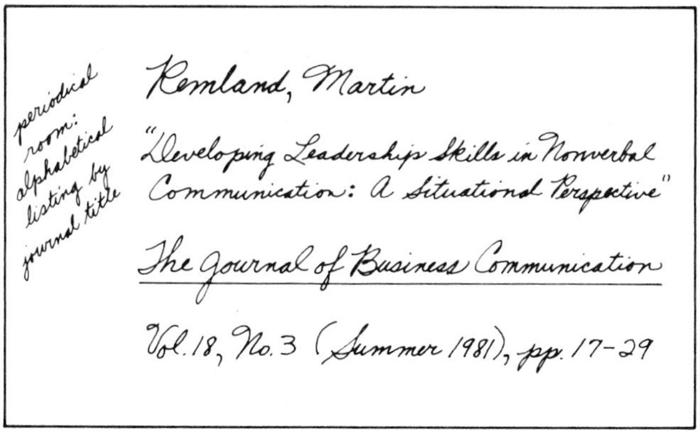

FIGURE 4.7 *Bibliography Card for a Magazine Article*

If you are not sure what information you will need to reference your source, take down as much information as you can. This will sometimes include volume numbers for books, editors' names for anthologies or collections, translators' names, edition numbers, and section numbers for newspapers.

Taking Notes

Taking notes carefully is an important factor in using library sources wisely. Basically, you can take notes at three levels: the idea level, the support level, and the "sentence" level.

The idea level

Taking notes at the idea level involves determining the source's main idea and any major secondary ideas. In other words, you identify the controlling generalization and subgeneralizations governing the source's material.

Taking notes at this level really begins with the scanning and skimming of sources. Through scanning and skimming, you orient yourself to the source's perspective on your subject. You essentially ask, "What is the primary question the source deals with?" "What are the secondary questions?" "What are the source's answers to these questions?"

The actual notes you take at the idea level often take the form of summary. Consider the following directly quoted material:

> What happens when you play on a company softball team and you are injured? Are you entitled to collect workmen's compensation for a job-related accident? The general rule seems to be that a) if the injury occurred on your employer's premises, and b) you were on your lunch hour or regular recreation period, and c) your employer either expressly or by implication required participation or attendance at the function; or he derives a substantial benefit from your participation; or it is part of your contract of employment, you will probably get compensation. The recreation cannot be only for your own health or morale, but must be work-related.
>
> In a New Jersey case, a jeweler played softball on his lunch break with other employees on grounds behind his employer's building. When he was injured during a game, the court decided that the accident was work-related. The intershop softball competition was helpful in labor-management relations and was encouraged by the employer, who provided all the sports equipment. In a case in Colorado, however, a member of a gas and electric club recreation association was not given compensation when he was injured during a softball game. The games were held on public grounds after work, and although the company furnished the equipment and uniforms, the court felt the employer did not benefit except indirectly through the good morale of the employees.[2]

If you were taking notes, a summary of the preceding passage might read:

The key to collecting workers' compensation for an injury is to establish that injury, whether occurring in or outside of the workplace, as job-related.

Notes at the idea level can also take the form of a paraphrase. A paraphrase is a reworking of source material so that it appears in your own words. A paraphrase note on the same excerpt about workers' compensation might read:

To establish an injury suffered outside the work place as job-related, a worker must show the employer either required or benefitted from the activity involving the accident.

A paraphrase characteristically handles less material than does a summary and is usually less abstract. In other words, it deals with answers to secondary questions. More on paraphrasing in a moment.

The support level

Taking notes at the support level involves recording the information a source offers in support of its main idea. It involves asking "What types of evidence does the source contain?" (personal experience, interviews, experimental data, research) and "What information does the source contain that my reader needs to know?"

A paraphrase that records information at the support level might read:

Helm cites two cases involving workers' compensation. In one, the worker, injured during a game after work on public grounds, was denied compensation because the employer did not directly benefit from the play. In the other, the worker, injured during a lunch hour softball game, was granted compensation because the employer promoted such competition.

Such paraphrases, which record information at support level, usually make up the bulk of the notes taken in researching any given topic.

The sentence level

Taking notes at the sentence level involves recording the material *exactly* as it appears in the source's text—word for word, comma for comma, period for period. In short, it involves the direct quote. Knowing when to quote a source directly requires consideration of the stylistic concepts of appropriateness, accuracy, and conciseness.

In general, you should consider using directly quoted material when the source is:

1. appropriate, that is, when the person speaking is an expert or recognized authority on the topic or issue;

2. accurate, that is, when what is being said cannot be said any other way without distorting the meaning; and

3. concise, that is, when paraphrasing entails unduly lengthening the coverage of the material.

Taking notes as direct quotes should be kept at a minimum, because, as a rule of thumb, no more than one-tenth of the final paper should be directly quoted material.

Paraphrase vs. Plagiarism

Paraphrasing is converting the source's material into your own words with your own emphasis. In paraphrasing you should avoid the following:

1. covering the points in the same order as the source,

2. covering the points with the exact emphasis as the source,

3. using sentence structure similar to the source's,

4. using words or phrases identical to (without quotes) or similar to (with synonyms) the source's,

5. usurping the source's overall style, and

6. omitting direct or implied reference to the source.

If you can avoid these six pitfalls, you can usually avoid plagiarism, the illegal use of sources.

The specific examples in Figure 4.8 and 4.9 demonstrate the difference between paraphrase and plagiarism:

ORIGINAL.   (from P.V. Glob, *The Bog People,* pp. 84–85)

Even if many of the Early Iron Age men who have come to light in bogs can be reckoned to have belonged to the peasantry, this need not be so of them all. Some may have belonged to the priesthood, whose leading figures may have exercised secular power in greater or lesser tribal areas as chiefs or minor kings. As for the peasants, the examination of the young girl from Domland Fen at Windeby in Schleswig showed that she could suffer from deficiencies in diet over the winter months, and this deficiency must have been characteristic of the north of Jutland no less than the south. Yet as many discoveries indicate, the peasants were not poor.

Thus in an Iron Age house at Ginderup in Thy, North-West Jutland, a hoard of current Roman coins was found. In such a context the find is unique and calls for special explanation. . . . The treasure, buried in a hole dug beside the hearth, lay in a heap, as though the coins had all been contained in a

FIGURE 4.8   *"Paraphrase" One: Plagiarism*

purse. The owner must have hidden the hoard and not revealed its hiding place before his death.

first sentence almost identical in construction to original opening

synonymous transition; identical sentence construction

Even though most of the Early Iron Age bog people may have been peasants, some may have been priests who had

identical comparison

secular power <u>like</u> that of chiefs. In terms of the peasants,

identical verb

a young girl found in Schleswig showed signs of diet defi-

synonymous transition; comparable sentence construction

ciencies. But this does not mean the peasants in general

identical adjective *synonym*

were poor. For example, in a house in Thy, a bunch of

compressed but essentially identical sentence construction

identical verb

Roman coins was found buried beside the hearth, the

identical sentence construction

owner dying before revealing its location.

points covered in same order as source and with the same emphasis

no credit to source

FIGURE 4.8 *"Paraphrase" One: Plagiarism* (Continued)

overt reference to source (assumes previous reference to book title)

According to P.V. Glob, Early Iron Age peasants may have had poor diets, especially in winter, but they also could possess significant monetary wealth, as did one Thy householder who secreted a stash of Roman coins in the earthen floor.[3]

one sentence capturing the essence of the Glob passage

second source acknowledgement, possibly used so the reader could get the details Glob uses from the source itself; in any case, page numbers for outside material are usually given through such footnotes

wording somewhat close to original but presented within different sentence construction and with a different emphasis — in conjunction with the contrast between poor diets; "Early Iron Age," "winter," "thy," "Roman coins," all represent identical word choices, but in this case are justified because they fall under the category of <u>common</u> <u>knowledge</u> or <u>common</u> <u>usage</u>. What other sensible way is there to indicate the "Early Iron Age," for example?

FIGURE 4.9 *Paraphrase Two: Legitimate Source Use*

When paraphrasing, you would do well not to look at the material you are working with. You should read, reflect, paraphrase, and then re-check.

▶ **EXERCISE 4.6**

Paraphrase the passage below from *Summerhill: A Radical Approach to Child Rearing.*

> Children who are freely brought up about sex matters have an open mind about so-called vulgarity. Some time back, I heard a vaudevillian in the London Palladium who sailed very near the wind in a breezy Elizabethan manner. It struck me then that he got laughs from his audience that he couldn't have got from the Summerhill crowd. Women shrieked when he mentioned ladies' undergarments, but Summerhill children would not consider such remarks at all funny.
>
> Once, I wrote a play for the kindergarten children. It was quite a vulgar play about a woodcutter's son who found a hundred-pound note and ecstatically showed it around to his family, including the cow. The dumb beast swallowed it, and all the family's efforts to get the cow to drop the note proved futile. Then the boy conceived a brilliant idea. They would open a booth at a fair, and charge a shilling for two minutes of attendance. If the cow dropped the money during someone's attendance, that person would win the money.
>
> The play would have brought down the house in a West End music hall. Our children, however, took it in their stride.[3]

After checking that you have used your own order, your own emphasis, your own sentence structure, your own phrasing and your own style, you are ready to place a footnote at the end of your "plagiarism-proof" paraphrase. ◢

Using Notecards

Taking notes at any level does not have to involve using actual notecards, but the task is much easier if you do. Using notecards allows you to reorder material without having to recopy or cut-and-paste.

A key factor in making such notecards work is cueing them with headings and sometimes subheadings. These headings should reflect the main subject or idea presented by the card's notes. For example, a cued notecard for the paraphrase about workers' compensation might appear as on the following page.

Besides being cued for main ideas, notecards should also be tagged for the source and page number where those ideas were found. (See Figure 4.10, for example.)

Eventually, these notecard cues can indicate how to group or sequence the parts of your material and therefore can suggest how to arrange

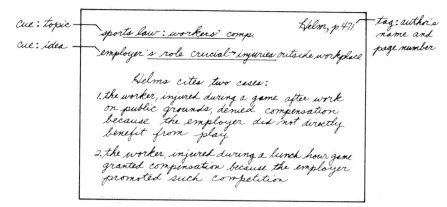

cue: topic

cue: idea

tag: author's name and page number

sports law: workers' comp.   Helm, p.471

employer's role crucial→injuries outside workplace

Helms cites two cases:

1. the worker, injured during a game after work on public grounds, denied compensation because the employer did not directly benefit from play

2. the worker, injured during a lunch hour game granted compensation because the employer promoted such competition

FIGURE 4.10   *Cued Notecard*

your paper. For example, let's say you have six cards cued for the topic "sports law: workers' comp." Of these six, four are cued for the idea "employer's role crucial," and two are cued for the idea "compensation amounts vary." A two-part structure emerges from these cues: one part dealing with *how* compensation is awarded in the first place and a second part dealing with *how much* compensation is possible. (Further connections between the interrelatedness of parts and the selecting of arrangement are discussed in Chapter 5, pages 139–41.)

Notecards facilitate the comparison of sources. They help answer these questions: "What information does this source contain that others don't?" "What information does the source share with other sources?" Notecards also help answer: "What information offered by each source supports my tentative controlling generalization?" "What information falsifies it?" "Does the source information overall compel me to change my tentative controlling generalization?"

Consider, for example, the grouping of notecards in Figure 4.11 on page 118.

The grouping of these notecards establishes which ones share common approaches to the subject "sexism in language." The grouping also suggests comparison/contrast or argument as possible forms of arrangement. Depending on the writer's tentative controlling generalization, the grouping might also suggest a change in the writer's approach. For example, had the writer begun with the tentative controlling generalization, "Male chauvinism is promoted by the language we use everyday," he or she might consider supporting a new train of thought represented by the alternative generalization, "Attempts to revise the sexual bias out of language will do little to purge sexual bias from society."

Furthermore, the grouping might suggest that the writer consider the question, "Does sexism in language promote sexual bias in society or does it merely reflect the bias that is already there?" Answers to this question might suggest additional tentative controlling generalizations.

The type and number of notecards you take varies with the composing context. Some writers, in fact, find rather complex systems of notetaking helpful. For example, consider the sample notecards in Figure 4.12 and 4.13.

Using notecards in this way facilitates both the consideration and reconsideration of controlling generalizations, of groupings of material, and of detail selection.

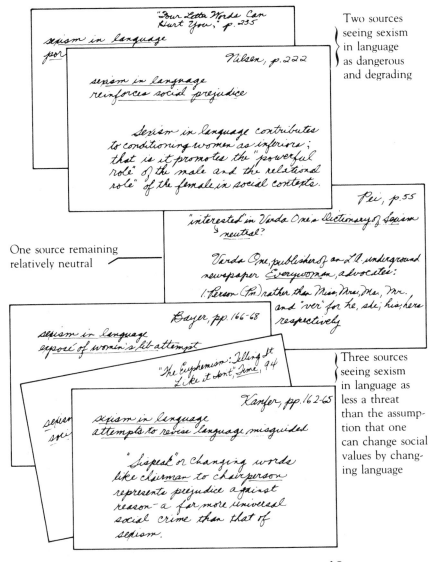

FIGURE 4.11 *Notecard Groupings Suggest Arrangement of Support*

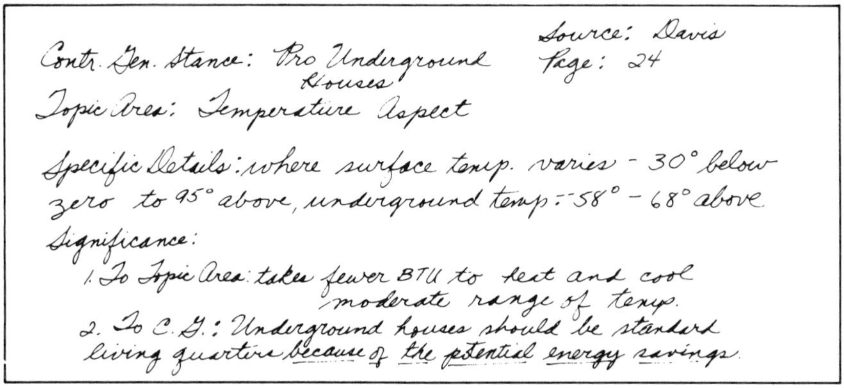

Source: Davis
Page: 24
Contr. Gen. Stance: Pro Underground Houses
Topic Area: Temperature Aspect
Specific Details: where surface temp. varies - 30° below zero to 95° above, underground temp: 58° - 68° above.
Significance:
1. To Topic Area: takes fewer BTU to heat and cool moderate range of temp.
2. To C.G.: Underground houses should be standard living quarters because of the potential energy savings.

FIGURE 4.12 *Sample of Complex Notetaking*

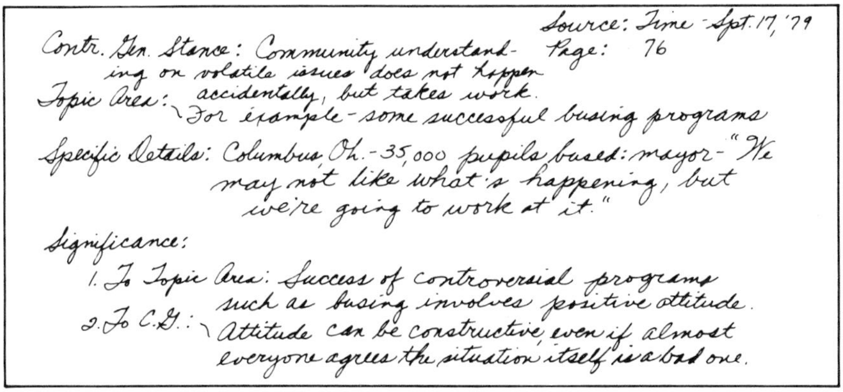

Source: Time - Sept. 17, '79
Page: 76
Contr. Gen. Stance: Community understanding on volatile issues does not happen accidentally, but takes work.
Topic Area: For example - some successful busing programs
Specific Details: Columbus Oh. - 35,000 pupils bused: mayor - "We may not like what's happening, but we're going to work at it."
Significance:
1. To Topic Area: Success of controversial programs such as busing involves positive attitude.
2. To C.G.: Attitude can be constructive, even if almost everyone agrees the situation itself is a bad one.

FIGURE 4.13 *Sample of Complex Notetaking*

Incorporating Source Material

Eventually, you will have to incorporate your chosen source material smoothly into your text. Assume, for example, that you begin with the following source material:

> "Maim" is the modern equivalent of the old word "mayhem," and some have long been inclined to abandon the earlier word entirely. . . .
>
> To cut off, or permanently to cripple, a man's hand or finger, or to strike out his eye or foretooth, were all mayhems at common law, if done maliciously, because any such harm rendered the person less efficient as a fighting man (for the king's army). But an injury such as cutting off his ear or nose did not constitute mayhem, . . . because it did not result in permanent disablement, but merely disfigured the victim.[4]

In incorporating the above material, you may paraphrase, selectively quote, or directly quote the passage.

1. In most cases, *paraphrase* is the primary method of source inclusion.
   a. In the English common law, a person could be prosecuted for maiming another only if the act were malicious and the injury prevented the victim from serving in the nation's military.
   b. According to Perkins, disfigurement alone is not mayhem.
2. Quoting just key words or phrases to enhance the paraphrase is also an effective writing strategy.
   a. You could slice off a person's nose but not gouge out his eye under English common law, for the former "merely disfigured" your victim while the latter made him "less efficient" as a soldier.
   b. Perkins points out that crippling a person is mayhem "if done maliciously."
3. A direct quote, if used at all, should fit naturally into the text.
   a. The definition of what constitutes a particular crime is not always without political overtones. For example, mayhem was a crime in England, ". . . if done maliciously, because any such harm rendered the person less efficient as a fighting man. . . ."
   b. The entire Perkins selection could be introduced by an introductory phrase: The definition of mayhem reveals some surprising aspects of English common law.

►EXERCISE 4.7

Using the Process Sheets on pages 121 and 122 as guides, locate a variety of possible sources (personal, social, library) on the topic you chose for Exercise 3.13. Then scan and skim the sources, form a tentative bibliography, and take notes.

Your instructor may ask you to submit this material as "prep" work, or ask you to write a quick draft on the basis of that material, or both. ◢

LOCATING INFORMATION

What information can I find about my topic through personal sources? What do I know about my topic? What information does my journal contain? Can discussions suggest? What contributions can my friends make?

What information can simulations supply?

What information can I gain from "social" sources? What information can an interview provide? A survey?

What questions preface an interview or survey? What questions determine interview or survey quality?

What information does the library have on my topic?

What information does the card catalog reveal? The *Reader's Guide?* Other indexes?

What should I remember about notetaking and plagiarism before I start taking notes from my sources?

NOTETAKING

What is the primary question the source addresses? The secondary questions? What is the source's main idea? Purpose? Audience?

What types of evidence does the source offer? Of this evidence, what is crucial to the understanding of the topic? To the support (or falsification) of my controlling generalization?

Is there any material in the source that warrants a direct quoting on the grounds of appropriateness, accuracy, or conciseness?

How can the sources themselves be grouped?

Does the source material suggest a change for my tentative controlling generalization?

NOTES

1. Dr. Meredith Moore, Washburn University, contributed to the material on interviewing.

2. Alice K. Helm, ed., *The Family Legal Advisor* (New York: Greystone Press, 1974), p. 471.

3. A.S. Neill, *Summerhill: A Radical Approach to Child Rearing* (New York: Hart Publishing Company, 1960), p. 232.

4. Rollin M. Perkins, *Perkins on Criminal Law,* 2nd ed. (Mineola, New York: The Foundation Press, Inc., 1969), pp. 184~85.

5

DISCOVERING ARRANGEMENTS

After you have researched your topic, you face several tasks: forming a final controlling generalization, selecting the information to support it, and arranging the parts of your support in relationship to each other and to the controlling generalization.

These tasks help you fulfill the reader's expectations that your writing be unified, supported, and coherent. (See Chapter 2.)

FINALIZING THE CONTROLLING GENERALIZATION

As shown in Chapter 3 (page 89), tentative controlling generalizations can be formed from the primary question that a topic raises. Controlling generalizations, however, can also suggest themselves during the course of your search for information. For example, let's say your purpose is to examine the much-assailed U.S. educational system for an audience of both high school students and college freshmen. You are interested in the topic question, "What do high school seniors taking composition courses think about writing?" and you have proposed the tentative controlling generalization that, "High school seniors taking composition courses do not take writing seriously." Let's say further that you have decided to use a survey to test your controlling generalization.

After receiving permission to do so, you distribute the survey to two separate high school composition classes of twenty seniors each. You later collect and tabulate the results. While you would have to study *all* the results of the survey in making judgments for your paper, let's, for discussion purposes, outline and discuss the data gathered from a few select questions:

1. Do you plan to go to college?

yes 19	no 0	unsure 1	Baker's
yes 15	no 1	unsure 4	Parks'
34	1	5	Totals

4. How much do you think the study of writing in high school will help you in college or in your career?

not at all	1	2	3	4	5	a great deal	
1	1	0	5	10	2	1	Baker's
2	2	2	12	1	0	1	Parks'
3	3	2	17	11	2	2	Totals

8. How important is correct grammar when you are writing a letter to apply for a job?

not at all	1	2	3	4	5	a great deal	
0	0	0	2	8	4	6	Baker's
0	0	4	12	2	1	1	Parks'
0	0	4	14	10	5	7	Totals

FIGURE 5.1 *Survey Results*

What do these numbers mean? Remember, first, that the numbers relate to the primary question, "What do high school seniors taking composition courses think about writing?" and to the secondary questions (introduced in the survey), "Do you plan to go to college?" and "How important is correct grammar when you are writing a letter to apply for a job?"

In response to the secondary questions, you can make the following statements: a majority of students from both classes think higher education is important, although the percentage of college-bound students is higher in Ms. Baker's class than in Mr. Parks'. In addition, a majority of the students in both classes think writing will be only moderately helpful in college or in their future careers, although Ms. Baker's students clearly anticipate a greater benefit. Third, the students as a whole appear mixed as to how much writing will help them get a job; a majority of Ms. Baker's students think composition is quite important while most of Mr. Parks' view it as being of only average importance. Overall, the responses varied from class to class. It is important to note that polling different classes with the same survey did yield different results.

How does this information relate to the tentative controlling generalization that high school students do not take writing seriously? While the material does not refute the generalization altogether, it does seem to suggest a qualification, such as "Some high school students take writing quite seriously when it comes to letters of job application."

A separate alternative controlling generalization might also be prompted by asking the question, "Could I compare/contrast Ms. Baker's and Mr. Parks' classes in terms of attitudes toward writing?" That alternative controlling generalization might be, "Comparing and contrasting two classes' responses to the same survey about composition suggests that the more the students believe that writing will help them in school or on the job, the more seriously they will regard writing as a prerequisite for getting a position."

►EXERCISE 5.1

Assume that the same survey netted the following additional data:

9. In general, do you enjoy writing?

no	1	2	3	4	5	yes	
1	1	0	7	7	2	2	Baker's
2	1	4	8	3	1	1	Parks'
3	2	4	15	10	3	3	Totals

17. If you took the ACT today, do you think your score in English would be improved as a result of this class?

no	1	2	3	4	5	yes	
0	0	1	4	10	4	1	Baker's
1	2	3	10	3	1	0	Parks'
1	2	4	14	13	5	1	Totals

Using this data, answer the following questions:

1. What does this information mean? What are the primary and secondary questions involved?

2. How does the data test the tentative controlling generalization that high school seniors taking composition do not take writing seriously? Does it support the generalization? Does it suggest an alternative generalization?

3. When viewed together with the other survey results (page 125) how does it relate to the tentative controlling generalization? And does it suggest an alternative generalization?

4. How could this material alone, and with the other known data, serve as "representative" information of a controlling generalization?◢

When working with controlling generalizations, then, you will do well to remember that these generalizations can be formed outright (deductively) from the primary question or can emerge (inductively) from the information you locate, and that reformulation of these generalizations is a common occurrence in the composing process.

▶EXERCISE 5.2

For further practice in formulating a controlling generalization from a set of details, assume that you have taken the following notes from *Runner's World* magazine in your effort to answer the question, "What is important in running?" You tentatively think training is the key. Remember to check your controlling generalization for naming the topic, showing an attitude or idea about the topic, and setting an expectation.

1. Wells & Sandoval finished one-two in the Nike/Oregon Track Club Marathon, Sept., despite physical handicaps.
2. Rodgers won the Boston Marathon, 1978, "because he was *prepared* to win."
3. Rodgers' attitude is "Look out. Once I grab the lead . . . you're going to have to kill yourselves to catch me."
4. Goal setting in running must be realistic and specific . . . in terms of hours, minutes, seconds. Predict performance.
5. Visualization in running involves:
   a. seeing the wind as a giant's hand pushing you forward
   b. thinking of legs as pistons with no feeling or pain
   c. seeing self hit tape first—*positive expectancy.*
6. Be aware that negative input is garbage.◢

Some Precautions

In drawing up generalizations, you should keep in mind the following precautions. One is that when you are generalizing, you should try to avoid being absolute. As you may recall, this text has warned against posing broad questions during an interview because they don't allow the interviewee to recognize the complexity of a given circumstance or to make exceptions. The broad generalization, because it also uses words such as *always* and *never*, poses the same problem, a lack of flexibility. Secondly, you should be careful not to use a few "exceptional" details as the basis for a generalization; thus, you should do enough looking around or researching so that you can distinguish the *exception* from the *rule*. Another precaution you should take is to examine cause and effect relationships. Writers usually indicate causal relationships with transitions such as *accordingly, as a result, consequently, thus,* and *therefore.* A causal relationship may also be indicated by the "if . . . then" construction. For example, the following causal relationship is flawed: "If everyone would travel widely, then everyone would be better educated about situations around the world." To begin with, the causal relationship is based on the underlying generalization or major premise, "Everyone who travels becomes better educated." Is this really true? For *everyone?* This example also represents circular reasoning: everyone who travels becomes better educated; everyone should travel; therefore, everyone who travels will become better educated. Because the major premise and the conclusion are identical, the argument is circular, flawed.

►EXERCISE 5.3

With these precautions in mind, evaluate the information you have gathered to support your controlling generalization by considering the following questions:

1. What does the information itself mean? What primary and secondary questions does it deal with?
2. Does the information support my tentative controlling generalization? If so, in what respects?
3. Does the information suggest an alternative controlling generalization? If so, in what respects? What is that alternate generalization?
4. Which generalization (tentative or alternate) best characterizes my material?
5. What is the "final" generalization I want to use? (Even this final generalization may be subject to modification after you have chosen your overall pattern of arrangement, for the generalization will often predict how the paper will proceed.)◂

SELECTING SPECIFIC SUPPORT

Both audience impact and thematic emphasis influence the type of detail you select as specific support.

Detail Type

Chances are that many of the details you gather to support any given generalization will be neutral in nature. Such detail does not draw undue attention to itself. The data gathered in the student survey (pages 125–26) would be neutral in so far as a reader might expect such statistical evidence to emerge from survey analysis.

Details may also be stereotypical or atypical. In the following exercise, the writer has circled the details supporting the controlling generalization, "Elizabeth personifies 'class' with her possessions and actions."

DETAILS: (Parisian fashions) (disco dancing lessons) State University classes, (Motobécane ten-speed bicycle,) *Reader's Digest*, pin-ball, (Persian carpet,) 10 × 10 dorm room, pierced earrings.

The writer's selections are stereotypical; that is, they are selections that promote a conventional definition of what constitutes "class."

Now let's assume there are "classy" people with none of the conventional "classy" trappings. For example, in high school I once had a "classy" teacher, at least by my definition. The details I would associate with him include frayed shirt sleeves, flashing elbows; green, clanking Ford; a gap-toothed smile which he termed *sexy* because of something the medieval author Chaucer once wrote; a sly and ready chuckle; two room-mates, one of whom formerly studied architecture with Frank Lloyd Wright and the other of whom married the high school head cheerleader.

Thus, the details I would choose to emphasize when talking about my teacher are not those commonly associated with "class." It would tax my skill as a writer to show how each one of these atypical details truly "represents" the controlling generalization: "Mr. F. personifies *class.*"

►EXERCISE 5.4

(Circle) the stereotypical and <u>underline</u> the atypical details "appropriate" to the following generalization. If you mark a detail as atypical but thesis-supporting, then explain how the detail will work.

EXAMPLE: *green, clanking Ford* — Mr. F. has class because he is not concerned with purchasing a self image.

CONTROLLING
GENERALIZATION: Jack struck me as being quite eccentric.

DETAILS: Top hat, B.A., Camel cigarettes, married, radish sandwiches, pogo stick, pet bryozoan, pet dog, Pete Rose fan, glasses, works eight to five. ◢

Audience Impact

When selecting details appropriate to a given generalization, you will want to consider their immediate impact on the reader. You may want to pick stereotypical details because they are readily recognized or associated with a particular idea. Having immediately recognizable details would seem appropriate when, for example, the concept being explained or argued is particularly complex. These familiar details help to ease your audience into a difficult subject.

On the other hand, you may want to choose atypical details because they allow the reader to discover a new association. Having unexpected details would be appropriate when, for instance, the subject being discussed is familiar to the intended audience.

Finally, you may select neutral details because they best represent the information available on a certain topic, even though they contain neither the element of quick recognition nor the aspect of surprise for your reader.

▸ EXERCISE 5.5

Answer the following questions as specifically as possible.

1. Cite a specific case in your past reading or writing where stereotypical details were, or would have been, effective.
2. Cite a specific case in your past reading or writing where atypical details were, or would have been, effective.
3. Cite a specific case in your past reading or writing where a mixture of detail types was, or could have been, used. ◢

This discussion assumes audience to be an important factor in detail selection. Other factors include:

1. how specific and representative the details are;
2. how the details complement the final form of arrangement; and
3. what types of detail are available.

In any case, when selecting details, you would be wise not to ignore "inconsistent" details just because they do not at first seem to "fit." You may, indeed, end up eliminating them later on, but you also may discover that they, perhaps atypically, support your controlling generalization.

Emphasis

The relationship between the controlling generalization and its support is complex. The following samples show how a difference in emphasis in the controlling generalization itself can influence support choice and, in turn, can produce two entirely separate results.

These two student writers began with the same primary question: "Should I support the current freedom the press enjoys in the United States?" Each began with the purpose to persuade college educated and politically concerned readers to her point of view.

The first paper's controlling generalization concentrates on freedom of the press in terms of withholding the names of sources and supports the journalist's right to withhold such information. The second paper's controlling generalization emphasizes freedom of the press in terms of news interpretation and ridicules how one "news event" can precipitate two (or more) radically different news reports. This difference in controlling generalization has influenced the types of support offered. Because the first controlling generalization is basically "legalistic," the author supports it through documented legal precedent. Her choice of detail can be termed neutral. Because the second controlling generalization is about *subjectivity* in reporting, the author supports it through subjective or personal details. She fabricates an event, and then, from her research on Paul Harvey and Shana Alexander, predicts what each one's response to that event might be. Her choice of detail is atypical.

First student paper

Freedom of the Press

"The concept of freedom of the press is embodied in the First Amendment to the Constitution of the United States in the words, 'Congress shall make no law abridging the freedom of speech or of the press'."[1]

In spite of this long-observed principle, the Supreme Court has denied the existence of such a privilege. But successful journalistic investigative reporting depends on a reporter's right to protect his sources by withholding their names; thus, this right should be extended to every reporter.

It is true that this First Amendment right to protect sources by withholding their names has encountered legal opposition. The first example is of a reporter from New Jersey, Peter J. Bridge, who went to jail for twenty-two days because he refused to testify regarding "confidential information" he procured through investigative methods.[2] A second example is of a reporter for the *St. Petersburg Times,* Lucy Ware Morgan, who was sentenced to five months in jail unless she would reveal her sources for information about a grand jury story she had written.[3] A third example is of two editors and two reporters in Fresno, Calif., where a judge sentenced them to "indefinite terms" because they refused to reveal their source for a story that appeared in the *Fresno Bee* regarding a sealed grand jury testimony.[4] In addition to these three examples, there are many other reporters who were sentenced to jail for withholding sources.

Although the Supreme Court has denied reporters their right to protect their sources by withholding names, this First Amendment right has been recognized through statutes and a bill. Of course, there are those opponents who argue that allowing reporters the right to protect their sources by withholding names would encourage irresponsibility. But this statement "makes the grand presumption that the nation's press is just lying around waiting for passage of absolute immunity so it can commit all kinds of unheard-of atrocities on the American public."[5] Then, there are those who argue that a reporter, if allowed to protect his source, would take no risk; thus, his opinions would not be worth much.[6] This is an example of an error in logic for it offers no specific proof. And in spite of these arguments, eighteen statutes that grant partial immunities have been formed and a bill in New Jersey was approved on December 14, 1972, which says that a reporter does not have to reveal sources or information to any investigative agency.[7]

It therefore seems clear that a reporter should have the right to protect his sources by withholding their names. First, "confidentiality" plays a large part in a reporter's gathering of information. "Politicians, for example, are very reluctant to speak candidly to a reporter unless they are assured that they will not be quoted directly and that their names will not be disclosed as a source of the information."[8] Second, the decision to deny reporters of their First Amendment right would deny the public information necessary to make decisions on politics and other issues of public concern.[9] "And as the digging becomes less penetrating, the power to control thought drifts quietly into the hands of the few; the big lie becomes the accepted truth."[10]

NOTES

1. "Freedom of the Press," *Current*, Vol. 146 (December 1972), p. 27.

2. "Intimidating the Press," *Christian Century*, Vol. 89 (December 1972), p. 89.

3. "Threats to Freedom," *Time*, Vol. 102 (November 1973), p. 54.

4. "Denting the Shield," *Time*, Vol. 105 (June 1975), p. 69.

5. Peter J. Bridge, "The Public's Right to Know," *Current*, Vol. 247 (March 1973), p. 15.

6. Lewis H. Lapham, "The Temptation of a Sacred Cow," *Harper*, Vol. 247 (August 1973), p. 51.

7. Peter J. Bridge, p. 17.

8. "Freedom of the Press," p. 28.

9. *Ibid*.

10. "Intimidating the Press," p. 89.

Carolyn Koyanagi

Second student paper

Freedom of the Press

A news report informs us that former President Nixon traveled to Oxford, England to fulfill a speaking engagement. The ABC radio announcer on the eleven o'clock news informs us that Nixon was met by "five hundred egg throwing, jeering students." One hour later Paul Harvey tells us that Nixon was given a standing ovation by some seven hundred students. Later that same day Jim Hollis, WIBW reporter, tells us that, "In Oxford today former President Nixon was met with cheers and jeers." Each report is different, and we, the public, must decide which is accurate. Because news analysts have political biases, we must carefully scrutinize their reports concerning political figures.

In our imagination let us consider the following event as it might have happened in the White House in the early sixties. Half a dozen reporters are lounging about the first floor lobby awaiting news breaks concerning the latest government crisis. Coming up the hallway toward the elevator is a small entourage. President Kennedy and two Secret Service agents enter the elevator. Just as the elevator door is closing a reporter glimpses a "centerfold" brunette dressed in a shocking pink mini-skirted dress and laced-up black boots.

"Hey, did you see that?" the reporter asks his colleague. "Yeh, I saw THAT. She's probably our new Ambassadress to Liechtenstein and he is taking her upstairs to give her special instructions on how to handle Baron von Schmidtlein, . . ." They both laugh. Marty, another colleague, walks over and asks what the joke was. The tantalizing news spreads among the reporters like a brush fire on a windy hill. Among the reporters that particular day are Shana Alexander and Paul Harvey.

Shana Alexander is a representative of eastern liberalism. She is a Vassar graduate who now works as a contributing columnist to *Newsweek* and expresses cynical views about politicians. Also, she is a frontline ERA supporter. Paul Harvey, on the other hand, is a conservative midwest news analyst for ABC who quotes from small town papers, espouses Christian virtue and exhorts politicians to adhere to ethical moral standards. How does each react to Kennedy's "pink lady"?

Shana's first reaction to the event was embodied in a smile slowly spreading across her face. Her second thought was that the diplomatic corps' dress code had been altered completely. But an attitude of tolerance won out in her judgment. A little "hanky panky" surely should not affect our foreign policy. "Today at the White House President Kennedy took time from his busy schedule to personally conduct Caroline's new nanny through the family's living quarters. . . ." Her story went to press.

Harvey's first reaction to the "mystery lady" was shocked disbelief that our chief executive could be so indiscreet. His second thought was of poor Jackie and her innocent children. He muttered, "Well, when the cat's away, the RAT will play." At his typewriter he gathered material for the news broadcast. "Is there a crack in the castle at Camelot and is Jack a chip off the old block?" . . . begins his newscast.

Because we want to be intelligent we will strive to be informed about political events. In the process, we will have to store in our minds all the minutia we can gather on our reporters' biases so that we can evaluate their news reports.

Personally, I will throw away half of Harvey's hopes for ninety-nine percent sexual purity and keep one fourth of Shana's cynicism about actual performance. By adding to this my own prejudices and moral judgments, I will have a "sure fire" method for evaluating analysts' news reports.

Mary Jo Wodtke

➤ EXERCISE 5.6

Answer the following questions.

1. The Koyanagi paper makes use of neutral details. Is there a way the

paper could be improved by emphasizing atypical details? (In answering this question, generate at least one possible atypical detail in support of Koyanagi's controlling generalization and analyze its effectiveness.)

2. The Wodtke paper makes use of atypical details. Is there a way the paper would benefit from more neutral details? (Again, in answering, generate at least one possible neutral detail in support of Wodtke's controlling generalization and analyze its effectiveness.)

3. Is there any way either paper would benefit from having more stereotypical details, or are stereotypical details even possible with this topic? Explain. ◢

Selecting specific support is not a one-shot affair. Having initially designated the details you wish to use, you may later find it necessary to revise your selection, especially in terms of the paper's overall arrangement.

DISCOVERING PATTERNS OF ARRANGEMENT

When you have "finalized" your controlling generalization and have selected the details to be used as support, you are ready to unite your controlling generalization (your whole) with your supporting information (your parts) into some type of overall arrangement. What arrangement will you choose?

Sometimes arrangements can be imposed on material. For example, if you are assigned to write with a comparison/contrast structure, you can form a controlling generalization that predicts that structure and you can collect information that fulfills the expectations of that structure. (Review page 80.)

In other instances, arrangements suggest themselves during the composing process. They grow organically from the ideas and information present. The following discussion will note how arrangements can emerge as you write.

Clues in the Composing Context

Even early in the composing process, clues as to the final arrangement of a paper can present themselves; in fact, the composing context itself may suggest appropriate arrangements. An obvious instance where context determines arrangement is when a particular arrangement is actually assigned.

In a more general sense, both audience and purpose function as contextual elements that suggest arrangements. For example, let's say you are determining the audience's relationship to your subject, and you discover that your readers may need certain key terms defined. Therefore, you mentally set aside a portion of your final arrangement for definition even though you have not yet determined the overall arrangement.

Purpose similarly influences arrangement. If your purpose were to explain the different roles expected of the father by his teenage son, you would probably predict at the outset that your arrangement might be one of those forms traditionally associated with explanation. At this early stage, then, you could begin considering exemplification or comparison/contrast as arrangement options. Perhaps more importantly, you could eliminate some options, such as classical argument, because your purpose is to explain, not to persuade.

Clues in Your Reading

Your reading, important both to invention and to information gathering, can also suggest arrangement options. For example, assume you are writing on the subject, "The Effects of T.V. Viewing on Today's Elementary School Child." Assume further that in your reading you run across the following passage in Marshall McLuhan's *Understanding Media: The Extensions of Man:*

> . . . What disqualifies war from being a true game is probably what also disqualifies the stock market and business—the rules are not fully known or accepted by all the players. Furthermore, the audience is too fully participant in war and business, just as in a native society there is no true art because *everybody* is engaged in making art. Art and games need rules, conventions, and spectators.[1]

The context for this passage is McLuhan's belief that games, like media, are extensions of social human beings. The passage itself works through definition, offering negative details concerning what games *are not* and stating a comparison to art concerning what games *are.*

Although the McLuhan passage does not deal with T.V., it could suggest to you this idea: "Perhaps I could compare watching T.V. to working on an art project as activities and discuss the similarities and differences in the effects these activities have on elementary school children." In other words, the passage suggests comparison/contrast as a form of arrangement.

The passage could also raise the question, "What rules or conventions do T.V. programs follow and how do these influence children as spectators?" Here, a two-part structure emerges, dealing with *what* and then with *how.*

Each of these two arrangement options serves as a counterpoint to the cause-and-effect arrangement suggested by the subject itself.

Clues in Subjects

The subject itself often suggests its own arrangement. This suggestive power of subjects can be clearly seen in subject-splitting, in which the basis for the split often involves organizational forms. Consider the following:

The basis of division is *types* of mental functions; correspondingly, the suggested pattern of arrangement is classification.

The next example, although not as straightforward, works similarly:

Here the basis for division is the steps involved in star evolution; the suggested pattern of arrangement is process analysis. However, if the writer would want to focus on, say, the similarities and differences between the two red giant stages, the suggested pattern of arrangement would be comparison/contrast. Similarly, if the writer would want to focus on the nature of the yellow stage alone, the suggested pattern of arrangement would be definition.

Clues in Inventing from Premises

Using idea-sparring as a means of invention involves examining relationships between premises. Often these relationships embody conventional forms of arrangement, predominately comparison/contrast and cause and effect. Similarly, idea-shooting features comparative and causal analysis, with definition and process analysis playing major supporting roles. (See pages 70–72). In other words, during invention, traditional

forms of arrangement can serve as devices for both examining and generating ideas. These forms, in turn, can serve as the organizing principle of
the paper that eventually develops from the ideas generated. And, as will
be shown, these forms can also influence the final details you select to
support those ideas.

In addition, *how* ideas are joined during idea-synthesizing can suggest
arrangements. Consider the following:

SYNTHESIS: Current economic conditions and longstanding racial
                 discrimination led to the race riots in North Philadelphia
                 in 1966.

DISCUSSION: Because economic conditions and racial discrimination
                 are established as causes, the obvious pattern of arrange-
                 ment suggested by the synthesis is cause and effect. Yet,
                 because the two causes are joined by *and,* it is implied
                 that they contributed equally to the riot. An argument
                 may be conceived, therefore, concerning whether the
                 causes were indeed equal, and the paper might be struc-
                 tured as an argumentative analysis.

   Consider instead:

SYNTHESIS: Longstanding racial discrimination created a basis for
                 unrest in North Philadelphia, but current economic con-
                 ditions sparked the race riots there in 1966.

DISCUSSION: Here, the wording of the synthesis establishes economic
                 conditions as the catalyst causing the riots. These condi-
                 tions will presumably be the focus of the paper. How-
                 ever, because the current economic and longstanding
                 racial causes are joined by the coordinator *but,* they are
                 presumed to be equal in weight and therefore both de-
                 serving of discussion. The arrangement suggested by the
                 synthesis is cause and effect, with economic conditions
                 being discussed second. Perhaps a comparison of the
                 relative importance of the two causes is also in store.

   Consider finally:

SYNTHESIS: Although longstanding racial discrimination created a
                 foundation of unrest in North Philadelphia, current eco-
                 nomic conditions sparked the race riots in 1966.

DISCUSSION: As in the second synthesis, economic conditions are
                 seen as the catalyst causing the riots. However, because
                 longstanding racial discrimination is prefaced by *al-
                 though,* it is understood as subordinate to economic con-

ditions in this case and thus not as deserving of discussion. In fact, racial discrimination might be discussed only in the introduction or in a background section in the final arrangement. The final arrangement could feature a detailed listing or an enumeration of economic conditions responsible for the riots.

Clues in Primary and Secondary Questions

The wording of a primary or secondary question can call for a particular pattern of arrangement. For instance, if one of your questions is "Could I compare/contrast Ms. Baker's and Mr. Parks' classes in terms of attitudes toward writing?", your choice of a comparison/contrast structure would certainly seem in order. Similarly, if one of your questions is "Historically, has there been any change in long distance running styles?" (see page 84), your choice of narration—at least for the section of development answering this question—would seem appropriate.

Key words in primary or secondary questions can serve as clues to arrangements. For example, "What is the *meaning* of anachronistic futurist?", "What are the *types* of country music today?", "What are the *steps* associated with electing a President?", and "What *should be* done to preserve our National Parks?" are questions containing key words that suggest definition, classification, process analysis, and classical argument as respective arrangements.

Clues in the Relationship between Parts

Arrangements can also suggest themselves in the natural grouping of the supportive parts of your material. To discover these groupings, you might ask yourself questions such as "Do certain parts of my material all deal with *causes?*" If so, a cause-and-effect sequence might be in order. Similarly, the question, "Do parts deal with either a *pro* or *con* side of an issue?", might suggest traditional argument as a pattern. It might also suggest a classification or a comparison/contrast of the *pros* and *cons*. Mixed patterns may similarly present themselves.

In a very real sense, traditional arrangement options can be defined by the way they handle the relationship between parts. These options as products are covered in detail in Part III of this text. The following chart summarizes how certain arrangement options characteristically handle parts. The purpose of the chart is to provide a general context for arrangement selection; it is not meant to be a final, definitive statement of how arrangements work.

Process Involved	Effect	Representative Options
Selects one part for development	Isolates parts	Description Definition
Unifies several parts under one whole	Clusters parts	Classification Comparison/contrast Exemplification
Orders parts chronologically, procedurally, logically	Sequences parts	Narration Process analysis Cause and effect Argument

Within this context, you can discover clues about your final arrangement by watching how you begin to focus the supportive parts of your material. Do you find yourself focusing on the nature of one part? Do you find yourself grouping your parts according to their natures, their similarities, their differences? Or do you find yourself grouping your parts as representative examples of the same idea? Do you find yourself ordering your parts on the basis of time, steps, or logical progression? Each one of these questions points you toward a distinct set of arrangement options.

►EXERCISE 5.7

Briefly tell what arrangement(s) each of the following composing situations suggests. In your discussion, you needn't know the traditional name(s) for the arrangement(s) that you discover, but you should note basically what the major sections of the final paper could be doing:

1. You are writing instructions on how to play chess for readers who know how to play checkers.
2. You are writing a letter to your best out-of-town friend, trying to get him/her to come up for the weekend.
3. Your primary question is "What are some effective methods of coping with peer pressure?"
4. Your secondary questions include "What is the most effective method of coping with peer pressure?", "What makes a method *effective?*", and "Do these methods solve the problem of peer pressure?"

5. Your subject "Reporters: Journalists or Advocates?" evolved from the following subject-splitting:

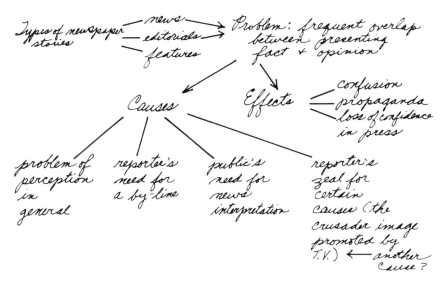

advantages of passive versus active solar power shows passive solar to be more cost effective."

7. Your synthesis is "The rewards of gardening are not necessarily measured in dollars and cents."

8. You are researching the varied adjustment problems that children of newly divorced parents face when you chance to see this saying: "Thom's Law of Marital Bliss: The length of a marriage is inversely proportional to the amount spent on the wedding."

9. In researching "The Nature of Sadat's Statesmanship," you are puzzled by the fact that many Egyptians prefer Sadat's successor to Sadat. In your attempt to learn more about the Egyptian people, you read the following comment in John Adams' article "On Expressive Communication in an Egyptian Village":

> If a speaker is a "friend," then what he says is generally accepted as "friendly." Even if the content is not complimentary, the listener assumes that his friend "doesn't mean what he says" or is "only teasing." If the speaker is an "enemy," then everything he says, however conciliatory, is suspect. The villager has few merely neutral relationships.

(Note: you might think about the nature of a diplomat's communication in general and of Sadat's in particular before addressing this item.)

USING AN OUTLINE

Whatever arrangement you choose for presenting your controlling generalization and its support, you can either plan or check your structure by using an outline. An outline characteristically shows coordinate and subordinate relationships between various supporting details, and between the controlling generalization and the support. An outline typically begins with the statement of the controlling generalization:

OUTLINE

Controlling generalization: *Karma, jñāna, and bhakti* represent three equal ways a Hindu may try to reach God. [3]

In this controlling generalization, the writer has established the topic (Hindu paths to God), the attitude (the paths are equally acceptable), and an expectation (the three ways will be discussed in more detail to follow).

In the subsequent development, then, the writer will probably want a general statement to introduce each category with its respective "representative" information. This statement, the sub-generalization, is indicated by large Roman numerals in the outline.

OUTLINE

Controlling generalization: *Karma, jñāna,* and *bhakti* represent three equal ways a Hindu may try to reach God.

  I.   First, the way of *karma* leads the Hindu to God through work.
  II. *Jñāna,* knowledge, provides the Hindu with a second path to God.
  III. Finally, the path of *bhakti* emphasizes neither work nor knowledge, but devotion.

Such sub-generalizations are *coordinate* in terms of weight or of emphasis. For example, let's say that the Hinduism outline proceeded as follows:

OUTLINE

Controlling generalization: *Karma, jñāna,* and *bhakti* represent three equal ways a Hindu may try to reach God.

  I.   First, the way of *karma* leads the Hindu to God through work.
  II. *Jñāna,* knowlege, provides the Hindu with a second path to God, while *bhakti,* or devotion, provides a third.

In this outline, the sub-generalizations are not balanced or of the same weight because the first covers one path and the second covers two. A second example of imbalance occurs in the next outline.

OUTLINE

Controlling generalization: *Karma, jñāna,* and *bhakti* represent three equal ways a Hindu may try to reach God.

   I.   First, the way of *karma* leads the Hindu to God through work.
   II.   *Jñāna,* knowledge, provides the Hindu with a second path to God.
   III.   The path of *bhakti* emphasizes neither work nor knowledge, but devotion.
   IV.   In many ways, Hinduism is a *dharma* rather than a religion because it emphasizes behavior rather than beliefs.

In this outline, the fourth sub-generalization is out of balance with the first three because it deals with Hinduism as a whole rather than with separate parts of Hinduism. In addition, the fourth sub-generalization is not predicted by the controlling generalization. For this reason it does not "belong." But while the fourth point may not serve as a sub-generalization in this case, it would still make a fine conclusion and could be incorporated at the end of the paper.

Because outlining is essentially a classification with Roman numerals representing the most important points, you can check the relative weight given to each respective point and rearrange material if necessary before presenting the finished product to the reader.

Outlines can also be used to check the logical relationships between the sub-generalizations and the supporting detail, as the outline in Figure 5.2 suggests. (See page 144.)

Although you are not obliged to use the exact wording of your outline in your final paper, you would be wise not to deviate from the arrangement reflected in a sound outline. Using an outline helps you stay "on point."

▶**EXERCISE 5.8**

Arrange the following generalizations into coordinate and subordinate relationships. Remember, generalizations are coordinate if equal in weight and emphasis; generalizations are subordinate if one represents a smaller part of the other. Remember, too, that major sub-generalizations may each be supported by minor sub-generalizations that also must be coordinate to one another but subordinate to the respective major sub-generalization. After you have determined the coordinate and subordinate relationships of the following generalizations, try to arrange them in outline form.

1. One reason college students should not patronize movie theaters is the outrageous prices.
2. Patrons elbowing each other for refreshments is unpleasant.
3. The poor quality of the movies should be yet another reason for students to avoid them.
4. Ticket prices have tripled in the past two years.
5. College students should avoid movie theaters.
6. Sequels frequently are pale versions of the original flick.
7. Another reason college students should boycott movie theaters is the unappealing atmosphere.
8. Movies too often rely on formula plots.
9. Patrons giggling during a show can be disruptive.
10. Concession items cost double what they would in a grocery. ◢

Some writers outline before beginning any sort of draft. Others outline to check a draft already in progress. In either case, the writer uses the outline to get a clear picture of the relationship between the controlling generalization and its support.

USING SECTIONAL BREAKDOWN

Whether you write a preliminary draft before or after an outline, you can view that draft as a series of sections, or expandable boxes, to be filled with the various parts of your support. These sections can represent divisions established by general writing practice or dictated by specific arrangement conventions.

General Practice

Sectioning an expository essay can sometimes involve nothing more elaborate than determining what belongs in the introduction, the body, and the conclusion. However, because the body of an essay characteristically involves some length and complexity, it often requires further sectioning.

Precise sectioning practices frequently govern other types of writing. In business writing, for example, negative messages usually contain these sections: an opening buffer, a section establishing the reasons for the negative message, a statement of the negative message itself, and a pleasant ending. In technical report writing, common sections for a description of a process include an introduction establishing context, a list of main steps,

Thesis: Lawyers should not advertise their services because this action would not significantly benefit the public.

I. It is true that those seeking legal services need assistance.

    A̶. The public does not utilize present available means. *—move to III ?*

   -? B̶. The public over-estimates the cost of legal services. *- this does not seem to fit concession*

II. Although the idea of advertising may seem beneficial to the public, if instituted, it would be misleading and deceptive.

    A̶. A code of ethics was established in 1908. *background- does not support* *misleading or deceptive*

    B̶. Advertising would commercialize the profession.

    C̶. Emphasis would be put on quantity, not quality. *again, this issue = not in sub- generalization* *- not sub issue*

 A. ←D. No two cases are exactly alike. *-keep--shows "misleading"*

 B. ←E. Compliance to standard fees would be impossible. *- keep --shows "deceptive"*

III. The public already has ample alternatives to advertising; therefore, if these were utilized more extensively, advertising would be unnecessary.

    A. Many people select lawyers from satisfied clients and business leaders within the community.

    B. Lawyer referral services exist to aid the public.

    C̶. More law directories should be published. *- this does not show current alternative*

    D̶. Interviewing candidates i̶s a necessity.

(should be viewed as)

move to conclusion

also move to conclusion this is a current alternative but would make a stronger recommendation?

FIGURE 5.2 *Using an Outline to Check and Revise Theme Logic*

a list of components, a description or analysis including definition and substeps, and a conclusion containing a summary and an evaluation. Similarly, progress reports for professional writing in general feature the following: statement of the problem, introductory background and significance, review of objectives, anticipated benefits of implementation, work plan progress, summary of project status, and plans for future activities.

These general writing practices offer you initial ways to sectionally organize your support as a whole. Other such practices may involve ordering section details in ascending importance.

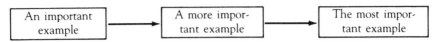

These writing practices, although general, are frequently tied to a specific writing context.

Specific Conventions

Although it is beyond the scope of this chapter to outline the sectioning that defines certain traditional forms of arrangement, it is important to note here that your choice of an arrangement can bring with it an "automatic" method of sectioning your draft material. For example, when you choose classification as a form, you section according to *types* of something. Each section deals with one type. When you choose classical argument, you predict having concession, presentation/refutation, solution and conclusion sections.

Such sectioning not only determines where your gathered material belongs, but also shows you where material might be missing. For example, let's say that you are forming a classical argument. You want to have a concession section, but have no material for that section. You thus discover the need to generate more information before you can complete the paper. Similarly, sectioning can tell you whether your development has balance, whether, for example, each *type* in your classification is equally detailed.

In any case, whether you are sectioning according to general practices or specific conventions, you might find the following questions helpful:

1. Do specific parts of my support resemble each other in content?
2. Do specific parts of my support overlap each other in content or coverage? If so, does this overlapping represent unnecessary repetition or desired reinforcement?
3. Does my support adequately "fill" my designated sections? OR Can specific parts of my support be eliminated?
4. Do specific parts of my support seem contradictory? If so, can the contradictions be resolved or accounted for?
5. More specifically, does the cueing of any of my notecards indicate some natural grouping of parts of my material? Some natural divisions or sections?

While sectioning, some writers find it helpful to devote a separate page to each new draft section so they can easily examine each section individually before linking the sections together into a coherent whole. Once the sections are determined and the detail marshalled accordingly, how to link the sections to each other becomes an important issue.

PROVIDING LINKS

Clear-cut organization, such as that planned or checked by outline, does not in itself guarantee the type of coherence expected by readers. Helping to promote coherence are also various linking devices available to the writer. In fact, sub-generalizations often serve as such links, as do topic sentences in paragraphs, and transitional phrases.

Sub-generalizations as Links

In a paper, the controlling generalization states the main idea. The rest of the information develops the idea and thus supports the generalization. Sub-generalizations link the controlling generalization with its support. These sub-generalizations usually contain four elements: (a) implicit or explicit reference to the thesis, (b) explicit reference to the support "at hand," (c) a transition, and (d) a "refinement" that gives additional information about the upcoming support. For example, let's take the controlling generalization: "Theoretically, nuclear power can be produced from either nuclear fission or nuclear fusion." One possible sub-generalization generated by this controlling generalization is:

$$\overset{c}{\Big[\text{First,}\Big]} \quad \overset{d}{\Big[\text{the method used currently,}\Big]} \quad \overset{b}{\Big[\text{nuclear fission}\Big]} \quad \Big[\text{produces}$$

$$\overset{a}{\text{needed energy}\Big]} \quad \text{and} \quad \Big[\text{unneeded nuclear waste.}\Big]$$

You will notice that the sub-generalization does not just state: first, there's nuclear fission. Instead, it offers additional information about nuclear fission in its "refinements."

▶EXERCISE 5.9

Label (a, b, c, and d) the four elements present in the following sub-generalization:

> Second, nuclear fusion, a method not currently utilized to produce domestic power, offers the potential of "waste free" energy once the technology is developed. ◢

▸EXERCISE 5.10

Form sub-generalizations for the following controlling generalizations. Include each of the four elements (a, b, c, and d). You probably will need to generate information for your "refinements" (*d*s). A dictionary might be helpful.

1. The terms aphrodite and transvestite represent two distinct sexual realities.
2. Counseling strategies can be cognitive, affective, and behavioral.
3. Major league baseball teams seem to be either a collection of "no-names" or a star-studded cast.
4. It should not be difficult to determine whether your pet rock is igneous, metamorphic, or sedimentary. ◂

Topic Sentences as Links

Paragraphs operate under the same principles as the paper as a whole; that is, they are unified around one main point and contain details to support that point. Paragraphs commonly represent subdivisions or subsections of the paper's arrangement.

In a paragraph, the topic sentence carries the burden of establishing the subject. It functions in the paragraph just as the controlling generalization does in the paper as a whole. Although it may appear anywhere within a paragraph, the topic sentence is usually found at or near the beginning. In this position, it may contain transitional links to previous paragraphs or subsections. Transitional links will be discussed shortly.

Sometimes, sub-topic sentences aid a paragraph's coherence by linking the topic sentence with its support, as in the following example:

> Part of Hilda's being a character involves her doing the unexpected. (Topic sentence) For example, in her younger years, she was an avid jogger, much to the surprise of the local school boys. (Sub-topic sentence) "Yep," Hilda revealed, "I used to run to and from the grocery where I worked after my husband died." The boys used to say, 'Look at that woman!' and wonder what I was doing. But I figured anything that was good for those boys that played football was good for me." (Supporting development, in this case direct quotes) Hilda also surprised me with the revelation that, at the age of eighty-nine, she repaired her own roof with the help of her granddaughter. (Sub-topic sentence) "Yep, I fixed it myself. Those repair

men didn't believe me where it was leaking, so I got up there through the attic . . . patched it up with some tin and tar." (Supporting development, in this case direct quotes)

Paragraph coherence is also aided by consistent emphasis and tense use. (Review pages 50– 51)

Transitional Phrases as Links

In addition to sub-generalization and topic sentences, transitional words and phrases can also give your writing coherence and unity. Transitional phrases can link:

1. controlling generalization to sub-generalization,
2. sub-generalization to sub-generalization,
3. sub-generalization to topic sentence (assuming the two aren't one and the same),
4. topic sentence to topic sentence,
5. topic sentence to sub-topic sentence,
6. sub-topic to sub-topic,
7. detail to detail.

In other words, transitional phrases represent a versatile means of getting the various sections of your paper to hang together.

In the following paragraph, for example, the various transitional phrases or markers are *underlined* (and optional markers are enclosed in parentheses). These markers increase coherence through enhanced continuity.

> Although Sergeant Marx's defense of Judaism appears to be determined by circumstances, his faith in man's dignity reflects an innate concern for human integrity. <u>For instance</u>, (for example, in the first place, first, demonstrating this) Marx several times expresses concern that he may have lost his ability to sympathize with others. Marx is aware that because of the war he has developed:
>
> > . . . an infantryman's heart, which, like his feet, at first aches and swells but finally grows horny enough for him to travel the weirdest paths without feeling a thing.[4]

After allowing the Jewish personnel to go to *shul* rather than making them participate in the G.I. party, Marx <u>therefore</u> (in addition, furthermore, consequently, secondly) feels amazement and happiness that he can sympathize with the "fellows" again. <u>In addition</u>, (furthermore, thirdly, in another case, later) Grossbart's comment that Marx is a "fine, decent man" touches Marx extremely. <u>Furthermore</u>, additionally, fourthly, also, in fact) the Sergeant's final decision to fix the orders so that Grossbart is properly assigned to the Pacific demonstrates Marx's concern for the integrity "of all of us." <u>Finally</u>, (lastly, in conclusion, it follows that) Marx's last statement shows his realization that a man who does try to preserve human dignity nevertheless remains a fallible human being. He concludes: "Resisting with all my will an impulse to turn and seek pardon for my vindictiveness, I accepted my fate." And so it often seems that doing our best remains inadequate, but still somehow worth the effort.

Such extensive use of transitional markers creates continuity. It also may create boredom. In fact, precisely because this writer is careful to use the same grammatical subject throughout the paragraph (Sergeant Marx, he, Marx, the Sergeant), she may reduce the number of transitional markers without adversely affecting continuity. It would be clear for the writer to say:

> After allowing the Jewish personnel to go to *shul* rather than to participate in the G.I. party, Marx feels amazement and happiness that he can sympathize with his "fellows" again. He is touched by the comment that he is a "fine, decent man." <u>And</u> Marx values the integrity "of all of us," so much so that he fixes Grossbart's orders and sends the corporal to the Pacific.

In addition to using transitions and maintaining a consistent grammatical subject, a writer may promote continuity by judiciously repeating certain words or phrases, as demonstrated in the following excerpt:

> . . . <u>After allowing the</u> Jewish personnel to go to *shul* rather than to participate in the G.I. party, <u>Marx</u> feels amazement and happiness <u>that</u> he can sympathize with his "fellows" again. <u>After hearing the</u> comment that he is a "fine, decent man," <u>Marx</u> is quite moved <u>that</u> he is seen as more than a Sergeant. <u>After fixing the</u> orders so Grossbart is properly sent to the Pacific, <u>Marx</u> reveals <u>that</u> his concern in doing so was for the integrity "of all of us." Yet, <u>after fixing the</u> orders, <u>Marx</u> also recognizes <u>that</u> trying to preserve human dignity does not make him infallible.

Note how patterned repetition and two key transitional links, "yet" and "also," maintain paragraph continuity.

One last comment on the Marx example is in order. Its topic sentence is really a strictly formed sub-generalization.

transition   *reference to previous sub and*
[Although] [Sergeant Marx's defense of Judaism appears to be
controlling generalization   *reference to current support*
determined by circumstances] [his faith in man's dignity] [reflects an
refinement
innate concern for human integrity.]

From this sub-generalization, both the previous sub-generalization and the controlling generalization can be constructed:

PREVIOUS SUB: Marx's defense of Judaism proves to be prompted by expediency (circumstances).

CONTROLLING
GENERALIZATION: Sergeant Marx ably defends both his Jewish faith and his faith in human dignity.

Such transparent arrangement of the paper helps the reader understand the writer's idea and how the writer's support relates to that idea.

In business and technical writing, headings and sub-headings often provide the reader with a quick visual appraisal of the writer's arrangement. Such headings also find their way into reports and term papers. However, in expository writing, writers generally weave their links directly into the fabric of their work.

The process of developing a system of links begins for the most part during the initial formation of any sub-generalizations and continues as the writer works to refine individual sections of the paper. Both the numerals and letters in an outline and the section divisions in a preliminary draft point to places in need of significant linking.

▶**EXERCISE 5.11**

Revise the following paragraph for increased continuity:

At a recent New Games Festival, games featured emphasized fun rather than competition. The New Games Foundation has its head-quarters in San Francisco. Competition characterizes most of the games now produced by manufacturers. The new *Mad Magazine* game states that whichever player loses all of his or her money first is the winner. Whoever loses best wins. Connie Strand, a reporter for the *Capital Journal,* points out that "Everyone was a winner" at the New Games Festival. People joined hands and tied themselves into a complicated knot. The games do not have any rules that cannot be altered by the participants. The New Games Foundation's slogan is "Play hard, play fair, nobody hurt." In the sports pages, a game-losing fumble becomes a "horrible nightmare." People are used to playing to win. At the New Games Festival, people worked together to keep a giant "earth ball" airborne. The New Games Foundation's address is P.O. Box 7901, San Francisco, CA. 94120.◢

⌐ EXERCISE 5.12

Analyze the following paper for links. In pencil *underline* the controlling generalization <u>twice</u>, any sub-generalizations <u>once</u>, and check (√) any additional linking devices.◄

Witchdoctor: The Complete Physician

Contrary to the average Western impression of the African witch-doctor as an evil potion-mixer or a gaudily plumed fraud, witch-doctors are actually knowledgeable ministers of religion and herbalists who are beneficial in their own settings.

As a minister of religion, the witchdoctor has the ability to commu-nicate with the spirit world. Through this contact he can find the cause of an illness or misfortune. In Africa, much often depends on the mood of the spirits. Thus, an illness could be blamed on an offended ancestral spirit rather than on an infectious microbe. Acting as a minister, the witchdoctor counsels the people on ways to worship the spirits. More specifically, he advises them on the type of sacrifice or ritual needed to get the spirits back into a good mood. Because the African is frequently deeply involved with his spirit world, many illnesses can be brought on by guilt or self-hypnosis. The witchdoctor assumes another of the minister's roles—that of a psychologist—in order to effectively clear up these psychosomatic complaints. For example, a person might come to the witchdoctor complaining of an aching body, a paralyzed limb, or mental turmoil. After it has been deduced that there is nothing physically wrong with the person, the witchdoctor might contact the spirit world to find the root of the problem. He might also use a technique similar to Freudian dream analysis in which the patient describes his dreams, free associates about them, and then listens to the witchdoctor's interpretation of them. Either way, the witchdoctor is able to determine which ances-tral spirit feels snubbed and the type of bribe it will take to placate the spirit. It may be found, for instance, that a patient has offended an ancestral spirit by failing to pay back a loan. If the patient pays back the loan to the closest surviving relative at the suggestion of the witchdoctor, the symptoms of the psychosomatic illness promptly disappear. The witchdoctor can clear up psychosomatic problems so well in such cases because of the African's total faith in the witch-doctor's ability to deal with the spirit world.

In addition to being a minister, the witchdoctor is a herbalist who knows how to identify, prepare, mix, and prescribe the herbs in his vicinity. Preparation of the herbs may require boiling, crushing, soaking, or drying. With his herbs, the witchdoctor can prepare medicines for snakebites, abdominal disorders, colds, toothaches, open wounds, and other common problems. Even though somewhat crude, the herbal treatments are medically effective. For example, witchdoctors have used a stramonium leaf as a cure for asthma and reserpine extracted from the rauwolfia root as a tranquilizer. Both stramonium and reserpine are familiar ingredients in the medicines used in the Western world for the same afflictions. Some of the witchdoctor's remedies and medicines are starting to find their way into official pharmacopoeia. Moreover, the combination of minister and herbalist proves especially effective in treating organic illnesses. If a patient came to the witchdoctor with an open wound, for example, the witchdoctor would dry the wound with herbs. He would also tell the patient that he had offended his grandmother's spirit and needed to sacrifice a chicken to appease the spirit. After sacrificing the chicken, the African would find his wound healing, and his mind would be at ease.

Linda Geiger

▶ EXERCISE 5.13

Write a paper growing out of one of the following composing situations. Include an outline and a sectioned preliminary draft as part of your prepatory work.

1. Read the Cowger and the Harris papers. (See pages 68 – 70 and 226 – 30.) Write a paper on an idea growing out of your reading.
2. Reread the Koyanagi and Wodtke papers. (See pages 131 – 33 and 133 – 34.) Write a paper on an idea growing out of your reading.◢

▶ EXERCISE 5.14

Write a paper featuring the evidence you gathered for Exercise 4.7 (page 120). ◢

The following Process Sheet should aid you when you're drafting your arrangement for Exercises 5.13 and 5.14.

DISCOVERING AN ARRANGEMENT

Are there any clues in the composing context that suggest arrangements?

Are there any clues in my reading that suggest arrangements?

Does the basis for my subject-splitting suggest arrangements?

Does how I examine the relationship between premises or how I join ideas into a synthesis suggest arrangements?

Does the wording of my primary or secondary question(s) suggest arrangements?

Are there any clues to arrangements in the relationship(s) between the parts of my material?

Does the sectioning of my material in my preliminary draft suggest arrangements?

154

NOTES

1. [Herbert] Marshall McLuhan, *Understanding Media: The Extensions of Man* (New York: McGraw-Hill Book Company, 1964), p. 240.

2. A diagram of the "Evolution of a Sun-Size Star" appeared in the December 27, 1976 issue of *Time.*

3. K.M. Sen, *Hinduism* (Baltimore, Md.: Penguin Books, 1967), p. 39.

4. Philip Roth, "Defender of the Faith," in *Story and Structure,* ed. Laurence Perrine (New York: Harcourt Brace Jovanovich, 1978), p. 157.

6

DISCOVERING STYLISTIC CHOICE

When you draft for arrangement (see Chapter 5), you address the reader's expectations that the paper be unified, supported, and coherent. When you draft for style, you consider appropriateness, accuracy, and conciseness. And, as established in Chapter 2, you can address these stylistic concerns by following these guidelines:

1. Adjust your level of usage to match your audience, subject, and purpose.
2. Distinguish between denotations and connotations in word choice and consider emphasis in phrasing.
3. Increase your vocabulary. Reduce passive and other wordy constructions. And maintain a single paragraph emphasis.

However, the experienced reader expects more from style than appropriateness, accuracy, and conciseness. This reader also expects that the writer's style will promote the familiar values of unity, specificity, and coherence. This chapter examines how you can make appropriate stylistic choices in your own writing.

PROMOTING UNITY THROUGH STYLE

Promoting unity through style involves devising a frame and selecting a perspective. A well-conceived frame and a consistent perspective function much like the setting for a jewel; they provide a context for your content and enable the audience to appreciate its full value.

Devising a Frame

In expository writing, the introduction and conclusion together provide a frame for the essay's message.

Using introductions to focus

The introduction establishes the focus of the paper and engages reader interest. If your paper has an explicit controlling generalization, you can establish your main idea and create reader expectations with one stroke. Recall that the controlling generalization states the topic, establishes an attitude or idea about the topic, and frequently sets up how the paper will proceed. Furthermore, the way the controlling generalization is presented can enhance the expectations. For example, compare the following:

1. "Art is basically either geometric or organic."

2. "How the *square artists* (I call them square because they seem obsessed with cubes, and they call me square because I think them so) fall into one category or pit, and the *organic artists* (the ones with the blossoming nudes) grow from a second."

The first controlling generalization seems to predict an objective analysis; the second, a subjective one.

Even without an explicit controlling generalization, the introduction can establish the paper's focus. In a natural narrative, for example, the introduction routinely sets up the main point as it ushers in characters and subjects and initiates the action. (See pages 5–6.) In other words, creating an introductory context can lay the foundation for the reader's discovery of the main idea that implicitly governs the text.

The following introduction by student Rick Jones combines narrative with controlling generalization:

> Several distinctively dressed gentlemen enter a plushly carpeted room carrying steaming mugs of cocoa. They sit down in soft, black, tall-back chairs and await the arrival of the secretary. Suddenly, the peaceful atmosphere is permeated by the clatter and confusion of the secretary and several of his aides carrying huge arm-loads of paperwork. A gigantic stack of papers is placed on the desk in front of each committee member. The Commission of Federal Paperwork begins another hectic and frustrating day of viewing thousands of pieces of governmental paperwork. This is only one minute example of how the United States Bureaucracy is becoming increasingly inept in its efforts to solve governmental problems.

Note how the calm of the gentlemen contrasts with the commotion of the secretary, introducing the idea of an inept, if not also inane, bureaucracy.

Using introductions to attract

Although your main idea should engage reader interest in and of itself, writers such as Rick Jones commonly employ various techniques to lure the reader into the text. Devices can range from incorporating narrative to constructing an analogy, from citing statistics to relating an anecdote, from asking a question to quoting a memorable statement. In fact, one method of engaging the reader is simply to use good specific detail. Compare, for example, the following excerpts:

1. Frustration is an annoying emotion. Bit by bit frustration mounts up to create agony and misery in what should be a pleasant situation. Although frustration can occur at almost any time, it is seen most clearly when a person attempts to type.

2. Birhaugh grms; ltn nac lrpllgo oj mrk . . . What? Again? Curses! I'm so FRUSTRATED when I try to type.

Because the specific detail visually portrays the writer's frustration, the second sample more successfully catches reader interest.

But specific detail alone does not guarantee a good introduction. The following example contains many specifics:

Nervously, mother was helping me unpack my new-for-college clothes including the wine color-coordinated sweater and skirt, which the newspaper ad acclaimed as the newest fall fashion. Also arranged and put away were the towels, blankets, Noxema, toothpaste, and assorted cosmetics required for nine months residence away from home. The conversation topic was a listing of ways to take care of myself. She was talking and I was listening.

Although specific, it establishes neither the focus nor the attitude of the forthcoming paper. In other words, the device being used to attract reader interest here has become an end in itself, instead of a means to an end.

In fact, integrating the interest-catcher with the main idea does cause problems at times. Consider the following:

"Hey man, that's a *bad* shot."
"That guy is really a *bad* dude."
"This place is really *bad.* "

Just how many times has American society changed words around? God only knows. There is no way I would want to be a foreigner living here in the states. ("That there would be one *bad* trip.") Heck, I have a *bad* enough time trying to keep up with the language now, and I have lived here my entire life. I think it is amazing how we can use words like love to mean hate and words like hate to mean love.

The difficulty in this excerpt arises from a possible double emphasis. Is the writer going to talk about the slang meaning of *bad* ? If so, the prose portion of the introduction is inappropriate, because it expands the focus to the regular meaning of *bad* and the paradoxical use of words in general. If, indeed, the focus is supposed to be on the paradoxical use of words, then the quoted portion of the introduction is misleading, for it seems to emphasize only the slang use of *bad.* An introduction should instead maintain a clear and consistent emphasis. Providing adequate links between the various parts of an introduction is therefore a necessity.

When devising an introduction, you would do well to start by asking, again, "What is the main point of my paper?" Your main point, whether expressed in an explicit controlling generalization or not, provides the focus for your introductory material.

You can then turn to other questions:

1. What would draw *me* into a paper on this subject? Would my audience in this case be attracted by similar devices or circumstances?
2. Which of the following interest-catching devices seems appropriate to my subject? To my audience? To my purpose?

questions	striking details, description
statistics	narrative or anecdote
quotation	startling or unusual facts
analogy	a representative example

3. Is there any portion of my information that could serve as raw material for one of the devices mentioned above? Will I need to generate additional material for the introduction?
4. What role will my controlling generalization play in the introduction?
5. If I decide to include both an interest-catcher and a controlling generalization, how can I link them together to form a coherent whole?

For further examples of finished introductions, see the narrative opening of the Alf Landon interview (page 231), the anecdote used in the comparison/contrast "The Bird and the Beast" (page 34), the summary opening to the progress report on Jessup (page 215), and the definition statement opening the technical description of a bhang (page 269).

Using conclusions to reinforce the main idea

The conclusion of a paper usually recaptures the writer's main point while encouraging the reader to think about the paper's ideas outside the context of the paper itself. Unless the paper is lengthy, the conclusion does not summarize the paper's content, although it may, without repetition, embody the controlling generalization and main points of the paper. For example, let's assume the conclusion of a paper read: "And so the intellectual heroes of these dramas may be said to have 'loved too wisely and not well.' " From this single sentence, the reader may deduce the paper's topic (the intellectual heroes in certain dramas), the writer's attitude (basically negative), and the overall procedure (discussion of several intellectual heroes and their inability to "love"). The single sentence thus embodies the previous content without repetition. The sentence also casts an ironic shadow across the content as a whole, for the original quote from Shakespeare's *Othello* is "loved not wisely, but too well."

The following excerpt illustrates several effective techniques that you might consider using in your own conclusions:

> I have tried the same experiment with members of my family. When I shriek hysterically "I love you" to my sister, she becomes upset and a quarrel ensues. When I whisper softly that I cannot stand her, she smiles coyly and answers, "I hate you too." Then we get along peacefully. Again, it was not so much what I said as how I said it. This is basically what McLuhan wants media experts to consider. How do media, such as radio and television, convey the message, and how are these media influencing us? Marshall McLuhan does not have the answers. He is merely, in his inimitable fashion, prodding others, the experts, to seek the answers. He explains:
>
>> I am in the position of Louis Pasteur telling doctors that their enemy was quite invisible and quite unrecognized by them.[1]
>
> McLuhan is the Pasteur of media.

In the first place, the conclusion above uses a *personal application* to reinforce the *controlling generalization* of the paper, which evidently is that media influence us as much by form as by content. Secondly, the conclusion briefly *analyzes* McLuhan's contribution to the above thesis and then *quotes* McLuhan himself. Finally, this conclusion uses *metaphor*, "McLuhan is the Pasteur of media," to reinforce the idea of McLuhan's *importance*. In sum, this conclusion variously deals with *significance:* personal, expert, and universal.

Drawing conclusions is quite similar to deriving controlling generalizations; that is, it involves assessing a body of material, in this case the foregoing paper. This assessment commonly contains an attitude or an idea about that material. It also commonly deals with the significance of the material and sometimes speculates as to future importance.

In drawing conclusions, you should take the same precautions as you did when deriving generalizations:

1. Avoid being absolute; allow for alternatives if possible.
2. Be careful not to base your assessment on a few "exceptional" or peculiar facts.

3. Examine logical relationships in general and causal relationships in particular.

And, as when deriving introductions, you should ask "What is my main point?" before you begin asking other questions such as these:

1. What is the significance of what I've written?
2. What do I want my reader to remember most? To think about?
3. Could any of the following devices be incorporated into an effective and appropriate close for my paper?

summary	statistics
quotation	personal application
analogy	general application
questions	specific detail
narrative	speculation

4. Is there any portion of my information that could serve as raw material for one of the devices mentioned in number three? Will I need to generate additional material for the conclusion?
5. Will my conclusion explicitly or implicitly contain my controlling generalization?

For further examples of finished conclusions, consult the remainder of the Alf Landon interview frame (pages 231–34), the statement of significance that closes the linguistics comparison/contrast (page 220), and the call to action that concludes the process analysis of computer procedure (page 235). From these conclusions, you might predict what the respective introductions are like before scanning the entire papers themselves.

Adapting introductions and conclusions for specialized audiences

Sometimes the process of composing a frame for your message is affected by specialized reader expectations. For example, in business and technical writing, the content or specific function of the introduction and the conclusion is often prescribed.

Business Writing.   In business writing, the introduction or first paragraph of a direct inquiry conventionally starts with the key question. The first paragraph of a prospecting application establishes the writer's central selling point in terms of reader benefit.

Similarly, the conclusion or last paragraph of a direct inquiry usually refers to the reader's next action and requires an answer by a certain date. The last paragraph of a prospecting application also asks for appropriate action and frequently contains a final sales "whip-back," or repetition of the writer's initial sales pitch.

Technical Writing.   Likewise, in technical writing, the introduction for a description of a mechanism characteristically features: definition, purpose, generalized description, and division of the device into components. The conclusion for such a description generally finds a causal analysis of the device in operation.

Formal Reports.   Formal reports often have introductions that establish the problem, the need, and the background involved, with the subject. The background portion, in turn, commonly notes the scope and limitations of the report, the sources of data, and the plan of presentation. The conclusion (sometimes placed immediately after the introduction in such a report) makes recommendations.

"Are there any specialized reader expectations concerning the frame for my message?" is thus a good question to ask. In any case, your frame should both orient and dispatch your reader.

▶EXERCISE 6.1

Construct a new and improved introduction and conclusion for either one of your quick drafts or for the student paper on pages 152–53. Use the following Process Sheets as rough guides to your composing.◄

▶EXERCISE 6.2

First redraft each of the following Process Sheets so that they refer to another person's introduction and conclusion.

EXAMPLE: What is the main point of *this paper?*
            Does *the writer* link the interest-catcher and the controlling generalization if both are present?

Then, use each Process Sheet to edit another student's introduction and conclusion. Make constructive suggestions for improvement if you find changes necessary.◄

INTRODUCTIONS[2]

What is the main point of my paper? What is my purpose? Who is my audience?

Which of the following interest-catching devices seems appropriate to my subject? My purpose? My audience?

questions	striking details, description
statistics	narrative or anecdote
quotation	startling or unusual facts
analogy	a representative example

What raw material do I have for my interest-catching device? What material can I generate?

What role will my controlling generalization play in the introduction?

How can I link my interest-catcher and controlling generalization together if both are present?

Will my introduction orient my reader to my subject? My purpose? Will it provide any contextual information necessary to my reader's understanding of my subject?

CONCLUSIONS

Will my conclusion explicitly or implicitly contain my controlling generalization? How so?

What is the significance of what I've said in the paper? How can I relate that in my conclusion?

Could any of the following devices be incorporated into an effective and appropriate close for my paper?

summary	statistics
quotation	personal application
analogy	general application
questions	specific detail
narrative	speculation

What raw material do I have for my conclusion? What material can I generate?

Will my conclusion provide a sense of closure for my reader? Will it, at the same time, prompt the reader to think about my ideas beyond the context of the paper itself?

164

Selecting a Perspective

By deriving a coherent and specific controlling generalization for your essays, you have already begun to select a perspective in terms of *arrangement*. When you select a perspective in terms of *style*, you consider point of view. Both the controlling generalization and point of view impose unity on your paper because they influence your selection of content.

Point of view may be defined grammatically, rhetorically, and contextually.

Defining point of view grammatically

Grammatically, point of view rests on the identity of the sentence subject. If the sentence subject is the one speaking, the point of view is first person. If the sentence subject is the one being spoken about, the point of view is second person. If the sentence subject is *that* being spoken about, the point of view is third person. Look at the following uses of grammatical point of view:

FIRST PERSON: *I* think *we* have lived here too long.
SECOND PERSON: *You* think *you* have lived here too long.
THIRD PERSON: *He* thinks *they* have lived here too long.

The composing context often determines your choice of person. For instance, report writers (and high school English teachers) characteristically prefer third person; business writers make extensive use of second person; fiction writers frequently speak in first person.

When choosing a grammatical point of view, you should ask, "Which point of view is appropriate to my composing context? To my audience? To my subject? To my purpose?" You should also be consistent after making your choice. Consider the following:

ORIGINAL: Although *he* cried loudly, *you* could tell the boy was not sorry.
REVISION: Although *he* cried loudly, *he* was not sorry.
ORIGINAL: A *person* has to endure some hardships as *we* go through life.
REVISION: *We* have to endure some hardships as *we* go through life.

OR

You have to endure some hardships as *you* go through life.

OR

People have to endure some hardships as *they* go through life.

Defining point of view rhetorically

Rhetorically, point of view identifies the place or perspective from which the writer or the writer as narrator is speaking. For example, a physical point of view might be the tree stump you're standing on to get a better view of the pasture below. A psychological point of view might involve the fact that you love such rural settings or that you've lost track of your hiking companions and you're anxious to relocate them. What you see and how you see it is affected by your point of view, and you describe the scene to your reader accordingly. Exercise 6.3 introduces the concept of differing rhetorical points of view and suggests how you might approach adjusting points of view.

☛ EXERCISE 6.3

This activity was designed by Jane Burgett to show "the difference between objective and subjective reality before the writer presents an account to a particular audience."

CHARACTERS: *Keith*—a football player
Mary—an adoring girlfriend
Dr. Kelly—an overworked, but concerned, dentist

SITUATION: Yesterday, June 7, at three-thirty Keith had an appointment with his family dentist, Dr. Kelly. He was to have a chipped tooth in his lower jaw removed. Despite Keith's objections, Mary insisted that she accompany him. After Keith and Mary waited for two hours in a crowded waiting room, a dental assistant ushered them into the "green room," one of the many rooms equipped with a dental chair and the other necessary paraphernalia. As Dr. Kelly prepared to remove the tooth, Keith insisted that he needed no anesthetic. Just as the doctor approached with the silver instrument to extract the damaged tooth, Keith fainted. After reviving him by splashing water in his face, Dr. Kelly decided to delay the pulling of the tooth in favor of a later date. Mary drove Keith home.

1. Look at the situation again. If Keith, Mary, and Dr. Kelly discussed the event at a later date, are there specific details about what happened that they could agree upon? List them.
2. Now imagine that you are Keith. Given your stature as a football

player, what concerns might you have had during this experience? List some concerns.

3. Imagine, on the other hand, that you are Mary, the adoring girlfriend. What might you be concerned with during the experience?

4. Finally, imagine that you are Dr. Kelly? What might have been your concerns?

5. Explain how a paper written by each of these characters might resemble or differ from those of the other two. ◢

As this exercise suggests, your point of view governs how you present details. Note how the following narrative uses distinct points of view to present "the photograph" as a detail.

The Photograph

Yellow gnarled fingers extended the photograph towards me. The snapshot, trembling slightly, showed an open coffin. My eyes avoided the corpse and focused on the white silk-like casket lining punctuated by tediously even rows of white satin-covered buttons.

She had foretold her sister's death the week before when I had come for my last harvest: a few closely bunched broccoli sprigs from among the already flowered yellow heads; four or five beets, purple and woody; a handful of tomatoes, green but not ripening. The corn stood already shocked to one side and the squash mounds leveled into a brown mulch. She had posted herself between the screen door and her cane, her white hair and pink skull bright with the low September sun. "She's gonna die," she announced. "It tore me up, seein' her. A time ago I offered to give her one of my rooms—free rent—but she said no. Said I'd be bossin' her." The screen door squeaked as she ventured farther out onto the concrete stoop. "And I can't even boss myself."

"She's in Green County—that's where my people's from. Has a little three-room house. Bought it herself. She worked at an insane asylum—got them folks everywhere, you know—but she quit work after she bought her house, because she could collect retirement. She says she has friends to take care of her—the Jardines—a good man but a cruel woman. And the man farms all day, so that leaves the woman."

The screen door squeaked again. "Well, I got a phone call, and it tore me up to see her. Bed sores. I ain't never seen such sores. Not when I took care of sick people. Before Bloomington ever had a hospital, I used to take care of sick people. I wasn't no nurse. I wanted to be but had no education, but I took good care of them. You have to be careful of wrinkles in the sheets—that'll give them sores, just wrinkles." She moved her cane in a smoothing motion on the white concrete. "Sores all over her backside. They don't use no bedpan. They've got one but it just sits beside the bed. They've got rags and old towels wrapped around her bottom. My sister takes the towels and dumps them in a paper sack the woman brings. This woman talks to people like I wouldn't talk to a dog. She gives my sister a bath everyday and says, 'Come on, I got to get you clean for the under-taker.' "

We had laughed at that, "Well, I told her all she had to do is wash her bottom. What do undertakers care about a little dirt . . . but them sores. It tore me up to see it." With stiff fingers she fondled her dress. "She wants to live, but she's gonna die."

She retrieved the photograph. "You know, seriously ill people breath through their feet," she said. "And that woman wanted to keep her completely covered." She adjusted her rimless spectacles and, looking at the photograph, saw a small schoolgirl in a hand-sewn ruffled white dress squinting against the light.

The key to the point of view in this selection is each person's percep-tion of the photograph. When handed the photo, the "I" sees a picture of a corpse in a white-lined coffin. The "I" then focuses on the lining itself with its "tediously even rows of white satin covered buttons." It is almost as if the "I" at this point is trying to imagine what the corpse will be seeing when the lid is closed.

The woman speaker, however, after retrieving the photo, does not see what the "I" has seen. Instead of a corpse in a white-lined coffin, she evidently sees "a small schoolgirl in a hand-sewn ruffled white dress." She apparently sees her sister in life and not in death, in memory and not in reality, in her mind's eye and not in the photograph.

▶ EXERCISE 6.4

What does this difference in point of view in "The Photograph" suggest to you as a reader? What is the writer's point of view in all of this? The writer's purpose? ◢

Exercise 6.3 and "The Photograph" both demonstrate that it is possi-ble not only to *have* more than one point of view on a subject, but also to *write with* more than one point of view on a subject. In other words, rhetorical points of view do not follow the same rules of consistency as do grammatical points of view. Rhetorical points of view unify through choice of detail for each perspective rather than through singularity of perspective.

It is then possible for the speaker's point of view and yours as the author to be at odds. For example, if your speaker says, "I was disappointed with my visit to a T.V. studio. For one thing, the 'sound stage' wasn't noisy at all, and for another, the characters kept on saying the same lines over and over," there is a gap between the naive expectations of the speaker and the presumably wiser perspective of you as writer. Such a gap creates an ironic tone.

The following excerpt from Phil Morris' "Writing for Fun, Fortune, and Fame" attempts such a tone.

> How one sees himself is somewhat atuned to how others see him. Keeping this thought in mind, the ambitious writer must present an appearance that will pave his road to goal attainment. The most obvious of first appearances concerns clothing. For the "writer-look" and for comfort during long hours at the typewriter, the cardigan or turtleneck sweater is universally acceptable, and a "must" for the garret writer who must endure cold temperatures. A man wearing the latter garment with neck jewelry emits an aura of questionable sexual preferences. The woman can achieve similar results by complementing the sweater with jeans and ski boots. . . .
>
> Smoking a pipe is a good special effect and, next to coffee-drinking, is a helpful stimulus to creativity: a MacArthur corncob, Danish Royale, or Meerschaum adds an individual quality. Unfortunately, pipe-smoking is still a male province; however, the female writer can express her individuality by smoking *Mores*. Lung cancer is always possible, but even this disadvantage can be a "plus" as will be apparent later. The last of the bodily accoutrements is glasses, an occupational disease that can just as well be an asset. Sooner or later the busy writer will have to wear them; sooner would be better, for the "intelligent" look. Horn-rimmed glasses are best. Some famous writers prefer the little "half-moon" glasses for their pleasing effect. . . . However it's done, the personal appearance must say WRITER. Don't *tell* the observer; *show* him!
>
> *Phil Morris*

How do we as readers know Phil is not serious? How do we know he is poking fun at stereotypes and at the notion that appearances "make the writer"? What is our knowledge of discourse allows us to bridge the gap between what the author is writing and what he is meaning? Certainly the rhetorical situation, "dress like this and you'll become a writer," suggests jest. The answers to these questions also involve contextual point of view, to be discussed in the next section.

Consider now the following exchange:

"I bought my grandmother a dishwasher for Christmas."

"How generous of you!"

"Yes. I charged it on her credit card and made the initial payment, myself."

"How generous of you!"

"Yes. And everytime she makes a payment now, she'll be able to think of me."

"How generous of you!"

As it is repeated in this conversation, the response "How generous of you" acquires an increasingly ironic tone. The conversation or rhetorical situation itself provides the basis or context for the irony.

Summing up rhetorical point of view, we see that it:

1. demonstrates the difference between objective and subjective reality, between fact and interpretation of fact;

2. acknowledges that having multiple perspectives regarding one event, person, object, and even idea is possible;

3. shows that the writer can at once present a subject from several points of view, and, in doing so, create a specific tone, such as irony;

4. allows for the writer to speak in a voice separate from his or her own; and

5. seems particularly appropriate in contexts employing first person narrative.

Although presenting such rhetorical points of view may seem particularly appropriate in composing contexts that use first person narrative, the ability to recognize and implement differing points of view is in fact crucial to creating reader-based prose.

As a writer, you must be able to put yourself in your reader's shoes. In business writing, this ability is termed *you-attitude,* or the presentation of facts from the reader's point of view. Compare the following points of view:

ME-ATTITUDE: We are shipping out your order on November 16.

YOU-ATTITUDE: You will receive your shipment of Candlelight Crystal in time for the Thanksgiving holidays.

You-attitude emphasizes and dramatizes reader benefits. In a less specialized sense, you-attitude involves fulfilling reader expectations.

When considering a stylistic perspective, you might find the following questions helpful:

1. Does my content suggest multiple points of view?

2. Would there be any advantage to presenting these multiple points of view stylistically? Or would it be just as effective to present them through arrangement, through clustering or even sequencing?

3. Would first person narrative be appropriate to presenting my material?

4. What would distinguish one point of view from another stylistically?

5. Do I want to create a gap between what I am saying and what I actually mean? If so, what would be my purpose? How would my audience respond?

Defining point of view contextually

Contextual point of view involves the existing relationships between writer, reader, and subject.

In determining your relationship to the subject, you can ask subjective questions such as, "What personal assumptions does my subject include?" "Why does my topic seem relevant to me?" and "How well does my main idea reflect my social and/or ethical beliefs?" These questions help you determine how you approach your subject interpretatively and help define your perspective as author.

In defining your relationship to your audience, you can ask questions such as, "*Who* is the audience in relationship to me? Is it an instructor? A peer?" "*What* is the audience in relationship to me? Is it hostile? Objective? Educated?" "Does my audience share my world view?" These questions help you determine how to approach your audience. They help determine, for example, whether using irony would be appropriate and effective.

In assertaining the audience's relationship to the subject, you can ask questions such as, "*How well* does my audience know the subject?" and "What assumptions does my audience hold concerning the subject?" These questions reveal, for example, how abstract you can be or how concrete you will have to be in handling the subject.

Contextually, then, point of view plays a definitive role in the following sequence:

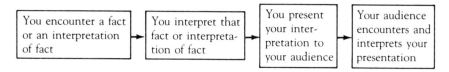

| You encounter a fact or an interpretation of fact | You interpret that fact or interpretation of fact | You present your interpretation to your audience | Your audience encounters and interprets your presentation |

Summarizing the use of point of view

The overall consequence of stylistic point of view is that it affects how details are presented.

Writing from a distinct grammatical point of view affects whether the detail is approached from first, second, or third person. Compare, for example, the following, paying special attention to the apparent correlation between grammatical person and rhetorical point of view:

ME-ATTITUDE: *I* expected the *tool* to be used, not to be put away in the closet.

YOU-ATTITUDE: *You* can use this *tool* to scrape off old paint from round surfaces such as chair legs.

IT-ATTITUDE: The *tool*, with a curved blade at one end and a sharp point at the other, was designed for scraping old paint from round surfaces.

Writing from a distinct rhetorical point of view influences your emphasis. When writing from the viewpoint of a child, for example, you might emphasize a toy's color, texture, and size, whereas when writing from a parent's viewpoint, you might emphasize the toy's price, educational value, and safety. Similarly, when writing from the viewpoint of an incumbent public official, you might choose to emphasize single digit inflation, whereas your opponent might choose to emphasize double digit unemployment. A more objective point of view would consider both factors.

Contextual point of view defines existing relationships between self, audience, and subject. As such, it affects whether you can best present the detail in a straightforward or an ironic manner, in an objective or subjective fashion. Contextual point of view highlights the interpretative aspect or value of the detail: how you see it, how the reader sees it, how you both can see it.

Each type of point of view unifies by offering a stylistic center of gravity:

Point of View

	Grammatical	*Rhetorical*	*Contextual*
Unifying Perspective	A grammatical "person" presents the detail.	A psychological perspective filters the detail.	A situational perspective informs the detail.

PROMOTING SPECIFICITY THROUGH STYLE

Promoting specificity through style commonly involves using concrete language, but it can also entail using such devices as dialogue, lists, tables, and graphs.

Using Concrete Language

Chapter 2 established the distinction between the conceptual, the general, and the specific in terms of detail. The language used to convey such detail can similarly range from the abstract to the concrete. Abstract words are conceptual; they deal with ideas, with things that cannot be seen, heard, smelled, tasted, or touched. For example, "freedom" and "anxiety" are abstract words.

Concrete words are specific; they deal with things accessible to the senses. "Growl" and "wagon" are concrete words. Compare also the following examples:

ABSTRACT: His *generosity* impressed her.
CONCRETE: His *$1,000 donation* impressed her.

ABSTRACT: Motorists enjoyed *comparative freedom* on the turnpike.
CONCRETE: Motorists enjoyed *an 85 M.P.H. speed limit* on the turnpike.

In each of these pairs, the concrete language specifies what the abstract language means in these particular cases.

Context can influence the concreteness of language. Take, for instance, the different writer/reader assumptions that affect this closing to a business letter: "Please send me this information *as soon as possible.*" Here, "as soon as possible" really represents a concept and, as such, is abstract. You as the writer may think "as soon as possible" means something concrete, such as "by next week" or "by return mail." However, your reader, possibly overburdened by requests, may think it means something more abstract, such as "when I get to it" or "within thirty days." Consider, then, an alternative: "Please send me this information by *February 16.*" Here, although "February 16" is not a "sensual" term, it does specify a definite length of time for your response, stands for a precise objective, and therefore is concrete, leaving less room for error in interpretation.

Using concrete language does not always guarantee a specific interpretation, however. For instance, look at the following expressions:

1. What's your 10–20? Come on.
2. Gimme 10–36.

The terms "10– 20" and "10– 36" are specific and represent concrete, or relatively concrete, realities. Yet, for those unacquainted with C.B. jargon, "10– 20" and "10– 36" become as abstract as the terms "beauty" and "truth." For the uninitiated, "10– 20" and "10– 36" may represent the idea of talking in code.

▶EXERCISE 6.5

Discuss in a sentence or two the *concreteness* of each of the following italicized phrases. To what extent does the audience determine how concrete a term is?

1. *"See you later, alligator."*
2. That *schnook* puts everything on the *back-burner.*
3. Cut all the *hearts and flowers!*
4. That *acid head* sure has a lot of *chutzpa.*
5. Terry really *took me for a ride.*◢

For concrete language to increase specificity, it must increase specificity *for someone* in a *certain situation*. Consider, for example, the following:

1. The patient exhibited paranoid behavior, and is therefore clearly schizophrenic. (Personal assessment of client)
2. The patient displayed attitudes which seemed to be persecutory and suspicious in nature as his comments were very accusing toward people, since he said the people were 'no good' and that they were trying to poison him. These feelings of the patient appear to be paranoid in character and are therefore indicative of schizophrenic thinking.[3] (Revised assessment for clinical report for fellow staff members)
3. This patient distrusts people in general, calling them 'no good.' He also thinks people are out to get him, saying that they are trying to poison him. Patients expressing such feelings of suspicion and persecution are often classified as paranoic. But because these delusions of persecution are combined with feelings of omnipotence (he feels he knows what everyone is thinking), this patient could also be classified as possibly schizophrenic. (A second revised assessment for the patient's permanent record, accessible to staff and lay persons)

In selecting concrete language, you might find the following questions useful:

1. Does my material primarily express an idea, or does it support an idea? (Is it part of a controlling generalization or sub-generalization, or is it part of the detail that explains them?)
2. If the latter, how concrete is the language that conveys that information? Can it be made more specific? How so?
3. Will my audience need a more specific presentation of material?
4. Does my context demand a more specific presentation?

Using Dialogue

Using dialogue is actually a specialized form of using concrete language. Dialogue or direct discourse is more specific than indirect discourse because it dramatizes the statement involved:

> She said that she was disgusted with him.

> "You disgust me!" she said.

The second statement puts the reader at the scene of the action.

As is the case with other stylistic devices, using dialogue is not appropriate to every context. The clinical report writer (page 174), for example, felt that dialogue was unnecessary, perhaps because the *interpretation* of the patient's behavior rather than the behavior itself was the focus of the writing. Dialogue is most effective in situations in which "hearing" the person talk is just as important as knowing the content of what he or she said.

Using Lists

Using lists is another way to promote specificity. In prose, items may be lined up one after another in a simple series:

> English majors must take courses in *Chaucer, Shakespeare,* and *Milton.*

Or in a more complicated structure:

> English majors must take courses in Chaucer, featuring the *Canterbury Tales;* in Shakespeare, covering the range of achievement from history, to comedy, to tragedy, to romance; and in Milton, touching on both major poetry and prose.

In any case, such series are generally embedded within the text.

However, you can increase the impact of a series by creating a list:

1. English majors must take:
   a. Chaucer, *The Canterbury Tales;*
   b. Shakespeare, selected dramatic works; and
   c. Milton, major poetry and prose.

Lists visually highlight the material covered and are used extensively in business and technical writing.

When constructing a series or a list, you must make certain that the items featured are grammatically identical. This grammatical unity is called *parallelism:*

NOT PARALLEL:	Jim felt his career had been damaged by drink, having the wrong type of work habits, and the fact that his training had been too elementary.
PARALLEL:	Jim felt his career had been damaged by his drinking too much, his having poor work habits, and his getting inadequate training.
PARALLEL:	Jim felt his career had been damaged by excessive drink, poor work habits, and inadequate training.

Using Tables

Tables, like lists, visually highlight selected material. Tables allow you to handle large quantities of data clearly and efficiently. Look closely, for example, at the table in Figure 6.1

Table 1: Wind Chill Chart

	THERMOMETER READING (degrees F.)						
Wind Speed (mph)	30	20	10	0	−10	−20	−30
	EFFECT ON EXPOSED FLESH						
0	30	20	10	0	−10	−20	−30
5	27	16	6	−5	−15	−26	−36
10	16	4	−9	−21	−33	−46	−58
15	9	−5	−18	−36	−45	−58	−72
20	4	−10	−25	−39	−53	−67	−82
25	0	−15	−29	−44	−59	−74	−88
30	−2	−18	−33	−48	−63	−79	−94
35	−4	−20	−35	−49	−67	−82	−98
40	−6	−21	−37	−53	−69	−85	−100

FIGURE 6.1 *Sample Table*

If you were to convey this data in prose form, you might end up with a paragraph something like this:

> Wind chill factors are determined on a sliding scale involving the actual thermometer reading (degrees F.), the wind speed (m.p.h.), and the resulting effect on exposed flesh (degrees F.). If the thermometer reading is 30 degrees and the wind speed 0 m.p.h., the effect on the flesh is 30 degrees. If the thermometer reading is 30 degrees and the wind speed is 5 m.p.h., the effect on the flesh is 27 degrees. If the thermometer reading is 30 degrees and the wind speed is 10 m.p.h., the effect on the flesh is. . . .

As a reader, which would you prefer in this case: table or prose? This is an important question for you as a writer to ask when you are dealing with a quantity of facts and figures.

When incorporating tables, or any other similar visual aid, into your text, you should provide a brief prose interpretation of the device, unless to do so would insult the reader's intelligence.

▸ EXERCISE 6.6

Assume that you are going to make a table reflecting the outcome of an opinion poll. Your raw data indicates that 75% of the men and 50% of the women answered "yes" to question one; 20% of the men and 25% of the women answered "no" to question one; and 5% of the men and 25% of the women polled answered "no opinion." For question two, the figures were 85% men, "yes"; 65% women, "yes"; 5% men, "no"; 30% women, "no"; 10% men, "no opinion"; 5% women, "no opinion." Construct the table, generating your own headings. ◂

Using Graphs

Graphs are another way of visually enhancing specificity. Although graphs come in many forms, they tend to organize data in much the same way that arrangements organize the parts of a paper's support. That is, graphs isolate, cluster, and sequence data. Consider the pie graph in Figure 6.2:

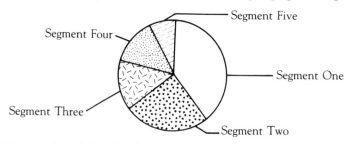

FIGURE 6.2 *Sample Pie Graph*

This pie graph presents its segments in order of decreasing size, beginning at 12:00 o'clock and moving clockwise. Because it deals with 100 percent of something, this graph can be said to isolate one set of factors for examination. Questions associated with such a pie graph include: What percent of the total amount is devoted to each aspect? and How is the total divided?

Now consider the bar graph in Figure 6.3:

Sample One   —————————

Sample Two   ———————————————

Sample Three   ——————————————————

L_____L_____J
0   50

FIGURE 6.3   *Sample Bar Graph, One Variable*

Because it implicitly deals with comparison, a bar graph can be said to cluster factors for examination. Questions associated with such a bar graph typically include: How far did each item progress? and How much did each item cost?

Bar graphs can also represent more than one variable per sample, as Figure 6.4 shows:

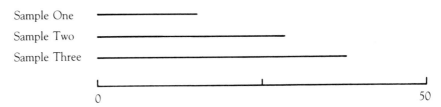

Sample One | Variable A | Variable B |

Sample Two | Variable A | Variable B |

L_____L_____J
0   50

FIGURE 6.4   *Sample Bar Graph, Two Variables*

Such graphs are particularly suited to showing causal relationships.

Finally, bar graphs can be used to compare total percentages to total percentages, with each bar functioning as an elongated pie:

Sample One | A | B | C |

Sample Two | A | B | C |
                  Units

FIGURE 6.5   *Sample Bar Graph, Variable Percentages*

Bar graphs may be oriented horizontally or vertically.

The line graph in Figure 6.6 represents another way of presenting data:

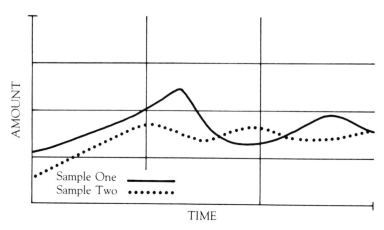

FIGURE 6.6 *Sample Line Graph*

In this type of graph, variables occupy both the vertical and the horizontal axis. Because such a graph usually represents changes occurring over a given time span rather than discrete data sets, it can be said to sequence factors for examination. The line graph in Figure 6.6 also features some clustering; the trends revealed by the data are being clustered. Questions associated with such a line graph include: How has the production of these items grown in the past year? Is the general progression upward or downward for these samples? What is the projected movement of these samples? (Projected trends are usually indicated with dotted lines extending from solid ones.)

▶EXERCISE 6.7

Decide what type of graph would be appropriate for each of the following situations. Construct a rough projection of what each graph would look like.

1. In doing a paper on the changing nature of the American family, you collect data on three types of couples: (1) those who choose to have children right away, (2) those who choose to postpone having children, and (3) those who voluntarily decide not to have children. You find that since 1960, the number of couples in

category (1) has decreased slowly but steadily while the number of couples in categories (2) and (3) has risen unevenly but steadily, and that the greatest increase has occurred in category (3). Category (1) had the greatest number of couples, but is fast being challenged by categories (2) and (3) in that order.

2. In examining the local mass transit system, you discover that it offers various fare options. Without passes, the fare is 50¢ a ride on fixed routes. With fixed route passes, the fare is $8.50 for 20 rides. Regular fare for Dial-a-Ride is 75¢ a ride. With a senior citizen pass, however, the Dial-a-Ride fare is $12.00 for 20 rides. And non-senior citizen Dial-a-Ride passes cost $13.00 for 20 rides. (When you construct your graph, you will have to convert this data into comparable figures—for example, cost per ride.)

3. As part of a promotional campaign, your organization has decided to participate in a local run-a-thon. Your organization will donate 50¢ per mile if the participant runs 1 mile; $1 per mile if the participant runs 5 miles; $2 per mile, if 10 miles; and $5 per mile, if 26 miles. Although your organization stresses the importance of every contribution, it wants to encourage participation by experienced marathon runners.

4. In examining Roger Brown's campaign contributions you discover that 65% represented contributions of $1 or less. A smaller portion (15%) represented contributions of $2 to $5. Only 2% were for more than $20. The remaining percentage was equally divided between the $5 to $10 and the $10 to $20 contributions.

5. Now you want to compare the Brown statistics to those of Mary Green: 45%, $1 or less; 20%, $2 to $5; 15%, $5 to $10; 10%, $10 to $20; 10%, $20 or more. ◢

PROMOTING COHERENCE THROUGH STYLE

Chapter 2 established that emphasis in phrasing influences meaning. It showed how putting ideas together with coordinating conjunctions implied that the joined ideas were of equal weight, and how putting ideas together with subordinating conjunctions implied that the joined ideas were of unequal weight. It also showed how placement can moderate the effects of coordination and subordination. Chapter 5 noted that certain idea-combinings or syntheses often suggested patterns of arrangement.

Both chapters equated combining ideas with combining sentences; both assumed a close interrelatedness between how a sentence worked grammatically and what the sentence said rhetorically.

This section focuses on how sentence combining as a device can increase coherence in your writing. Before tying sentence combining to coherence, however, let's examine the technique itself.

Sentence Combining as a Technique

Sentence combining involves expanding and contracting kernel sentences, or sentences that contain one complete idea. Adding coordinate or subordinate ideas to these kernel sentences provides you with an effective way to shift emphasis and to achieve more clarity and economy in your writing. See how the kernel sentence is altered in the following combinations:

1. The officer struck the private. (Kernel sentence: one complete idea)
2. The officer struck the private, yet the private remained calm. (Coordinating sentence: two ideas, or kernel sentences, joined by a coordinating conjunction)
3. Because the private remained calm, the officer became embarrassed. (Subordinating sentence: two ideas or kernel sentences, joined by a subordinating conjunction)

Given the kernel sentences below, a wide range of combinations is possible.

1. The desk top is cluttered.
2. The desk top is strewn with pencils.
3. The desk top is smothered with papers.
4. The desk top is spotted with crumbs.
5. It also bears plants.

6. The plants are many.
7. The plants are different.
8. The plants surround the clutter.
9. The plants trap the clutter.
10. The plants hold the clutter on the desk.

VERSION ONE: The cluttered desk top is strewn with pencils, smothered with papers, and spotted with crumbs. It also bears many different plants that surround, trap and hold the clutter on the desk.

VERSION TWO: The many different plants surround the desk top strewn with pencils, smothered with papers, and spotted with crumbs. The plants trap the clutter, holding it on the desk.

In combining sentences, the writer may choose from a wide variety of options, including the following constructions:

1. The plants trap the clutter, *holding* it on the desk.
2. The plants trap the clutter *to hold* it on the desk.
3. The cluttered desk top is *strewn* with pencils, *smothered* with papers, and *spotted* with crumbs.
4. The cluttered desk top, *which* is strewn with pencils, smothered with papers, and spotted with crumbs, bears many different plants *that* surround, trap, and hold the clutter.

Grammatical subjects can also be varied:

1. *Trapping the clutter on the desk* is the job of many different plants.
2. *To trap the clutter on the desk* is the job of the many different plants.
3. *That the plants intended to trap the clutter on the desk* became obvious last week as the vines encircled a pen.

Besides having these options in sentence construction, the writer has options in emphasis; version one and version two of the previous example demonstrate separate emphases: the *desk* and the *plants,* respectively. In the following version, the emphasis rests neither on the desk nor on the plants, but on the idea of entrapment.

VERSION THREE: Entrapment was the plants' strategem as they surrounded the desk-top clutter. They held the strewn pencils, paper stacks, and crumb piles in a closing circle of green.

☞EXERCISE 6.8

For initial practice in sentence combining, combine the following sentences:

1. The parrot squawked.
2. It squawked loudly.
3. It squawked at a burglar.
4. It squawked, "Caught! Caught!"
5. The burglar jumped.
6. The burglar saw the parrot.
7. The burglar laughed.
8. He said, "Not! Not!" ◢

After you have finished Exercise 6.8, ask yourself the following questions:

1. How do I begin my version? How do I end?
2. Which words do I eliminate? Which do I add, if any?
3. Do I emphasize the parrot? Do I emphasize the burglar? Do I divide my emphasis between the parrot and the burglar?
4. How many sentences do I have? How long are my sentences?

After answering these questions, try writing a second version of the exercise, so that your answers are different.

When combining kernel sentences, you should avoid faulty parallelism and dangling modifiers. For instance, let's assume that you have chosen to combine the following sentences:

1. The pail contained sour slop.
2. The pail was emptied.
3. It was scoured by the farmer.
4. It was scrubbed by the farmer.
5. The farmer then refilled the pail.

Now, in your first combining attempt, let's say that you wrote, "Because it contained sour slop, the pail *was emptied, scoured,* and *had been scrubbed* by the farmer who then refilled it."

In constructing the series of verbs, you have made a parallelism error in that your verbs do not all have the same grammatical tense. You could correct the error by writing, "Because it contained sour slop, the pail *was emptied, was scoured,* and *was scrubbed* by the farmer who then refilled it." (It would also be correct to eliminate the second and third *was* here because they are understood to be part of the underlying structure.)

Now let's suppose that you had wanted to emphasize the farmer: "Containing sour slop, the farmer emptied, scoured, and scrubbed and then refilled the pail." In this sentence, "containing sour slop" is a dangling modifier. It will be interpreted by the reader as modifying "the farmer," resulting in the ridiculous notion that the farmer contained sour slop. There are several ways to correct this error:

1. Containing sour slop, the pail was emptied, scoured, scrubbed, and then refilled by the farmer.
2. The farmer emptied, scoured, scrubbed, and then refilled the pail that had contained sour slop.
3. Emptying the pail of sour slop, the farmer scoured, scubbed, and then refilled it with fresh slop.

(For more details on parallelism and dangling modifiers, you should consult your handbook or your instructor.)

When combining sentences, you should also be aware that length does not guarantee strength. A crisp sentence is almost always preferable to a convoluted one.

▶EXERCISE 6.9

Try to combine the following groups of sentences in a variety of ways. Check for economy as well as variety. Also, revise dangling modifers and faulty parallelism if either occurs in your combining. (The sentence group-ings indicate natural breaks in the emphasis of the sentence content. You may want to use these groupings as a guide to your sentence combinings.)

Energy Crisis

1. J. B. drives a pick-up.
2. The pick-up has eight cylinders.
3. The pick-up has air conditioning.
4. The pick-up has an automatic transmission.

5. J.B. drives at 70 miles per hour.
6. He makes jack-rabbit starts.
7. He is in a hurry.

8. J.B. talks on his C.B.
9. J.B. brags, "My truck makes 10 miles per gallon."
10. He says, "I'm going to get my fair share of gas, no matter what."

11. L.Q. drives a compact.
12. It has four cylinders.
13. It has no luxury options.
14. It has a standard transmission.

15. L.Q. drives at 55 miles per hour.
16. He drives defensively.
17. He is safety-minded.

18. L.Q. talks to his neighbor.
19. L.Q. states, "I don't believe there is an energy shortage."
20. L.Q. says, "I just want to save money and lives."

21. D.M. rides a bicycle.
22. The bicycle has ten-speeds.

23. The bicycle has a light-weight frame.
24. The bicycle is well-engineered.

25. D.M. rides his bicycle at 20 miles per hour.
26. D.M. races his bicycle at 50 miles per hour.
27. D.M. is a "bicycle nut."

28. D.M. believes America has an energy crisis.
29. D.M. thinks, "Americans will exhaust fuel supplies soon."
30. D.M. thinks, "Americans themselves are exhausted now."

Equality and Excellence[5]

1. Egalitarianism is an idea.
2. Egalitarianism involves rights.
3. Egalitarianism involves privileges.
4. It speaks to social issues.
5. It speaks to economic issues.
6. It speaks to political issues.
7. It speaks to legal issues.

8. Egalitarianism promotes equality.
9. Egalitarianism sprang from the American Frontier.
10. Egalitarianism existed in mining camps.
11. It involved setting tables.
12. It involved sharing silverware.
13. It involved having only one teaspoon.

14. Egalitarianism characterized the Jacksonian era.
15. It reached its heights in the Jacksonian era.
16. Trained personnel were considered unnecessary.
17. Special groups were considered anathema.
18. Individual competence was ignored.
19. Even licensing of doctors was lax.
20. To be lax was to be democratic.
21. To be "just one of the boys" was to be democratic.

22. Men are not equal in their native gifts.
23. Men are not equal in their motivations.
24. Men are not equal in their achievements.
25. Extreme egalitarianism ignores these differences.
26. It belittles talent.
27. It denies intelligence.
28. It ends striving.
29. It may end excellence.

30. "May the best man win" is an idea.
31. It involves striving.
32. It involves aspiring.
33. It involves competing.
34. It involves standards.
35. It involves America.

36. Andrew Carnegie was the son of a poor immigrant.
37. Thomas Edison had three months formal education.
38. Abraham Lincoln grew up in a log cabin.
39. Andrew Carnegie became an industrialist.
40. He became rich.
41. He became a philanthropist.
42. Thomas Edison became an inventor.
43. He took out over 1,000 patents.
44. He became famous.
45. Abraham Lincoln was elected President.
46. He fought to keep America one nation.
47. He became great.

48. Carnegie helped America economically.
49. Edison helped American intellectually.
50. Lincoln helped America politically.

51. Americans love the idea of equality.
52. Americans love the idea of excellence.

53. To love both is paradoxical.
54. "Can we be equal and excellent too?"

The Guerrilla

1. The guerrilla was curly-haired.
2. The guerrilla was unshaven.
3. The guerrilla sat in the mud.
4. The mud was deep.
5. It was oozing.
6. It was caked on his boots.
7. It covered his jacket.
8. It covered his pants

9. It soaked his T-shirt.
10. It smeared across his rifle.
11. It stuck between his fingers.

12. The guerrilla reached in his pocket.
13. He pulled out some paper.
14. He pulled out some tobacco.
15. He rolled a cigarette.
16. He cupped his hands.
17. He lit the cigarette.
18. The cigarette was foul-smelling.
19. It burned unevenly.
20. It burned with blue smoke.
21. The smoke drifted upward.
22. The smoke disappeared.
23. The smoke jogged a memory.
24. The memory was vague.
25. The memory was faded.
26. The memory had burning candles.
27. The memory had laughter.
28. The memory had a long table.
29. The memory had smiling faces.
30. The memory had a date.
31. The date was July 26.
32. The date was long ago.
33. The date was today.
34. The date was his birthday.

35. The guerrilla finished the cigarette.
36. He crushed the cigarette into the mud.
37. He was sixteen.◢

Sentence Combining and Coherence

The previous section suggests how sentence combining can promote variety and economy in sentence structure. But sentence combining can also promote coherence by increasing overall clarity. Compare, for example, the following excerpts:

1. One of the things I've learned is that you can't please everyone. At least you can't please everyone all of the time. This is a frustrating task if you try it. One example of this would be in what you say. What you say isn't going to make everyone happy all of the

time. You may tell your friend, "I'd rather not talk about T.J.'s divorce." Your friend might respect your tact. But he might not, too. You may tell your friend, "I'd rather not talk about T.J.'s divorce." This friend may get angry at your unwillingness to talk. This can be frustrating. And this is only one person. One person has many possible reactions. You can't please anyone all the time. How can you please everyone if not anyone?

2. Trying constantly to please everyone is a frustrating task. For example, if you tell your friend, "I'd rather not talk about T.J.'s divorce," he may either respect your tact or get angry at your unwillingness. And if you can't please one person all the time because of his many possible reactions, how can you please everyone?

The second excerpt is clearer because it has more combined sentences. It has fewer vague references, switches in emphasis, and unnecessary repetitions that bog the reader down.

Sentence combining can also promote coherence by establishing recognizable patterns of repetition designed to enhance meaning. Consider for example, the following:

When Kilroy graffiti first appeared around 1940, it was mostly restricted to fences and bathrooms. But somewhere along the line, Kilroy was recruited. He chalked his name on naval battleships; he splashed it across Pacific cave walls; he painted it inside Stalin's bathroom at Potsdam. Some G.I.s thought him to be an Air Force Sergeant who wanted to put the Infantry in its place. Others thought him to be an Infantry Sergeant who wanted to put the Air Force in its place. But whoever he was, Kilroy sparked rivalries. When Kilroy graffiti appeared on a Marshall Islands atoll, it occupied its own large sign:

NO GRASS ATOLL, NO TREES ATOLL,
NO WATER ATOLL, NO WOMEN ATOLL,
NO LIQUOR ATOLL, NO FUN ATOLL.
AND, an anonymous pilot added, NO KILROY ATOLL. WELL, a mysterious writer appended, I JUST DIDN'T PAUSE ATOLL. KILROY.

Liz Block

When analyzed, the preceding excerpt shows a correspondence between the way the sentences are structured and their content. See the analysis in Figure 6.7. Such correlation between style and content can help the reader understand your message.

When... { ① <u>When</u> Kilroy graffiti first appeared around 1940, <u>it</u> was
it { mostly restricted to fences and bathrooms.

But... ✗ { ② <u>But somewhere</u> along the line, <u>Kilroy</u> was recruited.

series of three ③ { He chalked his name on naval battleships;
he splashed it across Pacific cave walls;
he painted it inside Stalin's bathroom at Potsdam.

directly parallel "couplet" ④ { Some G.I.'s thought him to be an Air Force Sergeant who
wanted to put the Infantry in its place.
Others thought him to be an Infantry Sergeant who
wanted to put the Air Force in its place.

But... ✗ { ② <u>But whoever</u> he was, <u>Kilroy</u> sparked rivalries.

When... { ① <u>When</u> Kilroy graffiti appeared on a Marshall Islands atoll,
it { <u>it</u> occupied its own large sign.

series of three ③ { NO GRASS ATOLL, NO TREES ATOLL,
NO WATER ATOLL, NO WOMEN ATOLL,
NO LIQUOR ATOLL, NO FUN ATOLL.

directly parallel "couplet" ④ { AND, an anonymous pilot added, NO KILROY ATOLL.
WELL, a mysterious <u>writer</u> appended, I JUST DIDN'T
PAUSE ATOLL. (KILROY.) ⟷ *non-parallel element emphasizes the subject of the paragraph*

① *When and where Kilroy graffiti appeared.*

② *What Kilroy was doing at the time (in ①).*

③ *Specific ways Kilroy appeared.*

④ *The rivalry Kilroy provoked.*

(The sentence combining in this paragraph produces an almost symmetrical excerpt.)

FIGURE 6.7 *Example of How Coherence in Style Promotes Clarity*

►EXERCISE 6.10

Select one of the following options:

1. Write an expository essay (three to five typed pages or equivalent)
on some type of communication. (Body language, for example,

would be a general type of communication.) Focus the essay any way you wish. Be sure to include library sources as part of your support and to have a clear sense of audience. Use the following Process Sheet when considering the stylistic presentation of your material.

2. Write a report (three to five typed pages or equivalent) on how a company (of your choice) would benefit from using computers. Assume that you are a communications consultant. Focus the essay any way you wish. Be sure to include some type of "outside" source material in your report and to have a clear sense of audience. Use the following Process Sheet when you consider the stylistic presentation of your material. (Your company may be fictional, just as long as you have its specific characteristics clearly in mind.) ◢

USING STYLE TO PROMOTE UNITY, SPECIFICITY, AND COHERENCE

What is the main idea of my paper? Its purpose? Its audience?

How can I use my introduction and conclusion together to frame my message? To orient my reader? To establish the significance of my paper?

Which devices are appropriate for my introduction and conclusion? Does my reader have any specific expectations concerning my frame?

What grammatical point of view (person) is appropriate to my subject? My purpose? My audience?

What rhetorical point of view is appropriate? Would presenting multiple points of view be appropriate and effective? If so, what would be the best method of their presentation?

Contextually, is an objective or subjective approach preferable?

How can I promote specificity verbally? Through concrete language? Through dialogue?

How can I promote specificity visually? Through lists, tables, graphs?

How can I use sentence combining to reduce vague references, switches in emphasis, and unnecessary repetition?

How can I use sentence combining to promote coherence through meaningful repetition?

PROCESS SHEET

NOTES

1. [Herbert] Marshall McLuhan, "Understanding Media: Extensions of Man," in *The McLuhan Explosion: A Casebook on Marshall McLuhan and "Understanding Media"*, eds. Harry H. Crosby and George R. Bond (New York: American Book Company, 1968), p. 21.

2. Edit sheet originally designed by Dr. Michael Flanigan, when Director of Freshman Composition, Indiana University, Bloomington, Indiana.

3. William T. Martin, M.Ed., *Writing Psychological Reports* (Springfield, Il.: Charles C. Thomas, 1972), pp. 27–28.

4. Nelda R. Lawrence and Elizabeth Tebeaux present graphic forms generically in *Writing Communications in Business and Industry*, 3rd. ed. (Englewood Cliffs, N.J.: Prentice-Hall, Inc., 1982).

5. Sentence combining content from John W. Gardner, *Excellence: Can We Be Equal and Excellent Too?* (New York: Harper & Row, 1961), pp. 11–20.

PART III

ARRANGING IDEAS AND EVIDENCE

7

PATTERNS THAT ISOLATE, CLUSTER, AND SEQUENCE

A NOTE ATTACHED TO A FINAL DRAFT

You know, if I had it to do over again and if this paper weren't due today and if I had time, I would change this whole paper around. Instead of presenting my reasons for a nuclear freeze in argument form, I would tell a story of this astronaut returning to earth in the year 2022 only to find a desolate wasteland. I would use descriptions of the horrible effects of the bomb to make my point against nuclear armaments. All the detail in this fictional account, of course, would be scientifically accurate.

In his note, Bill toys with the possibilities that a different arrangement would offer. As established in Chapter 5, such arrangements can be categorized according to whether they isolate, cluster, or sequence material. This chapter will present examples of papers organized according to each of these three arrangement groups. First, however, it will present an overview of how these arrangements work.

AN OVERVIEW OF ARRANGEMENT OPTIONS

Each pattern type—isolating, clustering, or sequencing—involves the writer's ability to categorize. Categorization is a thinking process that groups or separates ideas, generalities, or specific support in a meaningful way.

Categorization influences how we organize and interpret our world. For example, during a television interview conducted by John Chancellor, Bob Haldeman remarked that if Richard Nixon were guilty of anything, it was putting Watergate "in the wrong box," in the wrong category.

According to Haldeman, Nixon characteristically pigeon-holed problems as either public or personal; Nixon miscalculated and placed Watergate in the personal box.

When Nixon *categorized* Watergate as a personal problem, he evidently saw similarities between the break-in and perhaps a fraternity prank, a type of offense that could be handled without much fuss "in-house." Presumably, Nixon did not recognize that Watergate had much more in common with a felony, a type of offense that could not be handled privately and that demanded outside response.

When categorizing, a writer can group or separate. If grouping, the writer answers the questions, "What is the whole that governs these parts?" or "What do these parts have in common?" If separating, the writer answers the question; "What are the parts of this whole?" or "What distinguishes this part?"

Arrangements reflect the way the writer has categorized wholes and parts. If an arrangement *isolates,* it selects one part and forms an idea round that part. The purpose of such isolating is often to examine or explain the nature or use of that part to a less informed or less experienced reader. Figures 7.1 and 7.2 show two isolating patterns: description and definition.

Field of possible "objects"
to describe.

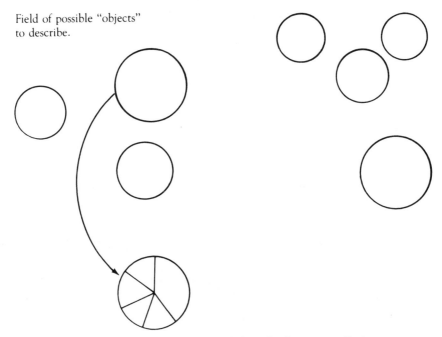

One object singled out for description. Each segment represents a characteristic to be described.

FIGURE 7.1   *Patterns that Isolate: Description*

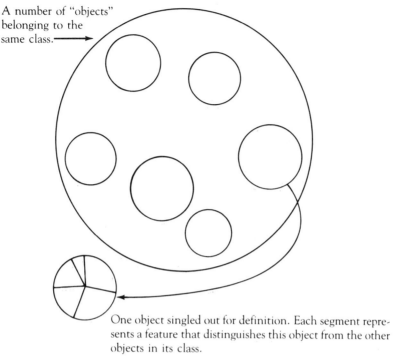

A number of "objects" belonging to the same class.

One object singled out for definition. Each segment represents a feature that distinguishes this object from the other objects in its class.

FIGURE 7.2 *Patterns that Isolate: Definition*

For example, if you were to choose to describe the vacant lot at Forty-third and Vassar, you would separate it from all the other vacant lots and detail its characteristics. In so doing, you might want to show your audience how it looks (a rusting junkyard) or how it is used (as a ball diamond for the neighborhood kids). You may also want to suggest an idea with your description, such as, "What a mess!" or "Let's clean this up!" or "This is the inner city" or "This is a good place to play" or "Let's preserve this ball diamond!" or "This is what it was like for me when I was growing up."

If an arrangement *clusters,* it groups more than one part together under one main idea. Figure 7.3 (see page 198) represents this process. For example, if you wanted to cluster vacant lots, you could do so according to type ("worthless" and "functional", for example). You could also group them as "examples of inner city blight" or "examples of playgrounds for kids."

If an arrangement *sequences,* it lines up parts chronologically, procedurally, or causally. Consider Figure 7.4 on page 199. If, for example, you wanted to use sequencing to deal with your vacant lot, you might show

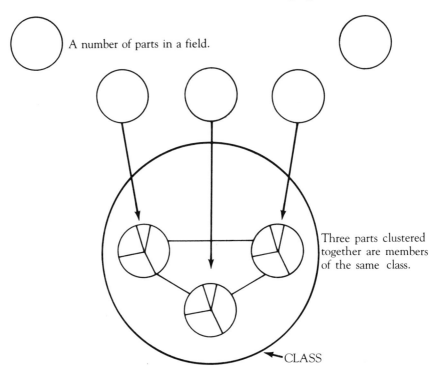

A number of parts in a field.

Three parts clustered together are members of the same class.

CLASS

FIGURE 7.3   *Patterns that Cluster: Classification*

how its appearance changed through time. You might also examine the causes contributing to its presence in the inner city.

PATTERNS THAT ISOLATE

Description and definition are two patterns of arrangement that isolate a part to discuss it. In description, you may detail a person, an object, a place, an event; you separate that person, object, place, or event from every other person, object, place, or event. You then write about those features that characterize your selected topic. The success of your description depends on your ability to perceptively categorize details as either belonging or not belonging to your selected topic. You then restrict yourself to writing about the features that "belong."

When you define, you may explain what a general or conceptual term means. You establish the *class* to which the term belongs before discussing its distinctive features, much as a dictionary definition might do. For instance, when *Webster's New World Dictionary* defines the word *griffon*, it states that a griffon is "a mythical animal [the *class*] with the body and hind

A number of parts in a field.

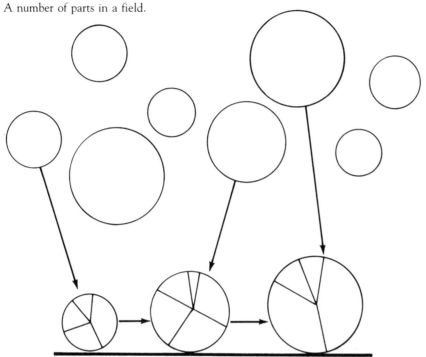

These three parts are singled out and lined up according to time
(past, present, future); process (step one, step two, step three);
or causation (cause, cause, cause).

FIGURE 7.4 *Patterns that Sequence*

legs of a lion, and the head and wings of an eagle [its distinctive features]."
Presumably, there are other mythical animals but none having the griffon's
body.

Let's move on to specific discussions of description and definition.

Description

Description isolates one person, object, place, event, from every other and
shows what the selected topic is like. Description is found in contexts that
solicit detail. Police reports, order letters, lab reports, leases, all require
description to be effective.

Description involves both purpose and point of view. For example,
let's assume that you have found an old wooden chest that contains these
items: a page ripped from Poor Richard's almanac (1798) with the motto:
"Want of care does us more damage than want of knowledge"; a chipped,
clay pipe that faintly smells of stale tobacco; a leather-bound, first edition

of Jonathan Edwards' *Original Sin* (1758) in "mint condition"; a musty, broken-backed copy of Michael Wigglesworth's *The Day of Doom* (1662) with newspaper clippings marking certain well-thumbed pages; a tarnished silver creamer, engraved with the name, Paul Revere; a wool card with sharp, broken teeth; a stained, homespun nightcap; and a cracked powder horn lined with smooth, silk-like black dust.

Now, if your purpose were to make some conclusions about the colonist who presumably owned the chest and its contents or about colonial life in general, you probably would want to detail all of the items. You could proceed by describing each item as you removed it from the chest, perhaps saving the most important find until last. Or you could group the items into different categories, such as those reflecting domestic concerns: the pipe, card, nightcap, powder horn, and even the creamer, and those showing intellectual interests: the almanac page and the two books. Or you could arrange the items on the desk top and describe each item in turn, moving from left to right.

However, if your purpose were to discover what the religious concerns of the chest's owner were, you would limit your study to the Edwards and Wigglesworth books, paying special attention to the marked pages in *Day of Doom*. Or, if your purpose were to financially gain from your find, you would immediately describe in detail the Edwards edition and the Revere creamer to an expert to assertain their authenticity and value. In any case, your purpose will provide a basis for including or excluding details and will thus suggest a type of unity or controlling generalization.

A description may be unified not only by purpose, but also by point of view. For example, the items in the chest could be described from a physical point of view, such as from left to right when arranged on a desk top, or from first to last as they are removed from the chest. Point of view may also vary according to the psychological relationship between the narrator and the things being described. A curious relative, a knowledgeable historian, or a burglar would have different points of view concerning the objects found in the chest.

▸ EXERCISE 7.1

Study the following details. Then select a purpose and a point of view, and write a description accordingly.

DETAILS: The following items were found in a damaged Y.M.C.A. locker: one unopened can of Spaulding handballs, two half-empty boxes of Sun-

maid raisins, a passport made out to Juan Trillo
(born 1947, Chicago, eyes brown, hair brown,
six feet, 185 pounds), a schedule for the air
shuttle from Baltimore to Washington D.C., a
current *Playboy*, two racquetball racquets, a
worn hooded sweatshirt, a passport—same
photo as on other passport—made out to John
Trilling (born 1947, Chicago, eyes brown, hair
brown, six feet, 185 pounds), a newspaper clip-
ping about Boston's "combat zone," a week's
worth of *Chicago Tribunes* detailing the Democratic Convention of 1968, brand new Adidas
running shoes, a dingy bath towel from the
Washington D.C. Hilton, a half-empty pack
of cigarettes, a slip of paper with these notes:
Jane, 334–4545; Alicia, 553–9800; Dwyer,
462–5771; and an empty, expensive, leather
overnight bag.

POSSIBLE PURPOSES: To present a complete character study of the
owner of these items; to speculate as to the
type of "athlete" the owner is; to establish
the owner as a suspicious character; to
show the owner as tied to the past; to establish the owner as a "womanizer."

POSSIBLE
(RHETORICAL)
POINTS OF VIEW

Through the eyes of the Y.M.C.A. custodian, of the woman who played racquetball
with the owner on a semi-regular basis, of an
F.B.I. agent, of a newspaper reporter. ◢

   Effective description operates by *showing* rather than *telling*. (Review
pages 26– 32.) The following excerpt *shows* not only in the visual sense,
but in terms of other senses as well.

hearing
sight
hearing

Clink-clank. Clink-clank. Clink-clank: the
measured pace of the sentry was marked out in un-
even metallic emphasis, until . . . clank, . . . clank,
. . . clank, only a dull ring interrupted the steady buzz
of the neon sign.

sight

Ca . . . fe. Ca . . . fe. Ca . . . fe. Through the
window a man could be seen, hunched over a steam-
ing coffee cup.

hearing and sight
smell sight taste
hearing smell touch
sight

Ca . . . clank, fe. Ca . . . clank, fe. Inside the cafe, the air smelled slightly of cigarette smoke and of vinegar, used to mop up the counter. At the counter, the man swilled the acrid liquid about his mouth, swallowed with a perceptible gulp, and settled comfortably down into the familiar, stale, almost sour odor of his woolen jacket which had scratched a red rash into his neck.

sight

Next to the counter, a glass case clung to the plaster wall. Inside the case, various posters hung at odd angles. The man, turning his head, stared at the nearest poster. A round-eyed girl with thick, black braids stared back at him from under large, block lettering: PLEASE NOTIFY if you know the whereabouts of Anna Bergen, born 1935, Dresden. . . .

sight
hearing

The man again faced his his coffee, sipped, swilled, swallowed, and then grunted. "It's 'bout time, isn't it?"

sight
hearing

The sallow-skinned cook glanced up.
The man fingered his cup. "For the 7:40?"

►EXERCISE 7.2

Describe one of the following subjects as perceived by the various senses. Remember to *show* rather than *tell*.

1. the contents of your purse or wallet
2. a picture in a magazine
3. your last meal
4. a prized possession (be sure you're looking at it) ◢

Effective description allows the reader to "sense" the subject as the writer perceives it. Thus, the reader can share in or identify with a subject that may be relatively remote from his or her experience.

In the following description by student Heather Mitchell, more is at stake than putting details in their proper place. Heather concentrates on creating a mental picture for her readers through concrete language.

Greasy Spoon

As I jerked open the broken screen door, I noted peanut shells, ashes, crumpled candy wrappers, and a not-so-fine layer of dirt covering the chipped linoleum floor. Towards the rear of the joint two waitresses sat on the counter facing the grill, one combing her hair, and the other smacking a wad of gum. Both wore dingy white uniforms that barely covered the tops of their thighs, and one had on a linty, grey sweater with a large hole under the right arm. After ten minutes, the waitress with the gum finally condescended to stroll over to the end of the counter to where I was. She took a pad of guest checks from her soiled pocket, leaned on one foot, smacked her Juicy Fruit, and said, "Yeah?"

"I'll have a coke and a hamburger please, and . . ."

"One burger!" she bellowed. "Anything else?" she asked, picking at a stain on her apron.

"Could I have that well done?"

She stared at me momentarily, smirked, and then shuffled back to finish her conversation with the other waitress.

The cook, meanwhile, who had been sitting on a stool engrossed in a well-thumbed *Hustler*, rolled his pudgy eyes. He then coughed and squeezed back to the grill and slapped a four-inch patty into the grease; he turned the sputtering meat only a few seconds later. He slid a bun on a chipped plate, slapped on a blob of mayo, and added a slice of pickle for good measure. As he licked the pickle juice from his fingers, he transferred the dripping hamburger from the grill to the roll, shoved the plate towards me, and abruptly returned to his reading. He grunted only slightly as I pushed the plate aside, left my dollar on the counter, and walked out.

Heather Mitchell

As suggested in Chapter 1, when readers encounter a written product such as Heather's description above, they see only the end result of the writing process. The following events may have contributed to that process.

MONDAY: Heather comes to class in a bad mood. She has had another disagreement with her roommate regarding cleaning duties. Heather thinks her roommate is a slob.

Heather's composition instructor gives the assignment, due next Monday, to write a 1-2 page description of a person, place, or thing, and to unify the descriptive details according to purpose and point of view.

Heather thinks, "This'll be easy. I'll just describe what a mess our room is to show what a slob my roommate is."

TUESDAY: Heather sits cross-legged in the center of her room and starts describing everything she sees, moving left to right, top to bottom. "To the top left are three athletic posters mounted on a bluegreen cinderblock wall. The first poster pictures a gymnast poised delicately on a balance beam, her left leg raised and stretched upwards and held by her left hand. . . ."

After detailing each of the three posters, Heather has six pages of notes and has lost her emphasis on what a mess the room is. She then decides to focus on the wadded kleenexes, crumby blotter, and stacks of papers and books that cover her roommate's desk.

WEDNESDAY: Fairly pleased with her efforts, Heather shows her description of her roommate's desk to her best friend. Her friend reacts: "You think that's bad. You should see my desks!" and promptly launches into a graphic description that makes Heather's roommate's desk seem immaculate by comparison.

THURSDAY: Having chucked her original description, Heather casts around for a new topic in her journal. She runs into this notation: "Today I ate, or almost ate, at the world's greasiest spoon. Lucky there was a MacDonald's nearby."

Heather thinks, "Now that *was* a mess. I could describe that!" She then begins jotting down details that illustrate what a mess the place was.

▶ EXERCISE 7.3

Write your own one to two page, specific description of a person, place or thing. Unify your description around a purpose and a point of view. Consult the Process Sheet on page 211 as a review of general description concerns.

Specific description is your acknowledgement of your reader's "right to know." It is your acknowledgement that generalities need specific support. It is your recognition that your reader probably does not see your subject exactly as you do. And it is your commitment to showing your perception of the subject as clearly as possible. Description is important not only as a pattern in itself but also as a means of relating the specific details that show your meaning in other patterns.

Definition

Definition, like description, isolates a subject. Definitions are primarily explanatory, answering the question, "What does this term mean to me?"

Definitions are often necessary to clarify what you mean by a conceptual term such as *courage* or a slang term such as *jive turkey*. Definitions may also explain specialized language or jargon. For instance, when my colleagues and I designed a flier to advertise a Sentence Combining Workshop, we decided to define what sentence combining meant to us. Figure 7.5 shows the interior portion of that flier. (See page 206.)

The flier establishes sentence combining in the *class* of techniques for teaching composition and distinguishes it as being based on transformational grammar and as dealing with kernel sentences. Thus, in "I.", sentence combining is defined in terms of form. Subsequently, in "II.", sentence combining is discussed in terms of function ("useful for . . ."). The technique itself is specifically demonstrated by the actual format of the flier, the Roman numerals being collections of kernel sentences and the Arabic numerals, various sentence combinations of those kernels. The puzzle motif,[1] although an imperfect analogy to the sentence combining process, indicates that in certain respects the solving of a puzzle parallels the combining of sentences. There is, of course, not merely one way that the kernels may be pieced together.

The flier, in short, defines what sentence combining means to *us* as writers and readers and not necessarily what it means to a primary school teacher of reading or to a college professor of theoretical linguistics.

The need to clarify through definition arises out of the fact that you are not identical to your audience. When you clarify, you strive to bridge the gap between you and your reader and to establish a means of identification.

In addition to clarifying what a term means, a definition can also show what a term doesn't mean. For example, the paragraph below defines the word "fortuitous." "Fortuitous" is a good candidate for definition, because it is many times used to mean "fortunate."

> *Fortuitous* does not mean fortunate, although it looks like it could. It even sounds like it could: fortuitous, fortunate. Fortuitous actually means accidental. It is thus more closely related to the word "fortune." Just as there can be good fortune and bad fortune, so also there can be fortuitous events that are good or bad. If I happen to meet a high school friend who I haven't seen in years, it is fortuitous. If I happen to twist my ankle getting on board a plane to Europe, it is fortuitous. If an event is fortuitous, it involves chance. And because fate can smile or frown, I need fortitude when considering the fortuitous. What should I think when a casual acquaintance bumps into me and says, "What a fortuitous meeting!"?

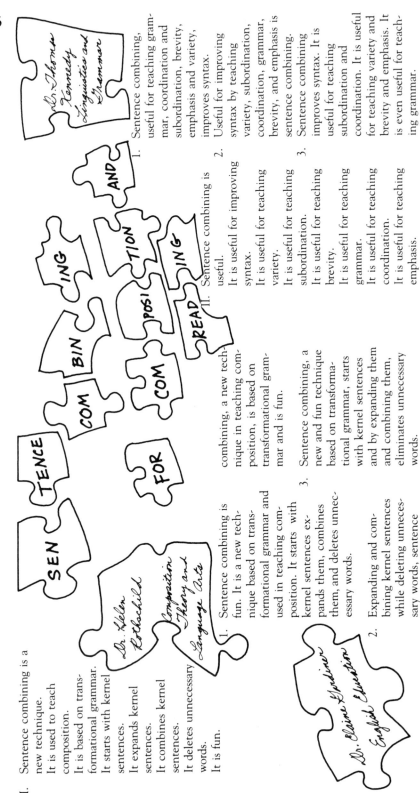

FIGURE 7.5 Flier Using Analogy for Definition

This section does not pretend to exhaust your options for developing a definition. For example, you could develop what a term means through an <u>analogy,</u> as in the flier example with its implied comparison between sentence combining and puzzle solving. An analogy defines the <u>unknown</u> in terms of the <u>known.</u> In fact, the word "analogy" itself offers us an opportunity to work with the definition process, as shown by Figure 7.6 (see page 208).

Whatever arrangement you choose, you establish the term's class and show its distinctive features. (A definition paper on the term <u>analogy</u> could contain a definition statement, a positive example, a negative example, and an analysis of use. The examples could be short or extended. In fact, a definition of the term <u>analogy</u> could contain an analogy. It could, for example, compare using an analogy with using prompt cards in a theatre production.)

The following essay written by student Lana Roth attempts to explore an issue through the definition process:

Held Hostage

Yellow ribbons everywhere: our hostages are home. But why *our* hostages? Why did the 52 Americans taken by the Iranians in November, 1979 become a national obsession?

Some people suggest, my history professor among them, that since Camelot left Washington in Kennedy's hearse, the press hasn't had a human interest story worthy of its mettle . . . or meddle. But now it has the Ayatullah Khomeini, *Time's* Man of the Year.

But it isn't only the press. It is us. Perhaps an answer to my first question will come by first answering a second question, "What is a hostage?"

class plus feature

According to Webster, a hostage is a person held "in a conflict as a pledge that promises will be kept."

restated class

A hostage is like the collateral insuring a loan. Like other forms of security, a hostage has some sort of built-in value. For the Iranians, that value was publicity. For the Americans, that value was their lives

features in this case

as "family." Without the hostages, the Iranians felt it impossible to air their grievances. Without the hostages free, Americans felt it impossible to be free themselves.

alternate class

Hostages are also a type of middleman. They stand in between two sides in a conflict. They are used by

feature in this case

both sides. But unlike other middlemen, such as those coming in between the farmer and the supermarket, the hostage has no power. In a college

Analogy

Definition statement 1.	A form of comparison [CLASS] that emphasizes the similarities between basically dissimilar objects or processes [DISTINCTIVE FEATURE]
Definition statement 2.	A logical process [CLASS] that predicts or infers future resemblances from existing resemblances [DISTINCTIVE FEATURE]
Definition statement 3.	A linguistic process [CLASS] by which new words conform to the pattern of established words [DISTINCTIVE FEATURE]

Definition example 1.	Mark Twain's comparison of becoming a river pilot and being a doctor, which makes the point that in both cases, knowledge destroys "romance" or idealization.
Definition example 2.	When the F.D.A. rules that because a new drug causes cancer in mice, it must cause cancer in humans.
Definition example 3.	If local can become localize, then final can become finalize. In children's speech: You are; you aren't. He is; He isn't. I am; I amn't.

Definition by negative example 1.	Unlike a comparison/contrast, which characteristically deals with objects or processes in the same class, an analogy commonly draws comparisons between objects or processes that do not share the same class. A comparison/contrast may discuss mice and rats (rodents), whereas an analogy may compare eating a hamburger with having a blind date.

FIGURE 7.6   Definition Process for "Analogy"

supporting features { lecture, Ramsey Clark, Attorney General under Johnson, stated that the hostages symbolized for the Iranians the former enslavement of Iran to the Shah and to American policy that kept the Shah in power. The hostages symbolized the Iranian people's former lack of power.

supporting features { The hostages also became a symbol of American impotence as the helicopter rescue mission failed at the cost of eight lives and as the negotiations dragged on and on without any results. It should be no surprise that Americans elected Reagan who had as his motto, "Make America strong again."

But I think it goes even beyond that. Americans were involved as a people, but they were also involved as individuals. My roommate couldn't watch a news report about the hostages without getting tears in her eyes, and her fiancé couldn't watch without wanting to "bust some Iranian in the nose." I couldn't watch, period. Why?

second alternate class { Could it be that we are all hostages in one way or another? Last year a fellow in my English class had to quit school and get two jobs to support his $10,000

supporting features { car. "I like the finer things in life" was his explanation. That car held him hostage, or his dreams of "finer things" held him hostage.

Now the 52 Americans are physically free. But psychologists say that the "returnees" may suffer psychological fallout from the experience for years to

feature in this case { come. The hostages may not be free yet, at least mentally.

Perhaps we have more in common with them than ever before.

Lana Roth

A definition expresses what *you* mean by a particular term. It is your recognition that language is complex and contains ambiguities of meaning. It is also your recognition that your reader will not always understand things exactly as you do. You therefore clarify through definition.

▶ EXERCISE 7.4

Write a definition paper, examining one of the following:

    1. a slang term, such as "preppie" or "hardhat" or "closet liberal"

    2. a technical term, such as "neurosis" or "critical path method"

    3. an abstract term, such as "hospitality" or "anxiety." ◢

More complicated examples of both description and definition are contained in the "mixed structures" portion of Chapter 8.

The following Process Sheet highlights the concerns of these two patterns that isolate a part or term to discuss it. Use the sheet the next time you have to decide whether isolating is appropriate to your material.

PATTERNS THAT CLUSTER

While the isolating patterns focus on one part (or term) for discussion, the clustering patterns deal with several parts unified under one whole. Although there are many possible clustering patterns, we will discuss only three here: classification, comparison/contrast, and exemplification.

Classification

Classification as an arrangement involves naming a whole, represented by the controlling generalization, and its parts, noted as categories or types in the sub-generalization. The trick in constructing a classification is to make the categories mutually exclusive (non-overlapping) and to concentrate on distinctions in *kind* rather than *degree*.

For example, let's examine the controlling generalization, "Woodworks, Inc. uses softwoods, fruitwoods, and hardwoods to make its fine furniture products." This generalization fails because it does not establish mutually exclusive categories. As the diagram in Figure 7.7 shows, fruitwoods are generally hardwoods:

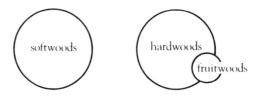

FIGURE 7.7

In a classification, or a division for that matter, the categories must remain distinct. As Figure 7.8 shows (see page 212), the categories do not overlap:

PATTERNS THAT ISOLATE

Is there one person, object, place, or event that I want to *show* to my audience?

If so, what will be my purpose in showing my chosen subject? My point of view?

What sensual details will contribute to my showing of the subject? What mental picture do I want to create?

Is there one term or concept that needs clarification?

If so, to what *class* or family does that term or concept belong?

What, in turn, are the distinctive features that separate that term or concept from every other?

Shall I discuss the term or concept by clarifying what it is? What it isn't? By using analogy?

Does my definition establish what the term or concept means to me and not necessarily what it may mean to others?

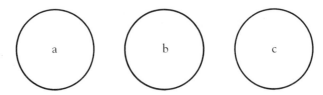

FIGURE 7.8

Each distinct category must also be an "equal" part of one whole. As Figure 7.9 graphically shows, the controlling generalization, "There are usually three types of materials used by Woodworks, Inc.: softwoods, hardwoods, and plastics," is not viable because "plastics" is not equal to "softwoods" and "hardwoods."

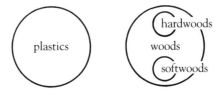

FIGURE 7.9

Furthermore, dealing with differences in *degree* rather than *kind* flaws a classification. For instance, in the controlling generalization, "Woodworks, Inc. always selects two types of woods in its quality furniture, hard and harder," it remains unclear where one category stops and the other begins. (See Figure 7.10.)

FIGURE 7.10

▸EXERCISE 7.5

Test the following classification statements for viability and rewrite the insufficient ones. You may need a dictionary.

EXAMPLE: There are usually three types of materials used by Woodworks, Inc.: softwoods, hardwoods, and plastics.

Woodworks, Inc. typically uses woods and plastics in its furniture.

1. There are three types of people in Chicago: whites, blacks, and businessmen.
2. Stacey could see advantages to both the subtle and the more obvious approaches to asking for a date.
3. Mechanic's wrenches come with hex, double-hex, six-point, and double-square openings.
4. Thrushes, veeries, solitaries, and bluebirds all belong to the songbird family, *Turdidae*.
5. The puzzle contained spheroidal pieces including circles, ellipses, and ovals, and trapezoidal pieces including squares, parallelograms, rhomboids, and triangles. ◢

An example of the classification in product form can be found on pages 152–53 in Chapter 5. In that paper, Linda Geiger examines the two types of roles a witchdoctor plays. A "behind the scenes" look at Geiger's paper (See Figure 7.11.) reveals how the classification grouping emerged from a series of notes.

1. Author views series of notes jotted down about various primitive cultures.

– In Mongolia, men and women alike practice target shooting from galloping horses.
– Some primitive Brazilian jungle tribes have a series of customs pitting males and females in ritual combat.
– In Kenya, Pokota keep birds from their crops by flinging mud balls from raised platforms.
– African witchdoctors use herbal treatments that are as effective as those of Western medicine.

2. Author selects the African witchdoctor as a focus and gathers the appropriate notes together.

– Witchdoctors use herbal treatments that are as effective as those of Western medicine: stramonium leaf → asthma; reserpine → tranquilizer.

FIGURE 7.11   *Notes for a Classification Paper*

– Witchdoctors communicate with the spirit world in dealing with psychosomatic illness.
– Witchdoctors also use dream analysis (Freud?)
– Witchdoctors recommend sacrifice and various "penances" in conjunction with treating illnesses.

3. Author groups witchdoctor notes according to how practices compare and contrast to those of Western medicine.

– Like the west: herbs contain medically proven ingredients.
– Like the west: psychological causes of illness considered when appropriate.
– Unlike west: doctor is also seen as a minister with spirit world connections.
– Unlike west: witchdoctor recommends extra-medical cures – like sacrifice.

4. Author regroups material according the witchdoctor's roles.

The witchdoctor's roles

minister

– communicates with spirit world
– advises on sacrifices
– contacts spirits in cases of psychosomatic illness
– uses dream analysis (Freudian?)
– recommends "penances"

herbalist

– prepares herbs
– uses stramonium leaf for asthma + reserpine for a tranquilizer (like Western Med.)
– dries open wounds, cures snakebites

5. Author articulates main idea behind current grouping.

Although we may find certain cultures primitive, we must not automatically dismiss them as without merit. The African witchdoctor, for example, joins the functions of physician and psychologist in his position.

FIGURE 7.11 (Continued)

214

Another example of how classification can appear in product form appears in the following report:

From November 1 to November 27, 1980, John Jessup has made mixed progress toward the installing of a wood stove in your mountain cabin, RR. #1, Loveland, Colorado. Jessup's progress can be rated adequate in terms of purchasing and intent, and inadequate in terms of actual installation completed and projected finishing date.

Work Completed
Jessup has done an admirable job in two areas of purchasing: obtaining quality materials and securing reasonable prices. Materials and costs are listed below:

1. Jotul wood stove, model 680 $496.00
2. Stove pipe, hardware (25 feet)   40.00
3. Stone for 4 × 6 hearth   30.00
4. Misc. materials   16.50

Jessup's intent is also commendable, both in terms of work procedure and attitude. Jessup is obviously bent on producing a quality product. His preparations are meticulous to the point of his leveling the plank floor that will support the hearth and stove. His measurements are precise. He has figured to 1/16 inch the location of the hearth and has charted the stove's placement with equal accuracy. The location of the pipe, the angle at which the pipe will enter the existing chimney, the number of feet of pipe needed, all these calculations plus detailed diagrams are kept in a separate notebook for ready reference. His commendable attitude is reflected in his comments, "If it's not done right, it ain't worth doing," and his contract: "If the cost of the project exceeds the original estimate, the overrun will be absorbed by the contractor. All labor and materials are guaranteed for ten years of normal use."

Work Unfinished
The major difficulty lies in the fact that only the purchasing and the initial measuring have been completed in these three or so weeks. Yet to be done are the laying of the hearth and the installing of the stove and pipe. Although it is hard to pin Jessup down here, he estimates that "barring unexpected problems" or "tourists," the installation would be completed by January 3.

Recommendations
Basically, you could be cool, aggressive, or exasperated in your approach. If cool, you could let Jessup proceed at his own pace and not worry about having a wood stove this ski season. If aggressive, you could renegotiate Jessup's contract so it stipulates a firm completion date with a penalty clause. If exasperated, you could fire Jessup and look for another contractor. Evergreen, Inc. (303–649–3000) or Big

Bill Clark (303– 567– 9112) are possibles. You could phone them for estimates. You might also contact your lawyer concerning your legal status in all of this.

▶ EXERCISE 7.6

Identify the various classifications contained in the preceding report by listing each class as a box and the categories of each class as branches under that box:

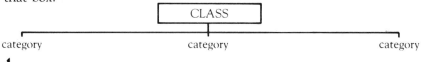

category   category   category

◢

Comparison/Contrast

Comparison/contrast answers the question, "How are these two parts similar and how are they different?" If possible, similarities should be shown and not merely stated. For example, instead of stating, "A and B are similar because they are both expensive," the writer should *show* that they are both expensive: "A costs $10 per quarter ounce, and B costs $600 per pound."

The basis for the similarity (or difference, for that matter) must also be parallel. For example, you wouldn't write, "A and B are both expensive, because A costs $10 per quarter ounce and B costs $600 per item. An "ounce" and an "item" are not measured on the same basis. They are not parallel and therefore cannot be compared.

Differences should also be developed. A good writer usually doesn't just write, "C is different from D in that while C has red hair, D does not." The good writer tells what D has instead: brown hair, bald pate, or expensive wig.

While all comparison/contrasts deal with similarities and differences, not all follow the same organizational pattern. Perhaps the various patterns possible within the comparison/contrast framework can best be demonstrated by taking a rough controlling generalization, such as, " 'Diploma' and 'Bachelor of Science' nursing programs have similarities and differences that led me to my present choice of curriculum," and by showing how the generalization and its sub-generalizations can be arranged according to various patterns.

First, let's take a look at Figures 7.12 and 7.13 to see two ways of following a similarities/differences framework.

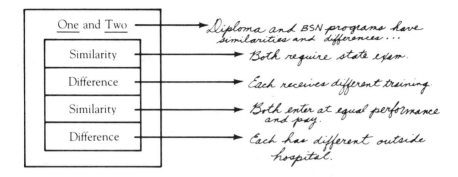

FIGURE 7.12   *Similarities/differences (mixed, alternating)*

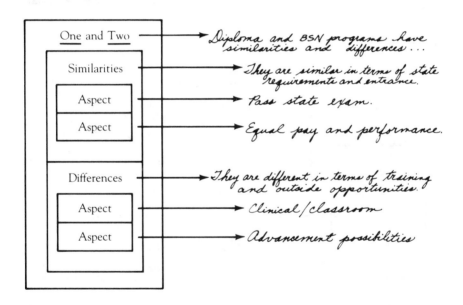

FIGURE 7.13   *Similarities/differences (grouped)*

In the similarities/differences patterns, the emphasis of the controlling generalization falls, appropriately enough, on the similarities and differences. The audience, in turn, perceives that your interest is not in the programs themselves as much as in their similarities and differences.

Now let's consider two half-and-half frameworks as shown in Figures 7.14 and 7.15:

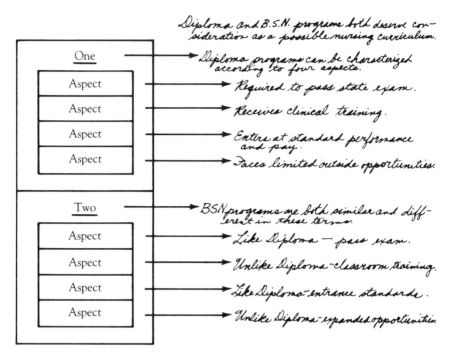

FIGURE 7.14 *Half and Half (mixed)*

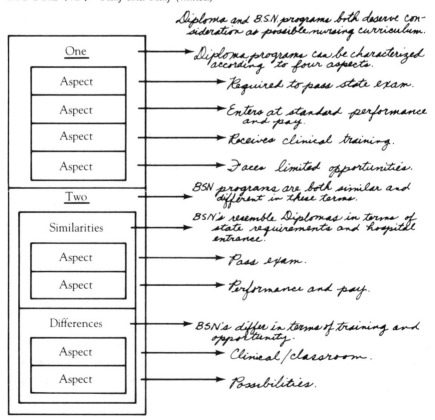

FIGURE 7.15 *Half and Half (grouped)*

In these structures, the emphasis of the controlling generalization falls on the programs themselves. The audience, thus, perceives that your interest is in explaining what each program is like. Within this framework, similarities and differences help in the explanation.

Finally, let's examine an "aspects" framework in Figure 7.16:

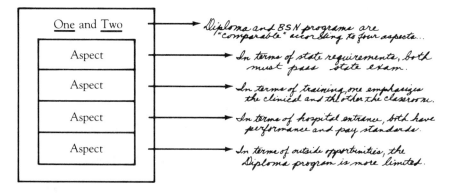

One and Two → Diploma and BSN programs are "comparable" according to four aspects...

Aspect → In terms of state requirements, both must pass state exam.

Aspect → In terms of training, one emphasizes the clinical and the other the classroom.

Aspect → In terms of hospital entrance, both have performance and pay standards.

Aspect → In terms of outside opportunities, the Diploma program is more limited.

FIGURE 7.16   Aspects (mixed)

In this arrangement, the emphasis falls not on the similarities/differences or on the programs themselves, but on the *aspects* involved in the comparison/contrast. The audience therefore perceives these aspects to be the key factors in your "choice of curriculum."

➤ EXERCISE 7.7

Start with the controlling generalization, "My two best friends have similarities and differences that show me something about myself," and generate sample details. Then, using either outlining or draft segmenting as a technique, arrange the controlling generalization and its support according to a similarities/differences framework, a half-and-half framework, and an aspects framework. Compose appropriate sub-generalizations for each arrangement. Note the difference each respective change in structure makes to your audience. ◢

The following sample comparison/contrast paper, written by linguistics student Robert Edwards, shows an interesting combination of the aspects and the similarities/differences frameworks. When you have finished reading Edwards' piece, turn to Morris' piece (pages 34–36) to compare arrangements.

Sound Correspondences between English and German

Any two languages which have developed from a common an-
cestor will exhibit both similarities and differences in their sound
systems, or phonology. Since modern English and modern German
are both lineal descendents of Indo-European and Proto-Germanic,
historical linguists can find many words of common origin (cognates),
having the same basic meaning, and exhibiting both similarities and
differences in pronunciation, especially of their consonants. The similarities can be attributed to the fact that certain consonant sounds
have remained unchanged in both languages over the centuries, while
the differences are the result of systematic sound changes in the
consonants of one or both languages.

In the following pairs of cognate words, the consonant sounds
are identical or almost so: finger/*Finger*, hair/*Haar*, bone/*Bein*, mine/
mein, blood/*Blut*, long/*lang*. This is because f, -ng, h, r, b, n, m, and
l have not changed their pronunciation in either English or German
for at least a thousand years.

Another set of cognate pairs shows an interesting difference:
drink/*trink-*, do/*tu-*, dead/*tot*, day/*Tag*, drag/*trag-*, door/*Tür*, deer/*Tier*.
The members of the pairs differ in that each English word begins with
a d-sound while its German cognate begins with a t-sound. The
sounds d and t themselves differ only in that d is "voiced" while t is
"unvoiced." Otherwise, they are identical in their articulation, both
being classified as "dental stops." This systematic correspondence of
d and t can be explained by studying the history of both languages.
In this case it would be revealed that in German, some centuries ago,
all initial d-sounds came to be pronounced as t, while initial d-sounds
in English remained unchanged.

Another example illustrates a sound change which occurred in
English: knee/*Knie*, knight/*Knecht*, knot/*Knot-*, knuckle/*Knöchel*. All
of the English words now begin with an n-sound, whereas the German
words begin with a kn-sound. Here English has changed and German
has not. In particular, speakers of English several hundred years ago,
began to delete the k-sound whenever it occurred before an n-sound
at the start of a word. The relative recency of this change is evidenced
by the k in the English spelling system, which was developed about
a thousand years ago at a time when the k was still being pronounced
and therefore written out.

A historical linguist could point out dozens of other systematic
phonological correspondences between the consonant and vowel
sounds of English and German, some as simple as these, others quite
complex. Where the modern sounds are identical or similar, they
attest to the close relatedness of the languages and the absence of
change. Where they differ, they witness the independent yet systematic changes of each. The cumulative effect of these changes,
along with changes in syntax, morphology, and inflection, is that

English and German, once the same language, are now mutually unintelligible.

Robert Edwards

Exemplification

Exemplification is a versatile form of arrangement that presents an idea or opinion and illustrates or "proves" that idea or opinion through a series of examples. This "proof" may take the form of various forms of evidence, including case studies, authoritative commentary, scientific studies, and personal experiences. To a certain degree, exemplification is a generic form of arrangement; that is, its concept of presenting examples to support a point is common to the procedure of other more specialized patterns. Exemplification can be used for a wide variety of purposes, including critical analysis and theoretical argument.

In the following selection, student Patricia Dillon argues her opinion that "Good people will have their turn in the world" through examples taken from personal experience and from literature readings.

A Turn in the World

I sometimes wonder what would happen in the world if only good prevailed. Could people actually learn to live without jealousy, competition, or cynicism? Though all people may never reach this state, there are some who are striving to convert the evil or injustice they see in their lives into something worthwhile. I believe that it is these people who will finally achieve significant goals in their lives. I remember many long and painful moments when I would stand and listen to my friend Matt quietly accepting berating insults from his father. I longed for him to shout back, just once. He never did. Today, my friend is successful in almost every aspect of his life. Matt is an excellent student, has plans of a career in business, and has a happy social life. Matt is an example of a person who was willing to endure hardships and injustice for something he thought was more important—harmony in his family. Because Matt was able to realize his desire for a better future, he constructively profited from the difficult times with his father.

Another example of a person who learned that he could somehow deal with the evil in his life was Henderson, from Bellow's *Henderson the Rain King.* There were many obnoxious traits in Henderson's personality. He spoke rudely in public, drank excessively, and often cared little for the feelings of his wife. However, Henderson soon became dissatisfied with his life as it was, and he decided to quest for a deeper meaning for his existence. He journeyed to Africa where he met Dahfu, the man who was an important influence on Henderson's future. Through Dahfu, Henderson was able to realize that by improving his day-to-day life, he could hope for a more successful future. Henderson began trying to change his life; one unsuccessful attempt to help the Arnewi people did not discourage him. He continued searching, and finally reached an inner peace and acceptance in his life. From this point on, Henderson began changing his life for the better. He decided to study medicine, a career he had long wanted to pursue. Henderson began to build up his life with new goals. By changing, Henderson was physically, mentally, and spiritually reborn. All of a sudden, he refused to accept the old monotony. He phoned his wife, surprising her by saying, "Honey, I aim to do better, can you hear? I've had it now."

Ivan Illych, the main character in Tolstoy's *The Death of Ivan Illych*, progressed in much the same way as Henderson. Originally, Ivan was an arrogant and self-centered man. He was of the highest class, never allowing those around him to get in his way. While in the Province, Ivan had an affair with a lady "who made advances to the elegant young lawyer. . . . It was all done with clean hands, in clean linen, with French phrases, and, above all, among people of the best society and consequently with the approval of people of rank." This was much of how Ivan's values were set. Where Henderson was able to learn the true meaning of his life during the quest in Africa, Ivan was only able to discover these things through his death. ". . . Ivan fell through and caught sight of the light, and it was revealed to him that though his life had not been what it should have been, this could still be rectified." Ivan realized that the material goals he had in life were no longer important, but he was late in discovering this. As he lay on his deathbed, he saw the animosity that existed between him and his family. He knew he would never have the opportunity to re-do his life, yet he wished to spare his family at least some pain. He longed to die, for he knew they were suffering much because of the length and difficulty of his death. Ivan found new hope in death; "in place of death there was light." Though Ivan's life had to be taken before he reconciled some of his evil traits, he was given a "time in the world." Through dying, he was born again, presumably to an eternal life.

One final character who followed the same rebuilding pattern as Henderson and Ivan was Louisa, a main character in Lawrence's *Daughters of the Vicar*. Louisa was raised by her family believing that she was a part of the upper society. She was not supposed to associate with the laborers or pit miners. However, when Louisa's family first moved into the town, she went out among her father's laborers giving piano lessons. Louisa showed an even stronger rebellion against the evils she saw in her family's ideals when she married Alfred. Her parents were strongly opposed to her "marrying-down." Louisa refused to follow her parents' wishes. "She was going her own way. . . . She had her fixed will to love, to have the man she loved." Louisa was searching for more than material or social status. She married the man she loved and began to live her own life—she had her "turn in the world." As the story ended, I was left with the feeling that Louisa was finally beginning her life. She did not have to travel to Africa as Henderson did, nor did she have to die in order to realize that whatever good she wanted from life would have to come from her own doing. Louisa learned at an early age that in order to achieve her desires, she had to transform some of the shortcomings in her life to achievable and worthwhile goals.

Through all these examples—Matt, Henderson, Ivan, and Louisa—I have come to believe that, as Dahfu said, "The noble will have their turn in the world." It is only through this exchange of materialism and evil for something constructive and worthwhile that man will find fulfillment in life and be given a chance to pursue deeper and more satisfying goals. When man does make this drastic change in his life, he will be given his "turn in the world."

Patricia Dillon

✔ EXERCISE 7.8

To examine exemplification more fully, answer the following questions about the Dillon paper.

1. Patricia cites four examples to "prove" her point. To what extent are the examples repetitious (say exactly the same thing)? To what extent does each example highlight a distinct aspect of the main point?

2. How does Patricia link her examples together?

3. Is there any reason that you can see for Patricia to cover her examples in the order that she does? Which example or examples are closest to your experience?

4. Underlying Patricia's argument are certain assumptions about what characterizes goodness, success, and satisfaction. What are these assumptions? How does each example show what goodness, success, and satisfaction are like?

5. Patricia uses examples from personal experience and literature readings. Are these types of examples appropriate to the main point she is making? ◢

Each of the clustering patterns discussed in this chapter arranges various parts around one whole. These parts can be types, categories; people, objects, places, events, similarities, differences, aspects; examples, illustrations, proofs. In any case, the parts are grouped together in a way meaningful to both writer and reader.

The following Process Sheet on page 225 highlights the concerns of the clustering patterns just discussed. Use it to decide which clustering pattern will work best for you by completing the following exercise.

▶EXERCISE 7.9

Start with the reader expectation that your final arrangement will have to be a classification, a comparison/contrast, or an exemplification. Also assume the expectation that your final paper will run approximately three pages typed or equivalent. Then generate and write a paper that will fulfill these expectations, along with the expectations regarding content and style already established in this text. ◂

SEQUENTIAL PATTERNS

Sequential patterns depend on a linear arrangement of parts. This linear sequencing can be based on controlling factors such as time, process, or logic, to name only a few. The following discussion of arrangements does not exhaust the sequencing possibilities.

Chronological Sequences: Narration

Narration commonly features a sequence of events in time. The relating of history and biography involves narrative, as does the telling of tall tales or the retelling of past events. Narrative does not have to follow a strict past-to-present order of events. For example, events can be related as flashbacks or with the actual sequence otherwise altered. If the order of events attempts to imitate the sequence as contemplated in a writer's mind, such as in "stream of consciousness" narrative, the order may become "imaginative" rather than chronological. (Discussing such imaginative sequences is beyond the focus of this text.)

The example of narrative by my former colleague, Michael Harris, (see page 226) features several time perspectives.

PATTERNS THAT CLUSTER

Are there various parts that represent types or categories of one whole?

If so, are these parts mutually exclusive? "Equal"? Do they exhibit differences in kind rather than degree?

Are there two (perhaps more) parts that have both similarities and differences?

If so, can both the similarities and differences be specifically developed?

What comparison/contrast pattern would most closely reflect the emphasis desired? Half and half? Similarities/differences? Aspects? Mixed?

Are there various parts that exemplify, illustrate, or prove one idea or opinion? (Or, can this idea or opinion be supported by more than one example?)

If so, to what extent are these parts or examples repetitious? To what extent does each highlight a distinct aspect of the idea or opinion?

Is the nature and ordering of the parts or examples effective in terms of purpose, audience, and subject?

▶EXERCISE 7.10

When reading the Harris narrative, keep in mind and try to answer the following questions:

1. How does the ordering of events depart from a strict chronological sequence? What was the actual order of events, as far as you can determine?
2. How does the present ordering of events affect you as the reader? What was Harris' purpose in presenting the events as they appear in the narrative? His main idea?
3. What strategies does Harris use to unify or link the separate events? What role, for example, does the title play? The father's profession?
4. The selection is a relatively long one. What function does each numbered section have? Could any section be eliminated without damaging the piece as a whole? Explain. ◢

Five Tableaux of My Father

An old dresser-locket of my mother's, containing five photographs, closing up or extending out like an accordian: I come across it while looking for something else. I pick it up and temporarily forget what I came for. . . .

I. The Race

My father returned home from his rounds one afternoon earlier than usual. I was out in the front yard, playing, restlessly alone. My father climbed out of his car, immediately sensed my desire for company, and walked over toward me.

"Wanna race?" he asked. At this time, there was a lot of contention among my two brothers and father and me over who was the fastest runner in the family. Each of us had been making vehement claims that he was the fastest. My father knew that I would accept a race such as this at the drop of a hat.

"Where to?"

"I don't know. Where would you like to race to?"

"Across the vacant lot to the Becks' yard." My father nodded agreement, trying to keep a straight face, and began to pull off his light brown coat. He was at a decided disadvantage. He had on street shoes and dress clothes; he even had a pair of surgical scissors loosely hanging out of his shirt pocket. How was he going to run a race in get-up like that? I, on the other hand, had on tennis shoes and play clothes. I looked over at him still getting out of his coat and then hanging it on a tree limb.

"Mark, set, go!" I shouted and took off for the Becks'.

"Hey! Hold on!" my father said, breaking out in a laugh, and chased after me. At the sycamore tree, just before you reach the vacant lot which separated the Becks' yard and our yard, my father caught up with me (he was actually the faster runner). Suddenly the surgical scissors bounced out of his pocket. He hesitated momentarily and I did too . . . then we both raced on. We finished in a dead heat, both breathlessly claiming we had nipped each other.

It seemed to me that at that point where my father lost his scissors and then only laughed and continued the race, he not only lost his chance to win the race, but he became at that point a young carefree boy again, like me. He had momentarily given up his profession in order to again reach boyhood and be on my level. As we walked together into the house, my father draped his arm around me and pulled me close beside him. He was looking down at me with his eyes soft and shiny, a radiant smile on his face. . . . He is wearing a similarly happy expression in one of the miniature photographs in my mother's locket which unfolds out five lengths (five photographs, all of my father) across her dresser. I sit there now, in her room, rapt.

II. Deer Hunting

Once, when I was thirteen, my father brought my brother Chuck and myself along with him on a deer hunt. Several other doctors and he had organized it. Among the group were Dr. Ken Barret and his two sons, Ross and John, a friend of John's whose name I've now forgotten, old Mr. Overman who owned Overman's New and Used Chevrolet, Toby Barret, Dr. Barret's brother, who was well-known around town for being an alcoholic, and fat old Dr. Bug who chewed cigars and never lit them because he couldn't understand the reasoning in burning good tobacco. The hunt was a one-day affair—getting there early in the morning before daylight, ranging through the woods at different widely-spaced points, and hunting all day.

The group had driven out in three or four cars. Every so often the caravan of cars would stop, and two or three hunters would step out and individually head out through the woods. My father and I were the next to last ones to get out (my brother Chuck was three years older than I—sixteen—so he could hunt alone). We stepped boldly into the woods as the other hunters had done, I following my father. It was very dark and quite cold and foggy. I carried my new 4.10 shotgun with both hands, being sure to keep it pointed down. I was primed for a full day of walking through the woods, hoping to myself to happen upon an idle buck day-dreaming in a clearing. However, after we got about twenty yards into the woods, my father abruptly halted and sat down under a tree. I sat down beside him. We sat and we waited in the cold, numbing darkness, wordless. So this is how you hunt deer, I thought to myself. . . . After a while, my father said, "It's going to be morning soon. Look." I looked out through the trees and saw the top of a great red ball rising over the flat, gray landscape.

My father and I just sat there, occasionally talking, sometimes pointing out a bird or a squirrel or a flower or a certain unusual type of tree—anything sufficiently exotic to be of interest. I see us there sitting beneath the tree, armed and girded up for the hunt, relaxed, peaceable, and wide awake to the woods around us. That was to be my last memory of my father. On the way home from that hunt there was a car accident and my father was killed.

III.   Report Cards

About halfway through my fifth year in school, a vivid thing happened between my father and me. Report cards had just come out and I had received straight C's, five of them. I even got a C in spelling, which was unforgiveable in our family. I brought my report card home and, like my two older brothers and one younger sister, I handed it over to my mother for inspection and approval. As it turned out, the other kids had chanced to have very good report cards this one time that I had done so poorly. My mother looked it over and said, "Hmmm . . . better go in and show it to your father . . ."

I brought the card in and interrupted my father from his book. He was reading Gibbon's *Decline and Fall of the Roman Empire* for the second time. "Dad?" I said, gently touching my knee against his black leather chair. He straightened up and took his pipe out of his mouth.

"Yes, son?"

I handed over the report card silently, looking very ashamed of myself. He looked it over and then looked up at me, then back down at the card again.

"You must not have put much effort into your school work this six weeks," he said. "Did you work very hard on this, son?"

"Yessir," I said. "I really tried hard."

"O.K., that's all I ask," he said and handed the card back to me. I was so pleased with my spontaneous sincere response and my father's acceptance of me, bad report and all, that I quickly decided to draw out the exchange.

"Dad . . . y'know . . . I'm not ashamed of myself about the report card. I think I'm just average, y'know, and C's are the best I can do. . . . I'm just cut out to make C's, even if Russ and Chuck can make A's."

My father looked up at me, very serious now. His eyes were narrowed and hard, then they relaxed. Even now I can see his expression, clear and in focus, arrested and permanent.

"Do you really believe you're just a C student, merely a C student? . . . 'cause if you do, maybe we ought to sit down and talk about it a little bit and figure out exactly what can be expected of you and from you from here on out. . . ." His tone was so understanding and his reasoning so patient and deliberate, that it made me go back and consider again what I had said.

"What do *you* think I am?" I asked.

"Well," he answered, "there's no doubt in my mind but that if you say you're a C student, then you must be what you say you are. But, I'll tell you something . . . if it was me, even if I *was* a C student, I wouldn't admit it . . . that's all the more reason to try for A's. Always attempt the most difficult, the highest there is, even if you're pretty sure you can't reach it. That way, whether you succeed or fail, you'll feel good about it afterward. You'll know you did your best. And that's all that counts. You think about it."

IV.   Casanova Kiss

When my father used to return home after making his rounds at the hospital, not infrequently we would have already sat down to supper. My father would call from the hospital and tell my mother that he'd be along shortly to join the family.

When my father walked in the side door—we always used the door at the side of the house for convenience: the front door was only rarely used: for dinner guests and the like—and then into the kitchen, he would be greeted with:

"Hi Dad!"

"Hiya Dad!"

"Hey Dad, how are you?"

"Dad, Chuck's been picking on me today . . ." etc. from my two brothers, my sister, and myself. He would smile at us and walk straight to my mother, take her in his arms as if he were Casanova and she were a precious statue, recline her to the point where she was almost parallel to the floor, and kiss her. This would of course elicit from us kids groans of disgust, catcalls, impatient pangs of hunger, and mad giggling—many various signs of uncomfortable reactions and repressed excitement, but which were meant in general to say, "Come, get on with it if you're going to do it. We're hungry." My father would feign innocence as if he didn't know what the trouble could be with kissing his wife. Then he'd again look down at my mother, still left dangling in his arms next to the floor, and say, "How are you, dear?" Stop. An old photograph. Now static.

V.   Miss Lilly

One summer afternoon, my father was slowly driving down our street—Quelqueshue Street, which was named after an old Indian tribe. He had finished his rounds quite early—it must have been a Saturday—and, as I say, was slowly driving down our street, happy, I suppose, in the expectation that he would have the whole evening off to spend with his family.

Down the street from us—about four or five houses down—lived the Glasgows: Mrs. Lilly Glasgow, the widowed mother, and her two spinster daughters, Helen and Hazel. Lilly must have been close to ninety, but she was as spry and cantankerous as an old billy goat. She was small and shrivelled up—like a wrinkled raisin, only she was lily white, with a shock of gray hair on top. The two daughters were school teachers: tall, thin, ashen-colored, close to sixty now, rather misshapen and poorly-looking, like trees or tall bushes that happened to grow up in a place where there was bad soil or little sunlight.

The mother, Lilly, loved to work out in the yard in her flower bed. We would often look at her, the other neighborhood kids and I, as we rode past on bicycles. Sometimes she'd speak to us; usually she wouldn't notice us at all. On this afternoon that my father was gliding leisurely down the street in his car, looking out the windows on either side of him, enjoying the bright sunny day, Mrs. Glasgow happened to be out in her front yard, with her back to the street, bent over digging in her flower bed. My father spotted her and immediately pulled his car up by the curb for a better look. Miss Lilly was *standing,* with her legs held straight, and was bent over at the waist with her tail stuck straight up in the air, instead of bending at the knees and crouching over the flowers, as most people would do it. Clearly in view to every passerby on the street was *everything*—from her lily white, bowed old legs to her white ruffled britches. My father laughed and called out a greeting to her!

"Good afternoon, young lady! You look mighty pretty today." Miss Lilly jerked around, just like an old hen, too old to lay eggs and too old to pluck and eat, and too wily and quick-witted to catch anyway. She hastily beat down her old dress till it hung down below her knees and stared at my father without saying a word, too shocked and outraged to even talk. They stood there staring at each other: the one, swivel-hipped around with her planter in her hand, still holding her dress tightly against her old legs; the other, smiling, almost apologizing for his visceral enjoyment of the situation. Miss Lilly tried to stare my father down, but she only succeeded in transfixing him, paralyzing him as he sat there in his parked car, the motor still running. Suddenly, her hard, taut expression softened and her eyebrows and forehead unwrinkled and her old toothless mouth gave way to a grin, involuntarily, as if she were beside herself with joy, but didn't want anyone to see it.

"Oh you, Dr. Harris! Don't you have any better sense than to fool around with us old women?"

My father laughed. His eyes were twinkling like they did when he was very pleased with something or someone.

"You'll never be too old for me, Miss Lilly," he said.

Michael Harris

For me as a reader, Michael's revelation of his father's death at the end of the second section creates a sense of loss and gives a new context or perspective from which to view the father's actions in the remaining sections. It also causes the seemingly innocent line, "You'll never be too old for me, Miss Lilly," to acquire a tragic, even ironic, meaning.

Narration frequently creates such contexts for readers. It frequently provides, for example, a frame for a specific account of an event, as can be seen in the following interview written by student Jan Hermann.

Framed by narration, her interview recounts an actual visit with Alfred M. Landon, nominated for the U.S. Presidency in 1936. In this write-up, narration functions much like the antecedent action of a play, introducing the cast of characters and providing initial background information. Further, narration also provides a *denouement*, the final discovery that "even rookies can interview governors."

Narrative answers the question, "How can I write about a past experience or event?" It also can answer the question, "How can I create a context for my subject?" And it can help answer, "How can I join separate elements of support?", also.

An Interview with Alf Landon

As I turned one of the brass handles of the enormous double doors, I realized there was no turning back. "I wonder if this is how Barbara Walters got started?" I silently pondered. Shutting the glass door, I was careful not to leave any fingerprints, for doing so would have definitely been the sign of a rookie. With pen and shorthand notebook grasped firmly (and sweatily) in hand, I approached the receptionist and professionally presented my name, rank, and serial number (well, my name anyway). She reassuringly replied, "Oh yes! Mr. Landon is expecting you. He'll be with you in just a minute." (A minute . . . sixty seconds . . . oh God!) I smiled politely and sat down in a dark brown leather chair in front of the fireplace. (Thank goodness it wasn't lit; my deodorant would have never made it!) As I glanced around the mid-sized but very businesslike room, I noted numerous pictures, cartoons, and plaques referring to Alfred M. Landon, Governor of Kansas in 1932. My nervousness quickly dissolved into admiration and curiosity. Yes, I found myself wanting to know more about this extraordinary man. "The Governor will see you now," the secretary stated. I followed her to a small office and halted in front of a cluttered desk behind which was seated Governor Landon. He rose and welcomed me. His eyes, smile, and handshake were a projection of warmth. "Perhaps this is his secret," I reflected. After introductions and being seated, I had no doubt that a most successful and highly interesting interview was in store.

QUESTION:	Mr. Landon, before discussing your political career, I have just a few questions regarding your personal background. Do you mind?
ANSWER:	Why no, go right ahead.
QUESTION:	How long did you reside in your home town of Marietta, Ohio?
ANSWER:	Beginning at age three, I lived there for about fourteen years.
QUESTION:	If your father, John M. Landon, was an oil producer in Marietta, what prompted your family to move to Independence in 1904?
ANSWER:	The development of oil in Kansas, of course!
QUESTION:	Were you interested in following your father's footsteps and entering the oil industry?
ANSWER:	No. Not primarily at that time.
QUESTION:	I understand you attended a law school. Which one?
ANSWER:	I graduated from the law school of Kansas University in 1908.
QUESTION:	Were you ever a practicing attorney? Any cases?
ANSWER:	The only client I ever had was the public! When I was Progressive county chairman in 1914, Victor Murdock was running for Senator. Well, I spent the day with him and long in the afternoon he said, "Alf, you oughta practice law. Come to Wichita, take on a good criminal case, and it will be publicized in the *Eagle*. The business is fascinating." I replied, "So is a poker game!"
QUESTION:	Upon graduation, what endeavors did you undertake?
ANSWER:	I worked in a bank and at the same time made oil deals.
QUESTION:	What influence did you have in the enactment of the Kansas oil proration law?
ANSWER:	Very much! I fought for its legislation. It was a hard fight with considerable opposition to small independent producers.
QUESTION:	May I inquire what your three children Margaret, Nancy, and John are presently doing? Any grandchildren?
ANSWER:	Margaret is now "Mrs. Mills"; Nancy is married also and lives in Wichita; John is working at a radio station in Fort Collins. I have twelve grandchildren and let's see . . . six great grandchildren.
QUESTION:	Do you still own your famous Shetland pony named "Red"?
ANSWER:	Yep, but he's getting pretty old like me!

QUESTION: I understand you're partial to a certain eating estab-
              lishment. Will you devulge its name?

ANSWER: You bet! I love to eat at "Tommy's Fine Foods." As
              a matter of fact, I just had lunch there today.

QUESTION: Didn't you just recently appear on the *Tomorrow
              Show*?

ANSWER: Yes, I did. I have done numerous interviews before,
              but that one was different from all others. I have
              even been interviewed by Eric Severeid you know.
              Anyway, The *Tomorrow Show* interview was unique
              in that I remained here but talked directly to Tom
              Snyder in California. We were both on the T.V.
              screen simultaneously. The telephone company
              built special towers in the front yard, and I had to
              wear a little bug in my ear. The interview was quite
              long.

QUESTION: In addition to an oil business, I understand you own
              four radio stations. Which ones? What are some of
              your frequent daily tasks?

ANSWER: I have forty-seven wells which each average about
              two barrels per day. I own radio stations in Topeka
              (WREN), Dodge City, Liberal, and Fort Collins.
              My main duties involve programming, news cov-
              erage, staff meetings, and in general, keeping track
              of what is going on.

QUESTION: What was your first stepping stone into politics?

ANSWER: Becoming county chairman for the Progressive
              party.

QUESTION: I noted that at one time you were Secretary to
              Governor Henry Allen. How long did you hold that
              position?

ANSWER: Oh, only for about two months. Allen's secretary
              was resigning, and I temporarily filled the position
              as a favor.

QUESTION: Could you briefly explain your relationship with
              William Allen White?

ANSWER: We met back in the early days and through the years
              continued a very happy association. William ran for
              governor in 1924 on the Independent ticket, and I
              supported him.

QUESTION: The thrill of victory was surely present when you
              were elected governor in 1932. What do you attri-
              bute your win over Woodring to?

ANSWER: Smart campaigning!

QUESTION: Your 1936 campaign slogan was "Don't Spend
              What You Haven't Got." How did this contrast
              with Roosevelt's slogan?

ANSWER: Roosevelt said inflation was a fool form of taxation.
                He supported a balanced budget. He said he was
                going to manage huge government bureaucracy. In
                addition, Roosevelt was opposed to the way welfare
                was financed. These issues are still present today.

QUESTION: Do you feel the actions of the Hoover Adminis-
                tration helped or hindered the Republican party at
                the '36 election?

ANSWER: Well, I don't think his activities helped a lot!

QUESTION: In 1938, you turned down an almost guaranteed seat
                in the senate. Why?

ANSWER: Mrs. Landon and I decided that we preferred the
                simpler yet more intelligent life of Kansas as com-
                pared to Washington.

QUESTION: What do you think of the stability of our political
                structure today?

ANSWER: Well, we must consider all factors such as inflation,
                our confused foreign policy, and federal bureau-
                cracy. I think the strength of our system has been
                proven by the proficiency that we exercise. How-
                ever, we still have plenty of problems ahead of us!

We both realized that the interview was completed, yet we
remained smiling at each other. The Governor mentioned that he
was indeed impressed with my possession of background information
and inquired whether I planned to enter the field of journalism. I can
assure you this reporter was highly flattered. As I thanked Mr. Alfred
M. Landon for the pleasant opportunity to speak with him, he made
me promise to mail him a copy of my final paper. When I exited the
now quite cozy office, I closed the great door behind me and inconspicuously pressed a tiny fingerprint on the virgin glass—proving even
rookies can interview governors.

                                                        Jan Hermann

▶ **EXERCISE 7.11**

As an exercise in narration, try to convert the question-answer portion of the preceding Landon interview into prose. ◀

Procedural Sequences: Process Analysis

Process analysis answers the question, "How does this work?" or "What are
the steps in this procedure or process?" The entire second section of this

text is essentially an analysis of the writing process. Process analysis commonly follows a step-by-step sequence. It is time-ordered in the sense that certain steps often must precede others. And it is sometimes the little preliminary steps, essential to the process, that are forgotten. For example, a student once wrote a graphic analysis of how to make a "super" peanut butter sandwich and forgot to have his readers open the peanut butter jar.

The following process analysis explains how to "log in" and "log out" on a computer. The writer's purpose goes beyond the procedure being discussed, however, as the conclusion shows.

Connecting with the Computer

Knowing how to use a computer is almost becoming a "literacy requirement" in this technological age. Here are a few A.B.C.'s to get you started.

Background

This university has several computer systems. The VAX system is the computer system available here for student use. This system operates all hours except from 7:00 a.m. to 9:00 a.m. daily, when it is "down" for routine checks and maintenance. System terminals can be found at various locations around campus, including the Computer Science Building, East Hall, the Library, and even most dorms. The main printer for the system is located in the Computer Science Building.

A terminal consists of a T.V. screen-like viewer and a typewriter-like keyboard. Some terminals also have deck printers, so you don't have to run over to Computer Science to get your printouts. Terminals on the VAX system are either A or B type. A complete list of where these terminals are located and whether they're A or B can be obtained from Computer Science, room 108. In room 108, you can also check out computer informational packets on such topics as "Useful DCL (Digital Command Language) Commands" and "Creating and Modifying Files Using SOS (the editor)."

Although there are various computer languages, including Fortran, Pascal, Wylbur, and Basic, you don't have to know any of these to log on and log off.

Preliminary Steps

1. Obtain your professor's signature on a VAX authorization form, so you can use the computer. Any professor can authorize your use if you plan on utilizing the computer "for instructional purposes."

2. Go to Computer Science, room 108. Obtain a list of terminal locations for VAX A and VAX B. Determine whether the A or the B locations are most convenient for you.

3. Go to the Computer Science accounting office, room 128.
    a. Present your VAX authorization form.
    b. Designate whether you want to use an A or a B terminal.
    c. Obtain a VAX username. A username identifies you as an authorized user to the computer. The name is prefaced by an AO or a BO, depending on whether you have chosen to use an A or a B terminal. A typical username would be: A012007.
    d. Designate a password. The password is the computer's way of identifying you individually. The password may be any word you choose. Let's say you've chosen the word "Lucky."
4. Using your list of terminal locations, find an empty terminal and be seated.

Steps in Logging On

1. Check to see that the terminal is switched on.
2. Hit the return [RET] key.
3. Type your username [A012007]. The "0" in this name is the number zero and not the letter "O" on the terminal keyboard. The "0" should appear "∅" on the screen as you type it. If you make a mistake, the computer will tell you that you have made a "user validation error." In this case, hit the return and try again.
4. Hit the return key [RET] key.
5. Type your password [Lucky]. This password will *not* appear on the screen. The computer does not show it to prevent others from using it. If you mistype the password, the computer will show: LOGIN ERROR, and you will have to hit the return key and try again.
6. After successfully typing the password, hit the return key.

At this point, the computer will show you a welcome message. It will then show you a dollar sign [$] "prompt." This is the signal that it is ready for you to begin your input.

Steps in Logging Off

1. Type "Lo."
2. Hit the return key [RET].

The computer will then show you the exact clock time you logged off and how much "computer time" you used.

After you see how simple it is to log in and log off, perhaps you will want to learn more about computer programming in general and about a specific computer language in particular.

When I was going to high school, I avoided foreign languages, because, I guess, I was afraid of them. So when I went to Europe last summer, I was reduced to a crude sign language in communicating. Now when I see other students afraid of the computer, I remember how I was about French 101. I also remember how I was in Europe, trying to ask directions to the "W.C."

So, with these instructions, I urge you to give it a try. You owe it to yourself in this technological age.

Jim Pace

(You will note that despite the meticulousness of the preceding analysis, the writer still could be more specific about where to get the VAX authorization form and how to "check the computer" [log in, 1] and switch it on.)

▶ EXERCISE 7.12

Write up a process analysis for one of the following: (1) how to operate a sewing machine, tractor, calculator, or camera; (2) how your system of notetaking or of cleaning up your room, car, or pet works; (3) how to be a good conversationalist. ◂

Causal Sequence: Cause and Effect

A cause, or reason, is something or someone that brings about a result or action. Causal analysis explores the questions, "Why did this happen?" and "What motivated this result?"

Some causes are "closer" to their effects than others. For example, you have to have a dog to have a dog bite. A dog is the direct cause of such a bite. But causes can also be remote. For example, remote causes can include the circumstances surrounding the event (or effect), the agent or person involved in or causing the circumstances, and the reasons causing that person to enter the circumstances in the first place.

The following dialogue illustrates various causes for one effect (a dog bite).

(My colleague walked into the office with his arm bruised and bandaged.)

"What happened to you?"

"I got bit by a dog." [The effect.]

"How did that happen?"

"The dogs were fighting." [The circumstance as a cause.]

"How did that involve you?"

"Well, I stepped in and tried to separate them." [The person involved in the circumstance.]

"Why did you do that?"

"I was taking care of the dogs for a friend. Besides, I didn't think I would be bitten." [The reasons for the person becoming involved in the circumstance.]

Notice that in answering the question, "How did you get bitten?", my colleague does not launch into a graphic description of the dog's teeth piercing his flesh. He assumes that I'm interested in more remote causes.

In identifying causes, you might ask the following questions:

What is the effect I'm concerned with?

What are the circumstances involved?

Who initiated or entered into these circumstances?

Why did that person initiate or enter into these circumstances?

In causal analysis, it is necessary to examine each cause to be sure it contributes to the effect. In this regard, you should not necessarily equate distant or remote causes with time. Just because something happened six years ago doesn't make it a distant cause. Likewise, you should guard against thinking that just because something follows an event in time, that "something" was caused by the event. Just because John didn't drink before marrying Mary, but now drinks heavily, does not mean that his marriage "drove him to drink."

In the following paper, student Yong Kwet Loong examines various causes of the current jogging trend.

Running for Fitness and Fun

Remember the good old stone age days when people used to run? Yes, back in those prehistoric days, our forefathers, who didn't have to go to college then as there were no colleges, were running barefoot all over the surface of mother earth with tyrannosaurs, pterodactyls and other pesty creatures hot on their heels. Horses, trishaws and automobiles hadn't been invented then and a pair of good strong legs was a very practical asset. Today, millions of leap years later, planet earth has changed; volcano smog, acid lava, and flying volcanic rocks have, for the most part, been replaced by industrial pollution, acid rain, and Skylab. Man is still running as hardily as ever though. Today, however, man is fastidiously running for fun as well as for fitness.

Man's tinkering with the miracles of nature has brought about scientific discoveries that have made life on earth easier, so much so that his physical well-being is being seriously affected. Fatty, high calorie foods and lack of physical exercise have caused severe repercussions on man's life span.[1] Fat is becoming a household word and despite heavy tax burdens, undertakers and morgue proprietors are getting progressively richer through increased business. Thus, with the ingenuity that is commonly attributed to human beings and African chimpanzees, people are becoming conscious of their fat and blubber and are beginning to wage war against fat and unfitness by taking up running. Bob Glover, in his book *The Runner's Handbook,* observes:

> Suddenly, Americans by the tens of thousands, are stripping off their clothes, pulling on shorts, lacing up shoes and running. They run everywhere: in City Parks, along rivers, lakes and oceans, up and down mountains; in gyms and field houses. They are running for their lives. They are running because their friends are dropping dead from heart attacks. They run because they are fat, scared or tense. They run because their lives are sedentary, made too easy by machines.[2]

Thus, with fitness and physical well-being as a cause, the running crusade began.

In 1972, the Fitness Institute of Toronto administered exhaustive tests to 4,021 men and 1,675 women and proved that man's sexual activity depends largely on his physiological age—that is, his degree of fitness.[3] This discovery proved to be a big incentive for people, especially senior citizens, toward taking up running. Sam McConnel is sixty-seven years old and runs six miles a day. He says,

> "Most people over fifty don't have much sex, but running is a great contribution to the drive. I feel better today sexually than I did twenty years ago, and I attribute this to running."[4]

Aside from keeping a person fit and sexually active, running usually brings people who have been alienated by science and technology closer to mother nature. According to statistical research done by Martin Cohen in the May '74 issue of *Runner's World,* urban dwellers are more prone to take up running than suburbanites, because running takes a person out into the relaxing open country where clean, invigorating fresh air replaces smog and dust, and where the noise and chaos of city traffic gives way to the sweet tranquil sounds of a gentle breeze blowing through trees and to the singing of gaily colored birds.[5] Running is caused by a wish to escape.

In the midst of the running craze that has overtaken the world, I have myself participated non-competitively in this wonderful sport. Personally, I run for fun. The sheer ecstasy and exuberance of running, the feeling of my limbs and muscles striving to work as one is almost indescribable and certainly beyond my vocabulary of English words. Jogging lets my mind shut itself off from the weary tediousness and stress of life's routines. As my running shoes plod along a chosen path in rhythm with my frantic heart beats and labored breathing, I feel spiritually at peace with the world of nature that surrounds me. During those fleeting moments, despite the tons and tons of homework and lab write ups I have, I always feel good to be alive.

Running is a craze that has emerged in these contemporary times as a result of the tightly strung, cardiovascular diseased rat race society we exist in. Mankind's efforts to improve living through the use of labor-saving machines and devices has caused his health to deteriorate. Invariably, running for fitness and mental relaxation has become a need rather than a want for many people, and running today is certainly one of the most enjoyable and beneficial of fads I've seen.

NOTES

1. George Kirsch, "Running for Health and Beauty," *New Times,* March 1978, p. 18.
2. Bob Glover, *The Runner's World Handbook: A Complete Fitness Guide for Men and Women on the Run* (New York: Viking Press, 1978), p. 362.
3. Jade Batten, *The Complete Jogger* (New York: Jonathan James Associates, 1977), p. 179.
4. "Age and Running," *Runner's World,* January 1978, p. 14.
5. Martin Cohen, *Runner's World,* May 1974, p. 16.

Yong Kwet Loong

►EXERCISE 7.13

Examine Loong's paper in terms of the following questions. Jot down your answers on a sheet of scratch paper.

1. What would be the direct cause of running? What is necessary for running to take place? Is this covered in the paper?
2. Does the paper cover any circumstances resulting in the act of running?
3. Does the paper note any factors concerning the agent initiating or involved in these circumstances?
4. Does the paper mention any aspects motivating such an agent or person?◄

►EXERCISE 7.14

Generate and write a causal analysis of your own. Be sure to consider a variety of causes. Be sure also to take into account any specialized reader expectations. ◄

The Process Sheet on page 242 highlights the concerns of the sequencing patterns just discussed. Use it the next time you have to decide if sequencing of your material would be appropriate.

NOTES

1. Puzzle motif taken from Donald A. Daiker, Andrew Kerek, and Max Morenberg, *The Writer's Options* (New York: Harper & Row, 1979), cover.

SEQUENTIAL PATTERNS

Is there a chronological relationship between the parts of my material? Is there a history or a story involved here? OR Is there a need to provide a context for my material?

> If so, what time sequence best serves my purpose? Shall I use actual order, flashbacks, or some other order?

> If so, what context can my narrative provide? How can it be used to frame my material?

> How can various parts be linked?

Is there a procedural relationship between the parts of my material? Is there a process working here?

> If so, what are the steps in the procedure or process? Must certain steps precede others? What about preliminary steps?

Is there a causal relationship between the parts of my material?

> If so, what is the effect? The causes?

8

SPECIALIZED AND MIXED PATTERNS

Chapter 7 presents various isolating, clustering, and sequencing patterns of arrangement as separate, individual options. Often, however, these options are refined by specialized conventions or mixed in a paper's organization.

SPECIALIZED PATTERNS

Although there are many possible specialized organizational patterns only three will be shown here: the classical argument, the proposal, and the analytical report.

Classical Argument

Orators of ancient Greece argued in a prescribed manner. This manner of arguing comes down to us as a sequence of organizational elements, each having a certain function. These elements include the concession, presentation, refutation, and solution.

Although you can choose various arrangements when arguing an issue, this traditional form of argument is especially appropriate for discussing questions of policy, such as "Should I engage in pre-marital sex?" or "Should the Wilderness Act be ratified?"

The structure of the traditional argument can be shown by the following outline:

Controlling generalization: takes a stand on the issue established by the introduction.

I. *Concession:* allows the opposition its valid point(s) and proves both sides have been researched

    A.   } specific points of concession

    B.

II. *Presentation and refutation:* establishes opposition's weak points and *shows* how they're weak

    A. Presentation of weak points.

        1.   } points of contention

        2.

    B. Refutation of points in question

        1.   } author's analysis proving that points of contention represent weak points

        2.   in the opposition's argument

III. *Solution:* establishes the points supporting the author's controlling generalization

    A.   } specific points of support

    B.

This structure usually includes a conclusion that addresses questions of future action.

All arguments, however, do not follow this pattern, perhaps because two-thirds of the paper seems to be dealing with the opposing point of view. A common variation, then, is to alter the roles of certain sections as follows:

Controlling generalization: takes a stand on the issue established by the introduction.

I. *Concession:* allows the opposition its valid point(s) and proves both sides have been researched

    A.   } specific points of concession

    B.

II. *Refutation:* shows weaknesses in opponent's argument

    A.   } points contended with proofs of weakness

    B.

III. *"Presentation":* establishes strong points supporting the controlling generalization

    A.   } specific proofs of the controlling generalization

    B.

IV. *Solution:* speculates as to the future if the controlling generalization is accepted and/or shows how the controlling generalization can be adapted.

This structure would then conclude with a call for action.

Of course, even with this second argumentative structure, the organizational possibilities have not been exhausted.

There are various ways a writer can check to see that all the support material, however arranged, is contributing to prove the argumentative point. The following guide could be used:

Controlling generalization: _____ *should* (should not) be so.

Concession: Granted, those who say that _____ *should* (should not) be so have a point when they contend. . . .

Refutation: However, when those who say that _____ *should* (should not) be so say . . . , they are mistaken (misguided, deceived) because. . . .

Presentation: Moreover, _____ *should* (should not) be so because . . . .

Solution: If _____ *is* (is not) so, then. . . .

Conclusion: Having demonstrated why _____ *should* (should not) be so and having given you the resultant alternatives, I think finally that. . . .

Now that we have established the overall framework of the traditional argument, let's examine some of its elements in more detail.

The concession

One particular feature of a traditional argument is the *concession*. In the concession, you concede that your opponents may have valid arguments. The purpose is to demonstrate that you have researched both sides of the issue and to show that you are a considerate, fair-minded person. The concession is thus a strategy for developing audience rapport.

For example, the following concession complements the thesis: "Pornography should not be censored because it has social benefits."

> It is true that parents will continue to be upset when they accidently find that *Hustler* tucked under Junior's pillow or that ticket stub from an X-rated movie on Sis's bureau. In such cases, the benefits of pornography might not be readily apparent. Yet. . . .

Concessions are usually preceded by wording that indicates that a concession is being made, so that the reader will not misunderstand the writer's argumentative stance. Transitions such as "it is true that," "granted," and "admittedly" are often used to establish a statement as a concession.

The solution

Another traditional argument feature is the *solution*. It usually presents alternatives or a prognosis: "if . . . then." For instance, if your paper argues

that "Television programming for children should be significantly reformed," then your solution could propose methods of reform, such as the
elimination of male/female stereotypes or the reduction of violence. Specific recommendations, such as that children's shows should be modeled
after "Mr. Roger's Neighborhood" or "Captain Kangaroo," could be made.
The solution could also speculate on what would happen if children's
programming were not reformed or, indeed, if it were.

Argumentative emphasis

One particularly difficult aspect of argumentation that primarily affects the
central (presentation, refutation) portion of the paper is *maintaining the
argumentative significance of the details.* For example, it is not argumentative
to say "this is my data"; it is argumentative to say "this data proves my
point, because. . . ." The purpose of the former is to inform; the purpose
of the latter is to persuade.

In the following excerpts, student Ray Gonzalez struggles with the
problem of maintaining his paper's argumentative emphasis. Ray's thesis
is "Crime statistics should be regarded as inaccurate when they say lower
class juveniles commit more crimes than their middle or upper class
counterparts."

> . . . When criminal activity is brought to the attention of law enforce-
> ment authorities, the courts use diversion programs for the upper class
> juvenile delinquents to keep them from going through the judicial
> process. Parents and enforcement agencies would rather see the juve-
> nile examined by the private sector than by official agencies.
>
> Furthermore, it should be added that not only is the Juvenile
> Justice System at fault for using kid gloves on the middle to upper class
> delinquents, but so also are the parents of the youthful offenders.
>
> The parents try to conceal the delinquent behavior of their child
> and even go so far as to ignore any signs that something is wrong. The
> children are left morally adrift. The parents create an unconscious
> child with an inability to feel remorse.

In this first excerpt, Ray's argumentative emphasis on "why crime
statistics should be regarded as inaccurate" has apparently been lost. In the
second excerpt, he tries to restore the lost emphasis through selective
additions [marked by brackets].

> . . . When criminal activity is brought to the attention of law enforce-
> ment authorities, these authorities use diversion programs for the
> upper class juvenile delinquents to keep them from going through the
> judicial process. Parents and enforcement agencies would rather see
> the juvenile examined by the private sector than by official agencies.
> [This also keeps a criminal incident from being publicized, thus avoid-
> ing embarrassment for the middle to upper class parent. Whether it

be a non-violent crime which the youth has committed or one which causes major damage, both parents and courts seem more than willing to conceal the criminal activity.]

Furthermore, it should be added that not only is the Juvenile Justice System at fault for using kid gloves on the middle to upper class delinquents, but so also are the parents of the youthful offenders.

The parents try to conceal the delinquent behavior of their child and even go so far as to ignore any signs that something is wrong. The children are left morally adrift. The parents create an unconscious child with an inability to feel remorse. [Thus, when a middle to upper class youth does get into trouble, the parents become very surprised, and wonder where their parenting went wrong. If their child does appear in Juvenile court, the judge is also astonished, and willing to divert the offender to counseling and therapy rather than incarceration.]

Ray's revisions bolster his argumentative emphasis. Perhaps additional research would also have helped, although Ray, as a police officer, could have been basing his statements on personal experience. If so, more specifics from those experiences could have better established him as an authority on the juvenile justice system.

In general, it is not wise to base argumentative proof solely on personal experience, especially if that experience has remained "unexamined." We are too often mistaken in our impressions, too often naive in our assumptions, too often uninformed. Nevertheless, personal resources can often contribute a great deal to effective arguments.

The following paper by Sheryl Sweany shows how the traditional argumentative structure can be used to prove a personal point:

The Sex Business

Sex: it's one of those things we didn't talk about in the "olden" days. SEX: it's one of the biggest sellers on today's market. It is also one of the things that the public is up in arms over. People are protesting and complaining about too much emphasis on sex everywhere they look. The markets are flooded with sex paraphernalia, sex manuals, sex magazines, and sex flicks. There are people in organizations from church groups to PTA clubs that are shouting to the government and to the businesses that promote sex for tighter controls and stricter regulations on public sexuality. The government and the businesses are not, however, responsible for the expanding interest in promiscuity. The public is. The fact that so much sexual material is available does not matter. What does matter is that it sells. The public cry for decency is simply the voice of a loud minority. One only needs to look at the success of the "sex business" to see that it has the support of more than enough people to keep it alive. It is time for us to accept that it is the public that is making sex big business, not businesses forcing sexual material on the public.

Granted, if sexual and pornographic material were not available people would not buy it, but why should industries resist the temptation to turn a fast buck when public demand is so high? It is not as if this type of material is the only kind offered. The businesses that take advantage of public interest in sex, such as the movie, book, and music industries, also offer a wide variety of other types of interests. The fact remains that if sex didn't sell it would no longer be a part of these profit-making industries.

The public's obsession with sex has opened a new way for the music industries to pad their bank accounts. They are making hits out of songs with lines like: "Come on baby, do you do more than dance?",[1] "How can she lose with what she uses, 36-24-36?",[2] "They had one thing in common, they were good in bed.",[3] and "I'm on the hunt and everynight I'm hunchin'."[4] The music companies can produce them, but people are who make them hits. Songs concerning nothing but illicit sex are topping the charts. And don't think it is only "degenerate" rock and roll that concerns itself with sex. One of the top country songs of the year was about a woman named Lucille who left "four hungry children and a crop in the field" to get laid. Whether the subject is dealt with subtly or outright, it sells and sells well. Is the industry really to blame for making money on what the public wants?

The public has also made its interest in sex obvious to the book and magazine writers and publishers. *Mandingo,* which was a best seller for several months, was a conglomeration of "well-hung" black men and "wenches" that were constantly "pleasuring" and "pestering." That was best seller material! After that there was a rash of civil war books constructed along the same line. At least they had a general theme, but some of the public is apparently not interested in story. As long as a book contained explicit sexual excerpts it was a money maker. Book stores are full of books dealing with every type of sex from pre-marital, to extra-marital, to incest, to kink. Magazines are not being left out of this gold mine either. *Cosmopolitan* and *Viva* experimented with open frankness about sex and human sexuality. They received an excellent response in improved circulation. *Penthouse, Playgirl,* and *Playboy,* all top sellers, went even further. *Playboy* started it out with subtle nudity. The public response was so great that all subtlety was lost and the other magazines picked up the idea. The public wanted more and they got it, page after page.

The continued high ratings of television shows that incorporate sexual innuendos encourage networks to continue to use it. The TV industry must, of course, be more subtle, but sexual overtones are easily created. Take, for instance, M*A*S*H, a prime-time show, whose main character spends most of his time making passes at any and all females in sight. Even family shows throw in bits of implied sexual activity. Surely no one believes that when the Fonz goes out with the Hooper triplets that all he does is hold hands. Soap operas don't even bother to keep it implied. Everyone is sleeping with everyone else's husband, someone is always pregnant with the wrong man's baby, and the viewers love it! Some of the shows have run for twenty years. If that's not public support, what is?

The money that the public pours into the movie industry to support flicks involving sex is definitely not a deterrent to continued use. Every year dozens of cheaply made porno shows flood the theaters. Drive-ins thrive on movies like "The Cheerleaders," "Cheap Thrill," and "High Ballin'." Even the better-made films incorporate a little "action," just for effect. Burt Reynolds is one of the industry's biggest "sex sellers." He gets laid in every show he's in and almost all of them are box office hits. In his movie, "The End," he uses his impending death to get a "pity fuck" from Sally Fields. The audience loved it. If scenes like that didn't sell, they certainly wouldn't be included in a high-dollar, big-name show like that. The movie industry doesn't have to push sex material because the public is always ready, checkbook in hand.

Behavior modification works on industries too. The positive reinforcement of money is more than enough to keep them using sex as subject material. It is not the government who is responsible for controlling this material, not the industries who are responsible for it being wide-spread. It is the public who has given sex its place in society and only the public can change that, when and if. . . .

NOTES

1. Foreigner, "Hot Blooded."
2. The Commodors, "Brickhouse."
3. Eagles, "Life in the Fast Lane."
4. Lynard Skynard, "On the Hunt."

Sheryl Sweany

►EXERCISE 8.1

For practice in working with classical argumentative structure, draw up an argumentative "skeleton" for one of the following ten topics, using the guide on page 245.

EXAMPLE:

Controlling generalization: Swiss banks should not reform their policy of keeping accounts secret.

Concession: It is true that Swiss accounts are sometimes used to evade taxes.

Refutation: However, those who say that Swiss accounts can be used to "launder" illegally obtained money are naive concerning actual banking policy.

Presentation: Indeed, Swiss banks provide a valuable service with their secret accounts for three reasons.

Solution: If Swiss banks are not allowed to continue their policy of secrecy, misuse such as that which occurred during Nazi times could easily take place.

Conclusion: We should support secret accounts, even in the U.S.

1. Pre-marital sex
2. Trapping wild animals
3. Professional athletes' salaries
4. Food exports as a political weapon
5. Vegetarianism
6. P.E. requirement
7. Front-wheel drive cars
8. Draft registration
9. 55 m.p.h. speed limit
10. X-rated movies

(If you were to choose one of these topics for an actual argument, you would, of course, have to test your skeleton against researched data.)◢

▶ EXERCISE 8.2

Write a 750–1250 word argument stemming either from one of the topics listed in Exercise 8.1 or from a topic you generate. ◢

Proposals

Like arguments, proposals have a persuasive purpose. Proposals present a subject for consideration and attempt to convince the reader of that subject's value. A proposal may suggest that a certain subject or idea is worthy of investigation or that a particular solution should be tried because it represents the best way to address a given problem.

Conventionally, proposals contain the following segments:

I. *Introduction:* states subject and specifies *aims*

II. *Background section:* establishes the *significance* of the proposal from the writer's perspective or shows that a specific problem is in *need* of solution

III. *Text:*
   A. presents *method* of inquiry or procedure
   B. establishes the *scope* by setting the boundaries of the discussion or presenting a task breakdown
   C. offers a hypothesis in the form of an idea statement or *solution* statement
   D. discusses *feasibility* in terms of time/facilities/personnel/equipment/cost, etc.
   E. relates merits and/or *benefits* of the proposal

IV. *Conclusion:* urges action

Let's examine a few of these segments in more detail.

Background needs

The background *needs* section of a proposal is crucial because it represents the warrant for inquiry or change. In academic writing, the needs section commonly reviews the past research on the topic and then singles out an unexplored or underdeveloped area for further investigation. For example, much has been written about Taiwan. A proposal suggesting further investigation of Taiwan, however, could show that little has been written about the ramifications of a new U.S. arms policy towards Taiwan and, therefore, research into these ramifications is needed.

Background needs sections can also use a problem as a warrant. The following needs section written by student Gary McCoy establishes a four-fold need in arguing for the use of a new Data Page system for KGNI, a news-oriented radio station. The four problems presented are lost stories, a decline in ratings, a drop in advertising revenue, and a loss of image.

*Need for Data Page**

Many times the news team has been unable to get hold of our reporters as new stories have broken. Also, we have been unable to contact reporters to relay messages regarding stories, and to contact them about assignments. Within a normal working shift, five members of the news team are out on the streets covering various stories. But our present budget only allows us to rent three electronic pagers. Thus, we send some reporters out to work on stories without being able to get hold of them. This has caused us problems at times. Recently, we have been beaten out of stories of major significance

* McCoy took notes for this paper from "Beep! This Medium Has a Message," *Newsweek*, 98 (July 20, 1981), 58–59.

such as the Cinderella City Mall fire. We eventually got to the scene of the fire a half-hour late, but lost some of our listeners in the process who turned to our competition WGO. The WGO news team was there within five minutes, probably because all their reporters carry beepers wherever they go. With only three pagers available, we were also beaten by WGO when the county prison riot took place. We eventually covered the story, but missed out on our opportunity to report "live" from the scene.

Decline in Ratings

KGNI has taken a slide in the latest ratings book published by Arbitron, Inc. A significantly large number of listeners have tuned our news out. The Arbitron ratings put us a full seven points behind WGO in percentage of news listened to on the radio. Last rating period we were ahead of WGO by two points. Since WGO and KGNI compete almost exclusively on the coverage of live news events, the drop in ratings this period shows our lack of coverage during the two big news events. WGO has increased both the speed and accuracy of its reporting. This has given them a reputation as the station to count on when news events happen.

Loss of Advertising

A decline in our advertising revenue has resulted from our drop in the ratings. While overall station advertising has stayed even, the news department's advertising has dropped during our news blocks in the morning and evening hours. This correlates almost exactly with our drop in the ratings. Sales manager Jerry Jones feels that our declining revenues could be due to WGO's more aggressive news operation. He says the introduction of more pagers, could be part of a new bold and aggressive advertising campaign.

Miscellaneous Considerations

New Pagers should be more efficient than ones currently in use. Many times the Motorola pagers we now use have been inadvertently set off by microwaves and typewriters. Also, the Motorola pagers have a quite loud sound. Many on the KGNI news staff have had bad experiences when a pager has gone off in the middle of meetings. The paging in and of itself is not that disruptive; it is the obnoxious sound that is disturbing. A quieter model would help to create a better image of our station. A last improvement needed is some method of storing the message being sent. Many times it is hard for reporters to get to the phone immediately to call the station back. Some type of memory system would alleviate this situation.

In the next example, student Beth Hanna writes about the need for a C.P.A. firm to expand into energy audits. She brings out both national and company interests by listing her needs as *reasons*.

*Reasons for Incorporating Energy Audits**

Energy Facts

The present energy situation in the United States is receiving attention because of the news media, spiraling energy costs and numerous talks by United States leaders to persuade the country to adopt an energy program. The following facts can stress the importance of some form of energy conservation:

- Oil resources cannot be replenished. Because we are running out of oil, large price increases besides ones we have already experienced can be expected.

- During the oil embargo, the United States was importing 23 percent of its needs. In 1978, it was importing 45 percent of its needs. If present trends continue, the percentage is expected to increase.

- Free world consumption of energy has been doubling every ten to fifteen years. Third world countries are developing rapidly and will increase the usage rate.

- Coal can be an important factor in aiding the energy crisis, but increases the pollution problems. Also, nonreplaceable coal is expected to last from 100 to 400 years, depending on how it is used.

The future availability of our present energy resources is limited. We must develop new resources to replace these. Until new energy sources are developed, conservation of available resources is vital to the American economy.

Certified Public Accountant's Role

CPA firms are being called upon more and more to perform energy audits for their clients. CPA's are naturals for this type of service. The profession is trained to deal with the trade-offs between costs and benefits. Accountants' experience in financial planning and cost controls give them the ability to advise clients on controlling, conserving, and managing energy. CPA's also need to understand the client's business operation to perform financial audits. Therefore, *they* should be able to provide assistance to clients by identifying processes, facilities or production methods which are wasteful. They can also show clients how to reduce energy waste in non-accounting areas, such as lighting, heating and cooling.

Benefits to Hanna, Halma, and Knoot

Besides public utilities, Hanna, Halma, and Knoot will be the first to offer energy audits in the Mason City area. Energy audits will provide a useful service to the public, and Hanna, Halma, and Knoot

* Hanna took notes for this paper from Simich, Stevan, and Strauss, "The Energy Audit," *The Journal of Accounting,* 146 (Nov. 1978), 54–58.

can significantly benefit by implementing energy audits. The cost
savings attained by our clients will increase their net income, along
with new confidence in us. Other firms similar to ours in size and
clientele have expanded their client size within two years after incorporating energy audits. These mutual benefits are important reasons
to adopt energy auditing.

Beth Hanna

Answering the need

After the background or needs section, it is important that the proposal
show how the suggested research will fill the gap, how the suggested device
will address the problem, or how the suggested policy will involve the
reasons established in such need sections.

For example, Gary McCoy's solution statement that follows Exercise
8.3 proposes the Data Page in such a way that the device can be seen to
address previously established KGNI problems. The section also dramatizes
the proposed device by showing it in action at KGNI.

▶EXERCISE 8.3

As you read the following solution statement by Gary McCoy, list
how the presentation of the Data Page addresses point-for-point the problems mentioned earlier. Are there any problems not accounted for by the
solution statement? ◢

Proposed New Pager

After careful research with both our dealer, Mobile Page Inc.
and several others in the Denver area, it is recommended that KGNI
rent the Data Page. This new pager has just hit the American market
from Japan. It is an exciting new concept in beeper units. Besides
being light and compact like most current pager models, the Data
Page has several new features that make it superior:

1) It is much quieter, causing fewer interruptions and dis-
   turbances when it actually beeps;
2) It has a ten-digit lighted display, located on the pager, which
   makes it possible to send an encoded message with the page.
   The display either gives the person a telephone number to
   call, or a message which the receiver can decode:
3) It has a memory function which will store the message in case
   the reporter is busy.

In addition, the new Data Page is not difficult to hook up to the phone. "The message sender uses a push-button phone or accessory. He punches the individual phone number of the beeper unit, then taps out the ten-digit signal, which is relayed to the beeper." In terms of our news operation the system would probably work in a similar way. For example, when some big story breaks, Joe Henry, our news producer, would call a pre-determined number to activate the Data Page worn by Suzy Smith. When Suzy's pager beeps, then Joe would push numbers on the phone to send out the appropriate message to Suzy. Suzy would immediately see the message on her pager and then decode the message. After that Suzy would either call Joe at the station, or obey his message and run to the assignment. The introduction of the Data Page to our newsroom would make it easily adaptable to our style of reporting.

Feasibility

After readers have been convinced of the need for your project, policy, or project, they must be persuaded of its *feasibility*. In the next example, student Loras Goedken argues the feasibility of solar grain drying systems by mentioning ease of implementation and future cost savings.

Feasibility

Implementation

Employing free-standing collectors is one of the most basic applications of supplying supplemental solar heat to a corn dryer. The principle of the system is much like that of a solar collector for a home hot water heater. For the corn dryer, the solar collector can be of almost any height or width desired. The larger the collector, the greater the surface area it will have and the larger the total BTU temperature rise it will create. For each square foot of collector space added, the collector will gain an additional 1000–1200 BTU's per day.

The roofs and walls of agricultural buildings provide large flat surfaces that can readily be adapted for use as solar collectors also. The mechanics of this system (fig. 2) are such that the sun's rays, in striking the building's roof and facing wall, raise the temperature of these surfaces and warm the air beneath them. The heated air is then drawn out of the building's attic through a system of tubes and ducts by the bin fan. Blown into the stored grain, the solar heated air produces a temperature rise in the grain and dries it.

Modification Costs and Savings

While it is true that the cost of modifying a building just for the purpose of providing supplemental solar heat may be economically prohibitive, it is also true that when buildings are constructed to include the modifications for providing solar heat, the incremental material and labor costs are quite justifiable economically. For example, an Illinois farmer, Mr. Dale Sass, included a 4700 sq. ft. collector upon construction of a pole building. Costs for including the collector in the building were $4028, or $0.86/sq. ft. At an annual cost of $421 (includes depreciation), the collector saved 1330 gallons of LP gas valued at $483—a net savings of $62.

Consideration must also be given the fact that once construction is completed, the costs of the supplemental solar heat are fairly fixed. Fossil fuel prices are not fixed, so with the expectation that fuel prices will rise steadily over the life of the building, a larger net savings will be realized each year of operation.

In addition, the supplemental heat provided by such a system can be transported by air for use in a number of other farmstead applications including preheating ventilating air for livestock buildings and heating a farm shop. Grain drying alone does not have to recoup the whole incremental investment.

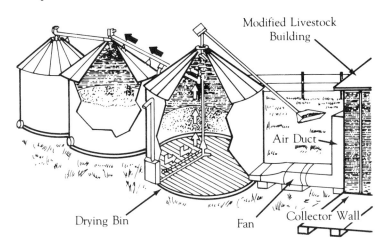

FIGURE 2:   *Grain drying system adapted to use heat from farrowing house solar collector-storage wall*

SOURCE: John Anschutz, Ralph Lipper, C. K. Spillman, and F. V. Robbins, "Drying Grain With Air from a Solar Heater Designed for Animal Shelters," *Solar Grain Drying Conference Proceedings,* U.S. Department of Agriculture, March 1979, p. 52.

Implicit in the solar grain drying example is also the argument that time is an important factor in implementing the proposal. The sooner the proposal is adopted, the sooner buildings can be constructed with solar drying systems installed and the sooner the farmer can reduce his or her outlay for increasingly expensive fossil fuels. This sense of urgency can be carried over into the conclusion that "the time to act is now."

The Goedken example also dramatizes the feasibility of solar grain drying systems by picturing one in action.

Benefits

The *benefits section* of a proposal outlines point-for-point how the proposal addresses the needs established earlier, unless the solution statement has already implicitly done so. In any case, the benefits section dramatizes the advantages of adopting the proposed project, product, or policy.

The following example, written by student Gary Armstrong, dramatizes the benefits of using a computer in a feeder pig operation by posing a question.

Benefits

The cost of the computer will be paid for in a short period of time when the computer is utilized to provide information that was nearly impossible to obtain by hand calculations. With this computer system, Growfast, Inc. can not only keep track of its accounts and stock, but it can also show what daily changes in our ration formula can be made to account for the price fluctuations in various foodstuffs.

For example, it's not at all uncommon for Growfast, Inc. to use a ration that has ten different feedstuffs with ten different protein values and ten different (and fluctuating) prices.

The computer could increase profits by figuring the complicated least-cost ration formulas on a daily basis. Or would you like to provide a 16% protein ration that would meet all the daily nutrient needs of our stock while accounting for such fluctuations in feedstuff prices as occurred between Wednesday and Thursday of last week?

In general, when writing a proposal you should anticipate and answer questions the audience might want answered and be sure to promise only what can be accomplished given any existing constraints, such as time or means.

➤ EXERCISE 8.4

Write a two to three page proposal for one of the following situations:

1. You have been assigned to do a term paper for your _____ class. As a preliminary step, you have been asked to provide a brief proposal of the topic you want to explore.
2. You want to propose the purchase of a _____ for the lounge of your dorm floor, fraternity or sorority house, or apartment complex. As your first step, you have decided to write up a

proposal of the suggestion for your supervisor/counselor/apartment manager to consider.

3. You want to propose a new policy regarding _____ at either your University or your place of employment. To do so, you must submit a written proposal. ◢

Analytical Reports

The analytical process involves breaking down an issue or subject to explore its meaning, nature, or function. (This process appears in the paragraph breakdown of draft work in Chapter 1.) You can analyze an idea, for example, to detail its aspects, explain its significance, or argue its merit. Similarly, you can analyze a product to detail its parts, explain its use, or recommend its adoption. You can even analyze a proposal (see previous section) to examine *what* its elements are, explain *how* it addresses a certain problem, or show *why* it should be adopted or rejected. Thus, this process can initiate reports that inform, explain, or persuade.

Analytical reports are similar in form to proposals with the text portion being less prescribed. These reports also feature "front and end matter" not characteristically found in proposals. The structure of such reports can be summarized as follows:

- title page
- table of contents
- synopsis or abstract

- introduction: the *why* and *how* of the report (purpose, scope, methods)
- text: breakdown of issue or subject
- conclusion: summary and/or recommendation

- appendix
- bibliography

Let's first discuss the main business of the analytical report, the analytical breakdown of the issue or subject, which suggests how to segment the text portion of the report.

Breaking down the issue or subject

This breakdown can occur deductively or inductively. That is, you can know enough about the subject at the outset to be able to predict how it can be broken down, or you can discover the breakdown while examining details about the subject. You can initiate the deductive breakdown of a subject by subject-splitting. For example, assume you have chosen to analyze the Mono Lake, California situation, where the basin is being tapped dry to provide water for the city of Los Angeles, 275 miles to the south. You might come up with the following breakdown through subject-splitting:

Mono Lake situation — *historical background* — *current details* — *environmentalist's position* — *the L.A. "Department's" position*

Notice that such subject-splitting here reveals some previous knowledge of the subject.

On the other hand, the breakdown of an issue or subject can also suggest itself during the research process. A breakdown similar to that achieved through subject-splitting could have emerged from the notes in Figure 8.1 on page 260.

Each breakdown in Figure 8.1 suggests the following organization for the text portion of the report: (1) a section defining the situation itself, (2) a section giving a historical background on the situation, (3) a section presenting the environmentalists' position, and (4) a section presenting the Department's position.

Given this textual breakdown, the introduction might establish that your purpose will show, for example, how one side represents the stronger position or will explain how each side uses conservationist-type arguments to support its particular point of view. Similarly, the report's conclusion could make a recommendation regarding the use of the Mono Lake basin or could present a summary of current thinking on the subject, depending on your chosen purpose.

Front and end matter

Such a report would be framed by front and end matter. A special feature often included in the front matter is the *synopsis* or *abstract*. An abstract is a brief statement of the main points of the report. It is sometimes distinguished from a summary in that the abstract notes the main idea and highlights the supporting evidence, whereas a summary often limits itself to the idea level. An abstract for the Mono Lake report might read as follows:

> Analyzing the situation involving Mono Lake, this report details current points of view regarding whether Los Angeles should continue to divert fresh water from the basin area. Highlighting the conservationist view is the feeling that the lake should be saved for the California gulls and migratory birds that depend on it for sustenance. Emphasized in the city's position are the facts that L.A. depends on

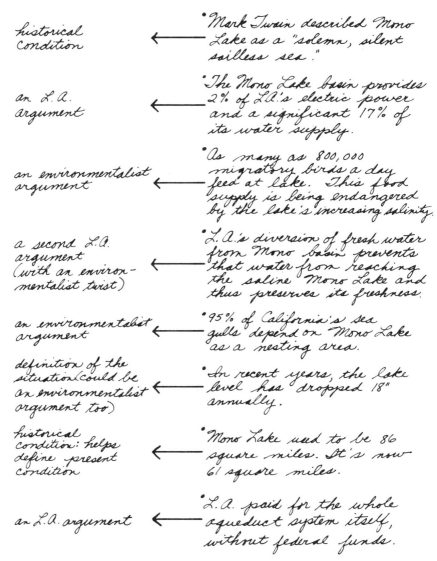

historical
condition
←———— •Mark Twain described Mono
Lake as a "solemn, silent
soilless sea."

an L.A.
argument
←———— •The Mono Lake basin provides
2% of LA's electric power
and a significant 17% of
its water supply.

an environmentalist
argument
←———— •As many as 800,000
migratory birds a day
feed at lake. This food
supply is being endangered
by the lake's increasing salinity.

a second L.A.
argument
(with an environ-
mentalist twist)
←———— •L.A.'s diversion of fresh water
from Mono basin prevents
that water from reaching
the saline Mono Lake and
thus preserves its freshness.

an environmentalist
argument
←———— •95% of California's sea
gulls depend on Mono Lake
as a nesting area.

definition of the
situation (could be
an environmentalist
argument too)
←———— •In recent years, the lake
level has dropped 18"
annually.

historical
condition: helps
define present
condition
←———— •Mono Lake used to be 86
square miles. It's now
61 square miles.

an L.A. argument
←———— •L.A. paid for the whole
aqueduct system itself,
without federal funds.

FIGURE 8.1   *Subject-splitting through Research*

the Mono basin for a full 17% of its water supply and that, by
diverting fresh water from the basin area, the city is actually pre-
serving the water from Mono Lake's natural salinity. The conclusion
suggests that how the courts decide the issue will have a far-ranging
effect on our view of water as a natural resource and "public asset."

The following report analyzes whether an industrial or a mechanical
engineer would better suit the needs of a certain business firm. The report,
written by student Fred Langdon, can be abstracted as follows:

This report examines whether an industrial or a mechanical engineer would better suit the needs of Magnepan, Inc. The report operates by correlating the educational characteristics of each curriculum with the responsibilities that the position entails. The report concludes that an industrial engineer would be more qualified to assume the responsibilities of the position. Some of the reasons were that an I.E. would be more qualified to manage human resources and that I.E. courses are oriented towards the needs of the position in general. An M.E., however, would have a better background to handle maintenance problems that arise in the production and testing equipment. The report concludes with the suggestion that perhaps both could be hired, given the fact that the position was vacated by a man earning $42,000 and that starting salaries for either engineer would amount to approximately $25,000 apiece.

This abstract would probably appear in a letter of transmittal prefacing the following report.

Staffing the Position of
Assistant Production Engineer

On November 15th of this year the board of directors of Magnepan Loudspeaker Inc. agreed to fill the newly opened position of assistant production engineer with an engineer from State University. It was tentatively agreed-upon to hire an engineer from either the mechanical or industrial engineering discipline. This report evaluates the qualities and characteristics of the mechanical and industrial, undergraduate curriculums at State University and then makes its recommendation.

Criteria

The criteria that will be used in evaluating each undergraduate program will be the responsibilities of the assistant production engineer at Magnepan Inc. which include: the monitoring and control of production levels, the maintenance of testing and production equipment, and the supervision of product shipping and handling.

A correlation between the responsibilities of the job and the aspects of each curriculum will be examined.

General Overview of Curriculums

Mechanical Engineering

The mechanical engineering program at State requires that freshmen engineers take a basic core of technical courses in mathematics, physics, freshman engineering, and English. These basic courses are similar to the seminars that are required of our mechanical technicians here at Magnepan. This core of courses is characteristic of all freshmen engineering programs at State; however, the mechanical engineering program requires more of a technical knowledge of engineering principles such as thermodynamics, fluid flow, mechanics of materials, heat transfer, electrical phenomena and dynamics.

Through the choice of various technical electives, M.E. students are allowed to choose an emphasis in specific fields of engineering such as vehicle propulsion, thermal environmental engineering, energy conversion and utilization, machines and systems, and materials and manufacturing. Because of the nature of our open position we would be looking for an M.E. specializing in one of these last two areas. M.E.s with this background in industry have activities that involve "production, operation, sales, and technical management".[1]

Industrial Engineering

As described in the section under mechanical engineering, the industrial engineering program at State includes the same basic core of technical classes as other engineering programs; however, the I.E. program is more oriented to the actual performance and efficiency of the overall industry itself. The I.E. program prepares a student in the areas of statistical analysis and financial evaluation for industrial activities such as assembling processes, inventory control, production machinery design, and production and plant quality control.

The I.E. program is basically a rigid one in that it does not allow broad elective areas for special topics like that of the mechanical engineering program. The I.E. is trained in areas of technical engineering, business and management functions, economics, and labor resources. I.E.s typically acquire jobs in areas of line management, cost and economic analysis, safety engineering, quality control and reliability, inventory and production control, work measurement, information systems design, and personnel supervision.

Responsibilities of Assistant Production Engineer

A correlation can be made between the responsibilities of the assistant production engineer and the mechanical and industrial engineering programs. The correlation can be visualized by reference to Tables 1 and 2 (see Appendix at end of paper) and the organization chart in Figure A. Tables 1 and 2 show courses that would be relevant to the individual responsibilities of the assistant production engineer. The identification number of the course is in parentheses and is followed by an "R" or an "E" indicating whether the course is required or can be taken as an elective. The flow chart (Figure A) will be referred to in the text that follows.

Production Level Monitoring and Control

The assistant production engineer is expected to keep accurate records of production levels during all phases of assembly of the Magneplanar speakers. Control over production must be maintained

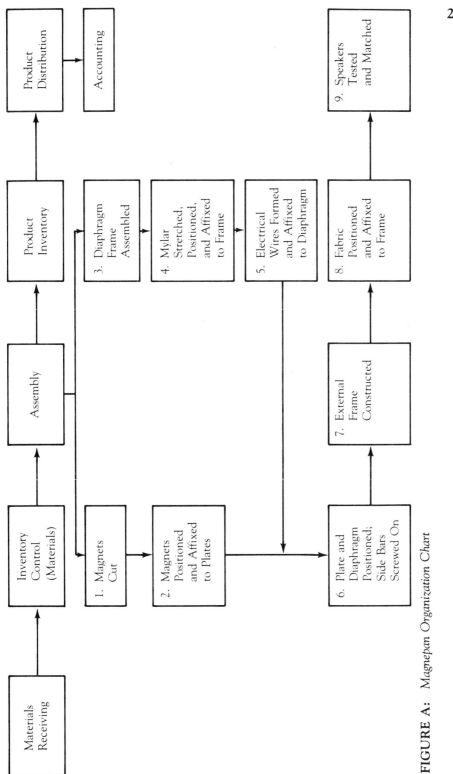

FIGURE A: *Magnepan Organization Chart*

by formulating and presenting solutions to problems that arise in the overall production process, in specific pieces of production machinery, and in the labor force.

In order to maintain understandable records the engineer must understand the technical process involved in assembling the speakers. By referring to the assembling portion of Figure A it can be seen that the assembly process consists of nine basic phases of construction. All of these phases require two operators of the machinery and one supervisor to oversee each stage. Thus, the first requirement of the engineer is that he be able to communicate with all of the supervisors. The engineer must maintain this communication in a two-way fashion with each supervisor so that production control can be maintained at each stage of development. The engineer must then interpret information that he receives from the supervisors and understand how *this* will affect the phases of operation.

Representative Example. On any one day, speaker assembly may be moving rather rapidly at stations 1 and 2 and rather slowly at stations 3, 4, and 5. Thus, we would be building up a surplus of metal plates with respect to speaker diaphragms. This problem is representative of a wide variety of situations that arise every day in the plant. The engineer must be able to realize that there is a problem and then react. For instance, he might take one laborer off of station 1 and put him in station 3 to speed up production of speaker diaphragms.

Backgrounds. An M.E. would be useful in these situations if our facilities were to be expanded for handling a large increase in production; however, Magnepan sees no high production demand in the near future.

M.E. courses that would apply to production level monitoring and control would be:

1. Industrial Automatic Controls (M.E. 411)—principles of automatic control; application of automatic control systems;
2. Mechanical Systems Design (M.E. 415)—methodology of manufacture and design of mechanical systems.

These courses were highlighted over the rest in this category because they are more representative of the responsibilities involved with production level monitoring and control. In general, courses in the M.E. curriculum deal with the design and automation of the machinery used in production. However all of the production machinery at Magnepan has already been designed and is in use; therefore, most of our production control will come from the management of our labor resources.

An I.E. background would be more appropriate for handling production level monitoring situations than that of an M.E. Important courses that would aid the I.E. in handling this responsibility would be:

1. Industrial Quality Control and Inspection (I.E. 361)—production data and statistical treatment of the data;

2. Methods Engineering and Work Measurement (I.E. 373)—principles of work economy and simplicity; methods for obtaining production data; and methods for treating variable situations;

3. Human Resource Management (I.E. 424)—employer and employee problems and solutions; organization and management of human resources; selection and placement of personnel.

These courses almost exactly fit the responsibility in this area.

Maintenance of Testing and Production Equipment

The responsibility of providing maintenance of testing and production equipment requires a fundamental knowledge of the mechanics, physical depreciation, and operation of the machines. Stations 2, 3, 4, 5, and 9 are critical stages in the production of the loudspeakers in the fact that delicate machinery requiring constant maintenance is in use.

Representative Example. Some situations that the assistant production engineer would be involved in would be measuring the factory air temperature and adjusting the glue temperature accordingly in applying the magnets to the steel plates. The tension of the mylar plastic must be adjusted in station 3 to account for thermal expansion due to the temperature difference between the mylar plastic and the glue used to affix the magnets. The same consideration in adjustments must be made in affixing the electrical wires to the mylar. All the adjustments just described would ultimately affect the testing and matching of speaker sets at station 9. The engineer must set the sound control instruments to account for differences in tension of the mylar plastic, changes in the magnetic field due to thermal gradients, and resistance in the electrical wires due to magnetic flux change.

Backgrounds. In understanding the maintenance of machinery, an engineer would need a background in areas dealing with magnetic flux theory, electrical engineering, heat transfer and thermodynamics, and machinery systems.

The only exposure the M.E. and the I.E. would have to magnetic flux theory would be in their study of Classical Physics (Phys. 223), so their background knowledge would be equal in this area. However, the M.E. would have more of a background in the other areas mentioned. Required courses for an M.E. as shown by Table 2 include:

1. Engineering Measurement and Instrumentation (M.E. 360) —design, selection, and operation of measuring systems; measurement processes and analysis of data;

2. Introduction to Electrical Machinery (E.E. 447)—magnetic circuits; operation, design, and control of d-c induction; synchronous and single phase machines; three phase circuit analysis;

3. Mechanisms (M.E. 310)—theory of machines; kinematic and dynamic analysis of mechanisms.

The most important of these courses would be Engineering Measurement and Instrumentation since this course would correlate perfectly with our needs in the area of maintenance of machinery. Also, it should be noted that the prerequisite classes to this particular course will also contribute to the new engineer's fundamental knowledge of machinery.

Reference to Table 1 will show that the I.E. doesn't receive a great amount of specific educational background in maintenance of machinery; the I.E.'s training in machinery would come from three course elective areas: engineering mechanics, electrical engineering, and engineering science. Each I.E.'s individual transcript would have to be evaluated in these areas to determine if the electives would be adequate for an understanding of maintenance of production machinery. Industrial Engineering Design (I.E. 441), which is required of all I.E.s, concentrates on equipment specification, plant engineering, and maintenance in a general sense. The lack of training in this area could contribute to inefficiency during the first six months while these skills are being learned; however, most of our personnel in this area need to be trained in-house due to the intricate equipment that we do use.

Product Handling and Shipping

Reference to Figure A will show that responsibilities in product handling and shipping involve keeping and updating the product inventory, distribution of speakers, and accounting of sales. All of these areas require a broad knowledge of inventory control systems, product economics, and accounting.

The engineer would be familiarized with our inventory storage and control system. He would also be working with general ledgers to record accounting data concerning the sales of our speakers to various distributors.

Backgrounds. About all that would apply out of the M.E. curriculum would be science and humanities electives in these areas; however, business and management electives would be more appropriate for handling these responsibilities.

The I.E. receives a background in areas such as industrial accounting (see Table 1), industrial engineering design, and material and project control. All of this gives the I.E. an advantage over the M.E. in product handling and shipping responsibilities.

General Overview and Recommendations

The most appropriate choice for the filling of our open position for the assistant production engineer would be an industrial engineer. This decision was reached by correlating the responsibilities of the assistant production engineer with the mechanical and industrial engineering programs at State University.

It appears that the industrial engineer should be able to assume specific responsibilities such as production level monitoring and control, product handling and shipping, and, with the appropriate individual background, maintenance of production and testing equipment.

In this last area it was found that the mechanical engineer would be more adept at handling technical problems with machinery; however, the I.E. does receive a large amount of technical training and would be highly qualified for our in-house training program in maintenance. The I.E. is also more suitable in dealing with our present needs which includes the management of our human resources.

One possible alternative that might be considered is the employment of both a mechanical and an industrial engineer. This would assure smoothness in filling our open position. Technical as well as business responsibilities would be covered. The maximum total salary of an industrial and a mechanical engineer would be $52,000 as compared with the salary of our leaving assistant production engineer of $42,000. (Salaries: Industrial—$25,000; Mechanical—$27,000).[2]

However, within the scope of this report, my findings show that an industrial engineer would be the best selection for our open position.

APPENDIX
TABLE 1

Responsibilities	Applicable Courses
Production Level Monitoring and Control	Industrial Accounting (Acct. 381) R
	Industrial Computer Technology (I.E. 209) R
	Work System Design (I.E. 274) R
	Industrial Operations Research (I.E. 312) R
	Methods Engineering and Work Measurement (I.E. 373) R
	Industrial Quality Control and Inspection (I.E. 361) R
	Industrial Methodology (I.E. 374) R
	Human Resource Management (I.E. 424) R
	Industrial Engineering Design (I.E. 441) R
	Material and Project Control (I.E. 341) R
	Engineering Economy (I.E. 404) R
Maintenance of Testing and Production Equipment	Engineering Mechanics Elective—6 Credits—R
	Electrical Engineering Elective—4 Credits—R

TABLE 1 (*Continued*)

	Engineering Science Elective—6 Credits—R
Product Handling and Shipping	Industrial Accounting (Acct. 381) R
	Industrial Engineering Design (I.E. 441) R
	Material and Project Control (I.E. 341) R

TABLE 2

Responsibilities	Applicable Courses
Production Level Monitoring and Control	Mechanical Systems (M.E. 311) R
	Industrial Automatic Controls (M.E. 411) E
	Manufacturing Processes (M.E. 322) R
	Mechanical Systems Design (M.E. 415) E
	Material and Manufacturing Considerations in Design (M.E. 520) E
Maintenance of Testing and Production Equipment	Engineering Measurements and Instrumentation (M.E. 360) R
	Introduction to Electric Machinery (E.E. 447) R
	Mechanisms (M.E. 310) R
Product Handling and Shipping	Science and Humanities Electives 11 Credits R

Reading Bibliography

1. State University, University General Catalog, 1981–1983.
2. State University Engineering Placement Office, Herb Harmison.

Fred Langdon

➤ EXERCISE 8.5

Write up how you think Fred arrived at the segmentation in his Magnepan report. In other words, what did his preliminary work dealing with organization look like? ◢

➤ EXERCISE 8.6

Write a five to seven page analytical report on a subject of your own choosing. If you have been assigned a "term paper" for a certain class, for example, you might be able to fulfill that requirement by writing an analytical report. ◢

MIXED OPTIONS

Sometimes the various isolating, clustering, and sequencing patterns presented in Chapter 7 become mixed in a paper's organization. Even though these patterns become mixed, one pattern or mode usually manages to dominate the paper's structure, with the additional patterns or modes playing supporting roles. The following monologue suggests how such mixing can come about, even within such a prescribed form as traditional argument.

How can I arrange my argument to prove that subliminal advertising should be banned from print media?

How can I, for instance, arrange my introduction? I can *narrate* how subliminal advertising is influencing the potential buyer or I can *describe* a sample ad that contains such advertising or I can, and should, *define* what subliminal advertising is.

How can I arrange my concession? I could admit that progress has been made in other media forms by *narrating* the case of drive-in theaters.

How can I arrange my refutation? I can *classify* the various objections to regulation and then *enumerate* reasons against these objections.

How can I add to the presentational aspect of my argument? I could *exemplify* what can happen if such advertising is used and show it as a *cause* of certain negative *effects*.

How can I arrange my solution? I could suggest a step-by-step *process* that the reader could use to effect a ban on such advertising.

How could I arrange my conclusion? I could *compare* the significance of the ban with the importance of printing ingredient labels on products. Even though there are *differences* here, the public has a right to know what it's getting.

The papers in the following section seem to be the end products of such thinking. Each paper uses a variety of arrangement options to present the chosen subject to the reader and to express the writer's ideas and purpose.

The first paper is a description of a waterpipe. In the paper, student Clark Candee uses description, definition, division (partition), and process analysis to show the reader the item.

Description of a Waterpipe

Description through
definition statement
of class and feature

A waterpipe (or bhang) is a device used for smoking tobacco which filters smoke by passing it through water. A drawing of a simple waterpipe is presented in Figure 1.

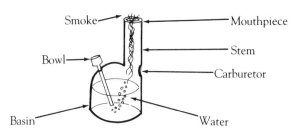

FIGURE 1: *A simple waterpipe*

Although many shapes and sizes are available, a typical waterpipe is about the same size and shape as a wide-based flower vase. Waterpipes may be made of either plastic, glass, or porcelain and are available in many colors.

Description through
division (partition)

The parts of a waterpipe are the mouthpiece, the stem, the carburetor, the bowl, and the basin.

Description and Function of Parts

Description through
detailing of parts

1. *Bowl:* The bowl is made of metal and is approximately the size and shape of a thimble. The bowl has a small hole in the bottom to allow the smoke to pass through to the basin. The function of the bowl is to provide a container for the tobacco. The bowl slides in and out of an indentation located on the basin.

2. *Basin:* The basin and the remaining parts of the waterpipe may be plastic, glass, or porcelain. The basin is a hollow enclosure about the size of a man's fist. The function of the basin is to provide a steady support for the waterpipe and to hold the water. The basin is filled with water to about half its capacity. (The water is the filtering element of the pipe. Water reduces the harshness of the tobacco by trapping tar and nicotine and by reducing the temperature of the smoke.)

Description through
detailing of parts

3. *Stem:* The stem consists of a hollow cylinder approximately one inch in diameter. The stem serves as a connecting link between the basin and the mouthpiece.

4. *Carburetor or "Carb":* The carburetor is simply a small hole about one-quarter inch in diameter located on the back of the stem. The carb controls the release of the smoke to the smoker's mouth. This function will be more obvious in the operating instructions which follow.

5. *Mouthpiece:* The mouthpiece is a round opening about one inch in diameter located at the top of the stem. The mouth is placed over the hole when the user is ready to smoke.

Operating Instructions

Operating materials: waterpipe (with basin half-filled with water), matches or lighter, tobacco, ashtray.

Operating procedure:

1. Place about a thimbleful of tobacco in the bowl and press it in gently with your finger.
2. Light a match (or lighter), hold the match in your left hand, and grasp the stem of the waterpipe with your right, covering the carburetor opening with your right thumb.

Description through process analysis

3. Place your mouth gently over the mouthpiece and touch the match to the tobacco in the bowl. Set the match in the ashtray once the tobacco is lit.
4. Apply a slow sucking action with your mouth. This action draws the smoke from the bowl, through the water, and into the stem.
5. Continue inhaling and remove your right thumb from the carburetor opening. This act will draw the smoke from the stem into your mouth.
6. Remove your mouth from the mouthpiece and exhale when desired.

Summary

The waterpipe has been described following the path of the smoke. The parts and their function have been described, as has been the operating procedure. Further information concerning waterpipes is available in bookstores and tobacco shops.

Clark Candee

▶EXERCISE 8.7

Given the nature of the item, why is it significant that the writer's purpose is to describe rather than, say, to persuade? Explain. ◀

The next selection by student Mary Boyd *defines* "success" by discussing its function. Boyd first argues against its commonly perceived function as the instrument or cause of character change. In so doing, Mary focuses on three categories of non-change in the successful director and actor, Woody Allen: loves, lifestyle, and fears. She thus uses *classification* as an overall framework. Within this framework, she uses *comparison/ contrast* to illustrate her initial point. She concludes by defining success as the *cause* of quite another *effect*. Can you spot these different arrangements?

▼ EXERCISE 8.8

While reading Boyd's analysis, keep in mind the following questions:

1. As a writer, Boyd is addressing a certain audience. Do you feel that you are a part of this audience? Have you, for example, seen any of the films she mentions?
2. What would you do to increase the effectiveness of this paper for an audience that may not have seen the films?
3. If you chose Woody Allen as a subject for a paper, how would you approach him as a "topic"?
4. How would you write a definition of "success" today?◢

The Basic Allen

Mid-year 1978, four Oscars passed from the stage of the Dorothy Chandler Pavilion into the hands of the creators, writers, and actors of *Annie Hall*. The Oscars merely confirmed what box offices had known for some time. The mastermind behind this touchingly warm and funny movie, Woody Allen, was a success.

Success is usually known as the "bitch goddess," because it commonly brings, along with fame and wealth, inevitable changes in personality and outlook. But success has not changed the basic Allen. Allen's loves, lifestyle, and fears have changed little since the coveted awards came into his possession. Success has not changed the interior Allen, although the strikingly different nature of his subsequent films, including *Interiors* and *Manhattan*, might indicate otherwise.

A comparison of two interviews on Allen printed nearly a year apart support my position. Jack Kroll's personable story from *Newsweek*, 24 April 1978, appeared prior to the release of Allen's depressing, serious drama *Interiors*. Richard Schickel and Frank Rich of *Time*, 30 April 1979, show Allen's viewpoints about a year later, during the premier of yet another movie, *Manhattan*.

Kroll's *Newsweek* interview provides a wide perspective on Allen and inevitably touches on the subject of Allen's lovers and friends, namely Diane Keaton of *Annie Hall* fame. Kroll declares Keaton to be "the most important of Woody's women." Possibly this is because Allen depends heavily on the freckled, chestnut-haired actress for a critique of his movies: "She's been a consistently clear mind and clear voice on every picture I've made." Allen, a director with a keen eye, is amazed at Keaton's sixth sense for beauty. "She has an utterly spectacular visual sense. I see many things today through her eyes, textures and forms I would never have seen without her." Allen is charmed by Keaton.

In this 1978 interview, Kroll also plays heavily on Allen's no-pleasure policy. "I'm anhedonic,"Allen insists. Allen's friend and producer Charles Joffe relates this story: "I felt badly that after the Academy Awards he could only say he was surprised. 'No joy?' I asked. 'I don't have time for that,' he said. I thought, what a shame he won't allow himself that joy." Even his closest confidant Keaton questions from where his fear of pleasure stems. Dozens of Allen's friends appreciate his deep generosity, but are puzzled by his self-denial of joy. Allen's second wife Louise Lasser summarizes this strange aspect of her ex-husband's personality by stating, "Life is difficult for Woody. He's one of the unfortunate tormented people."

In Kroll's interview, Allen elaborates on yet another fear that has shadowed him through his life. A sense of mortality lurks behind every door. Allen states, "I'm no fun to be with at parties because I'm very aware of this all the time." More deeply, Allen openly holds feelings of anger and rage that the human mind is so helpless where the issue of death is concerned.

More than a year later, the *Time* interview reveals little change in Allen. Allen still admires Keaton. Frank Rich broaches the subject of the educated and their ironies, and Allen states, ". . . someone like Diane Keaton, who had not a trace of intellectualism when I first met her, can always cut right to the heart of the matter." Allen still values Keaton's ability to perceive and interpret, whether it be people or movies. Allen still deeply appreciates Keaton's talent for discerning beauty, claiming she has "the eye of a genius." It appears that a year of extreme publicity for the two successful talents has only served to bring them closer still.

The no-pleasure policy is still in force, although there might be a slight difference in degree here. Allen sports the same plaid shirts and jeans in both *Annie Hall* and *Manhattan,* but he allows himself to pick up dinner checks and to have a cook and chauffeur now. Allen continues to insist he is anhedonic, however, even though his mission for self-denial might be abating slightly.

As in 1978, Allen continues to emphasize that "death is the big obsession behind all the things I've done." Allen maintains that "we have to go at it the hard way, and come to terms with the fact that the universe seems to contain only the grimmest possibilities." Yet, by accepting his fear, Allen may have mellowed, mellowed but not changed.

If success hasn't changed the basic Woody, it has given him the freedom to take risks. After *Annie Hall,* Allen took an enormous risk by producing such an intense and serious movie as *Interiors.* "Maybe a really logical person would feel that to do this just at the moment when I've achieved a certain recognition for doing comedy is suicidal, but I felt if I didn't do it, I'd never find out anything about myself." *Manhattan* co-star Michael Murphy made a similar observation, "Woody could have made a safer picture, like *Annie Hall.* This film [*Manhattan*] is a lot tougher, harder-edged. And it was a bold step for Woody not to be a hero."

Maybe Woody is inherently a risk-taker. Maybe he didn't need success to give him the freedom to take risks. But to me, success is that ingredient that gives me the freedom, or courage to take risks. If I had not had my first-grade teacher post my three-sentence narrative about "Swinging in the Park," as an example of good writing, I doubt if I would be in an advanced college composition course today. Success reinforces me; it does not change me, at least not yet.

Mary Boyd

The next paper, by student Joe Jordan, shows subtle arrangement variations within a causal sequence. Jordan uses narrative and classification to discuss cause and effect. Within his framework, causes become categories, and the effect is the "problem."

Pressurized

Narrative establishing situation (context)

Floating above the sweat-drenched heads of ten thousand screaming college students, a haze of marijuana smoke is pierced by sharp, glaring lights which beam down on one, lone performer. Not only does this rock star sing for his audience, but he also has control over them. The acid rocker yells; the crowd yells. The acid rocker claps his hands; the crowd claps its hands. When the star finishes and disappears behind the stage, the crowd pulls, as if magnetized, towards his back. In minutes the stage is overrun. Security guards are overtaken. A fire breaks out. Fights begin. Lost souls fall to the floor, unable to get up. The crowd is uncontrollable, animal.

Statement showing that situation is a problem; statement that problem is *effect; classification* of causes for the effect

A problem exists here. Students getting drunk, stoned, and assaultive is not right. Such action stems from two causes, both types of pressure: peer pressure and academic pressure.

Peer pressure is very persuasive. For example, the idea of being left out or the fear of missing something

Development of first
cause/category

worthwhile is crushing. If an individual decides to go out with the gang, he or she must then decide whether to drink "with the boys" or to sit next to them and drink a Pepsi. Next, this individual must decide about going to the concert or not. If the individual decides to go, he or she must decide whether or not to pass the community joint from his mouth to the next pair of lips. The individual is not obligated to do anything, but the possibility of not being accepted into the groups lingers insidiously. Consequently, he or she will drink, will attend the concert, and will pass around that joint.

Development of second
cause/category

Academic pressure exerts similar pressure. Attending fifteen lectures, writing two papers, having two chemistry labs, and taking two tests at the Coliseum in one week usually doesn't leave the individual too much time to relax. School is an institution of deadlines. As a result, a student has only a short period to take off the ceiling on his academic world and relieve the pressure. At this time, the person may let loose and live minute-by-minute. Without any pre-planning, this person will act outside his or her own boundaries. Later the student will go back to the books, but will take along the question, "Should I have acted the way I did?"

Summary of cause and
effect relative to
opening

The effects of pressure will vary from person to person. Although mass hysteria can involve many people at one time, everyone in the crowd cannot be blamed. Unfortunately, it only takes a few to fall victim to pressure to instigate the type of chaos seen at last night's concert. The same pressure, however, causes the crowd to have a short fuse in the first place.

Joe Jordan

▶EXERCISE 8.9

Jordan's paper almost follows a problem-cause-effect-solution sequence, commonly found in writing arrangements, but stops short of offering a solution. For practice, complete the sequence by writing a solution section for Jordan's paper. Reconsider both the problem and its stated causes before writing. ◢

▸EXERCISE 8.10

Write a three-to-five page paper with the "specialized reader-expectation" that you use a mixed pattern of arrangement. In mixing two or more options of arrangement together, you will probably find that one pattern or mode dominates.◂

NOTES

1. For convenience, details were taken from one source: Gordon Young, "The Troubled Waters of Mono Lake," *National Geographic*, Vol. 160, No. 4 (October 1981), pp. 504–25. The principles involved in the text's example, however, apply to situations in which the writer merely starts with the subject itself and not with an already written article.

PART IV

RECONCEIVING IDEAS

9 Discovery Through Revision

9

DISCOVERY THROUGH REVISION

We devote this separate chapter to revision, even though revision can and does occur throughout the writing process. Whether "in-draft" or "post-draft," revision is often not a systematic process. Reconceiving papers "proceeds by leaps and bounds, fits and starts, by insight."[1] Revision as a thinking process is hard to recapture on the printed page, yet the effects of revision can be examined in some detail.

IN-DRAFT REVISION

In extreme cases, in-draft revision can appear as the "revise as you go method." In the following example in Figure 9.1, the writer revises the lead sentence no less than nine times.

~~Revision is not a punishment, but an opportunity.~~

Have you ever known a person with a bad reputation? Was that rep always *undeserved* deserved? Revision has such a rep.

~~Revision is often an invisible process.~~ Because readers seldom see the drafts which eventually produce the final copy of a short story or essay or report, revision *seems* ~~can be termed~~ an invisible process part of the writing process. Because readers don't see revision, they sometimes assume it doesn't exist.

Up to this point, this text has pointed out that writing is recursive; that is, a writer can double back on what he or she has written and revise. *for example* A starting controlling generalization may not be the final controlling generalization.

FIGURE 9.1 *In-draft Revision*

Writing, reading, and revision are the "three R's" of ~~composition~~ *composing*

"How can I revise what I've just written?" is a question writers must always ~~ask~~. is a key question in composing.

Learning to ask question is a way of learning to compose. *Key* ~~Questions~~, *im* ~~important~~ ~~to~~ the composing process have been *previously* included ~~on~~ ~~the previously included~~ Process Sheets. This chapter deals with a question which underpins the entire composing process: "How can I revise what I've just written?"

Learning to ask questions is a way of learning to compose. ~~So far,~~ the Process Sheets in this text have included (key) questions ~~in the~~ *to various* composing process. *stages* This chapter deals with~~a~~ question which underpins the entire composing process: "How *improve?* can I ~~revise~~ what I've just written?"

The Process Sheets in this text have shown questions key to various composing process stages. This chapter approaches a question underpinning the entire process: "How can I improve what I've just written?" In other words, "How can I revise?"

FIGURE 9.1 *In-draft Revision (Continued)*

This method should appeal to those writers who enjoy treading water.

For the rest of us, in-draft revisions commonly are of two types: those revisions that affect what you are planning to say and those that define what you're going to do next in terms of composing "steps" or procedure.[2]

Revising Your Content

In-draft content revisions can be represented by the progressive changes your controlling generalization undergoes during the composing process. In Chapter 1, for example, the controlling generalization changes during an outline check. In the writer's outline, the generalization changes from "There are basically two types of guys that live on my dorm floor: ones that are easy to get along with and ones that aren't" to "There are basically two types of guys that live on my dorm floor: the pussy cat and the Don Juan." This generalization, in turn, experiences two post-draft revisions as well.

Early on, idea-synthesizing can generate similar changes in your controlling generalization. Consider the example in Chapter 3 in which the generalization changed from "Growing your own fruits and vegetables can save you lots of money" to "The rewards of gardening are not necessarily measured in dollars and cents." This change was triggered by a combination of idea-synthesizing and preliminary research.

Indeed, as suggested in Chapter 4, your search for support for a tentative controlling generalization can uncover information that falsifies that generalization and forces a change. The writer might begin with the main idea, "Male chauvinism is promoted by the language we use everyday" and, because of information uncovered, alter the generalization to read, "Attempts to revise the sexual bias out of language will do little to purge sexual bias from society."

Similarly, changing from an objective to a subjective stylistic presentation might also change the form of your controlling generalization. In short, whether you are generating topic ideas, searching for support, or planning your arrangement, your controlling generalization is subject to change. In fact, more than the controlling generalization undergoes revision. Your choice of subject, your clarification of your subject, your selection of detail, your mode of arrangement, your choice of style, all are revisable.

Revising Your Procedure

Another type of revision that occurs during the writing process is changing what you're doing to produce your draft. Simply put, you may switch from generating information to selecting an arrangement. The monologue in Chapter 1 suggests the fluid way a reader can shuttle back and forth among the "steps" in the composing process. (See pages 8–10.)

Such revision in procedure can also occur within composing steps. For example, you might decide to poll townspeople instead of college students in your survey involving "Attitudes towards Reagonomics." This switch might have been triggered by your desire to present the views of a less homogeneous population, or by a change in your chosen audience. In either case, it represents a revision in what you're doing to gather information on your topic.

▸ EXERCISE 9.1

Suggest a specific example for each of the following.
EXAMPLE: *an in-draft revision of an arrangement.* I might switch from a classical argument structure to a narrative structure because my reasons for supporting a "nuclear freeze" can be best shown by telling a fictional story about what the earth would be like after a nuclear holocaust and not by repeating and reviewing arguments presented by protestors. The fictional account would be factually based, but would appeal to emotions, not logic.

1. an in-draft revision of choice of subject
2. an in-draft revision of selection of detail
3. an in-draft revision of research procedure
4. an in-draft revision of what you're doing to increase stylistic specificity. ◢

POST-DRAFT REVISION

After you have a preliminary draft, you are ready for post-draft revision. Revision post-draft differs from in-draft revision in that the composing context has been altered. Instead of starting with an abstract set of assumptions, some pertaining to the subject but most not, you begin with a concrete draft that contains some of those assumptions now projected onto a particular subject and audience.

More specifically, instead of beginning with beliefs that might include "People are fundamentally good by nature" or "The way for the U.S. to prevent war is to be strong militarily," you begin with the premise or the controlling generalization that "Academic dishonesty is widespread on today's college campuses." This premise, in turn, may reflect the following assumptions:

1. As the writer, you think academic dishonesty is a problem. In other words, you project *your* values concerning cheating onto the subject. Your values may differ from those of people who might have a live-and-let-live attitude, or who might think cheating is "wrong" only if one gets caught, or who might view the whole academic process as a game anyway, where the end justifies the means.

2. As the writer, you nevertheless assume that a majority of your audience shares your point of view that cheating is a problem. For those "amoral few" who may not, you harbor the hope that they can be dissuaded. These assumptions about your audience involve the larger assumption that "People are fundamentally good by nature, (but if not always good, they are at least redeemable)."

Decentering

Having a draft as part of the composing context poses a problem with *decentering,* or the ability to look at what you've written from the reader's point of view. After you have completed a draft, you may lose the ability to put yourself in your reader's place because you think, "I've really put a lot of time and effort into this draft. Besides, it makes sense to me." In other words, your subjective investment in the draft prevents you from being objective about it.

To deal with this natural resistance to decentering, try to follow these suggestions:

1. Let the draft "rest" for a time (an hour, a day, a week).
2. Read the draft into a tape recorder and play it back.
3. Type the draft into a computer terminal and then view it on the terminal screen.
4. Ask someone else to read and comment on the draft.

These and other techniques help you step back from the draft and view it as *a* written product, not as *your* written product.

Like in-draft revision, post-draft revision involves changes in content and procedure. In fact, because post-draft revision really means producing a "new" draft, the two revision processes may seem identical. However, as any person who sews can attest, there is a great difference between creating a garment from scratch and altering an already existing one.

Post-draft revision involves evaluating what's already there, planning for change, and executing the planned changes. Post-draft revision may also involve the type of spontaneous shuttling back and forth so characteristic of in-draft revision.

Evaluating

Because unity, specificity, and coherence play such a crucial role in reader expectations and writer principles, you should focus on these aspects during draft evaluation.

Revising for unity

One of the first questions to ask during evaluation is "Is this draft unified?" A related question is "Does the draft end up addressing the primary question?" Answering these questions will involve checking the controlling generalization, reviewing the frame, abstracting the emphasis of each paragraph in the draft, and checking point of view.

Check Your Controlling Generalization. Keeping in mind that not all writing features an explicit controlling generalization, you can still scan the draft for an explicit or implicit one and then measure it against the primary question. The following preface to a student-designed instruction manual provides a clear statement of purpose as its controlling generalization:

Most new or beginning motorcycle owners/operators tend to forget that their two-wheeled vehicle is very similar to its four-wheeled relative, the automobile, in that both require periodic maintenance. Motorcycle drive chain adjustment is probably one of the most important maintenance procedures required to insure proper performance, stop premature part wear, and create safe riding conditions. Too tight a drive chain will cause premature wear on the sprockets and chain; too loose a chain will cause wear and may also cause an accident by becoming entangled with the operator or the moving parts of the motorcycle.

This manual is intended to provide simple step-by-step instructions for motorcycle drive chain maintenance. If the writer's primary question is "How do you perform motorcycle drive chain maintenance?", then the statement of purpose matches the question. If, however, the primary question is "Why is it important to perform motorcycle drive chain maintenance?", then the emphasis of the manual is off base. More appropriate would be a controlling generalization that, say, classified the reasons the maintenance was important (performance and safety), followed by an essay citing evidence.

If you discover that your controlling generalization does not reflect your primary question, you may be able to solve the problem by simply revising the question. Frequently, however, you will have to revise the draft significantly. Checking the entire draft to see if it answers one or several "primary questions" will determine whether a major overhaul is needed or if a minor tune-up will suffice. If the draft pursues more than one main idea, it probably needs substantial engine work.

Check Your Introduction.   When an explicit controlling generalization is absent, a review of the introduction often reveals the underlying main idea. What is the main idea of the following paragraph?

> Early in the mellowing spring, Jeff could be found effortlessly providing momentum for the potter's wheel where he perched. Soft, pliable clay flowed from one form to another with careful precision as the hours crept by like mere shadows, pausing only now and again when Jeff, leaning away from the clay and reaching upwards, gave new life to his back, knotted and taut with the underlying strain, not noticeable to a curious girl's eye. Many fine days were spent in the studio, clay dust floating lazily, almost unnoticed among the shafts of creamy sunlight. I would sit at the little wheel, watching Jeff, mostly unaware of my surroundings. . . .

In this introduction, Cindy Gammon appears to be addressing the question, "What was it like for me to be in Jeff's studio?" or "What was our relationship like?" If either of these were her primary question, then Cindy could relax. However, because she really wanted to answer the primary question, "What is Jeff like?", Cindy faces a problem, which she solves by revising the tense and emphasis of the introduction:

> Jeff, face aglow with the sun's remnants, can be found inside the high school, effortlessly providing momentum for the potter's wheel where he sits rhythmically kicking, his right leg thud, thud, thudding on the fly-wheel. . . . With no more notice than a deep groan, Jeff leaves off kicking. He grasps the sides of the wooden bench and leans to relax his thick back and chest. . . .

The new introduction focuses more emphatically on Jeff and thus better reflects Cindy's primary question and the subsequent development of her paper.

Check Your Conclusion.

Reviewing your conclusion also can tell you something about your paper's unity. Consider the following conclusion to a proposal, for example:

> By using the critical path method on future projects, Ford Construction will be able to reduce cost and increase efficiency. Since the industry as a whole is already moving in the direction of better control and scheduling, Ford Construction must use the means available to keep pace. It must implement the critical path method and a computer system that will work with it.

The preceding conclusion implies that there are two interrelated means available to "keep pace" with the construction industry as a whole: the critical path method itself and the computer system that ties into and effects that method. If the proposal that features this conclusion is unified around the method *and* the means for effecting that method, then the writer is okay. If, however, the writer has lost track of the double emphasis on method and means while writing the proposal, then he must reexamine his main idea. "Will the critical path method alone be a sufficient way of keeping pace?" is one question the writer might consider. If the answer is yes, then the writer might be free to organize the proposal around that single emphasis. If the answer is no, then the writer will have to make sure that the double emphasis on c.p.m. and computers provides the center point of the proposal.

Check Your Paragraph Emphasis.

Abstracting the emphasis of each paragraph in a draft is another way to evaluate draft unity. A detailed example of such abstracting appears in Chapter 1. (See pages 16–19.) Essentially, abstracting involves summarizing the main point of each paragraph and then checking for out-of-place, irrelevant, or missing ideas. For example, if the author of the critical path method proposal were to check his work, he might—through abstracting—find that his paragraphs progress in the following way. He:

1. establishes the importance of efficiency in the construction industry (the need);
2. shows the inefficiency of the bar graph method of scheduling currently used by Ford Construction (the problem);
3. defines the critical path method of scheduling;
4. compares the critical path method of scheduling with the bar chart method;
5. deals with the problem of updating schedules in general;
6. shows how c.p.m. can be adapted to computer use;
7. emphasizes the benefits of c.p.m. in terms of cost and efficiency;
8. reinforces the feasibility of adopting c.p.m. at Ford Construction;
9. concludes as we have shown above.

Given this abstract, the writer can assume that a double emphasis on c.p.m. and computer application is not necessary, since c.p.m. alone appears to upgrade efficiency. However, the writer might also see that he doesn't have a section in the beginning that establishes his purpose and that his fifth paragraph dealing with the problem of updating schedules in general might be out-of-place or even irrelevant at this point. Such an evaluation should help the writer move towards greater unity of purpose and subject in his revision.

Check Your Point of View.

Checking for point of view can reveal something about the unity of your draft as well. For example, let's say that you are writing a report from the viewpoint of a member of a dairy cooperative, Calf Savers, Inc. You are addressing a certain Mr. Shover, an experienced farmer who has recently suffered a 40 percent loss in his stock of young heifers. In writing the report, therefore, you must keep in mind two viewpoints: yours as a coop member and his as a farmer. These two viewpoints form the rhetorical center of your writing. This center influences how you pursue your purpose: to analyze what caused his loss and to suggest future preventative measures.

The following annotated excerpt demonstrates some problems a writer, who forgot this center, encountered.

What is the purpose of telling him this? Isn't he acquainted with the problem from his experience with his own herd?

Each year 20 percent of all dairy calves die before they reach 6 months of age. Death in young calves can occur as a result of various diseases such as pneumonia, scours, various bacterial infections and clostridial diseases. Diseases are often caused as a result of improper nutrition, in both the cow and calf, inadequate housing, improper care of young calves, inadequate ventilation, and lack of sanitation and vaccinating practices.

Improper Nutrition

Improper nutrition in the cow may cause the young calf to be born deficient in vitamins and minerals needed for a healthy animal thus causing the calf to be more susceptible to diseases. The calf may also be born smaller and weaker than normal causing it to be more susceptible to various germ causing organisms which lead to disease.

Are you implying, then, that this is part of this problem?

Improper nutrition in the calf may cause a lack of protein, vitamins and minerals in the body which are needed for normal growth and resistance to diseases.

Management Needed

The person responsible for calf raising is the single most important factor in calf survival and rapid and maximum growth of calves. Good management and proper care result in lower death rates, better health and more rapid growth. Earlier puberty and breeding provide economic advantages. Maximum growth is also obtained with early puberty.

Since he has a 40% death rate you are insulting him here; your purpose?

Feeding Practices

Persons feeding calves must know how much milk is being fed. Milk should be carefully measured before feeding. Calves should be nipple fed with a nursing bottle until 3 to 6 days of age and then bucket fed from 4 to 7 days on. An early change to bucket feeding results in fewer calves nursing each other which helps to prevent mastitis when heifers first freshen.

ditto

Practices involved in feeding should include regular cleaning of utensils used. A separate pail should be used for each calf and each pail should be cleaned between feedings. Grain and water buckets should be separated on opposite sides of the calf pen. If buckets are close together feed may be transferred to the clean water and may create a sanitation problem.

and you know he doesn't do this?

Importance of Colostrum

Presence of colostrum in the gut before and after 24 hours of a calf's age has a local effect in preventing the colonization of microorganisms, as well as the value of colostrum absorbed from the gut before 24 hours of age.

Colostrum is high in gamma globulin, Vitamin A and other nutrients and contains specific antibodies to fight diseases.

Studies show adequate colostrum ingested by calves reduces mortality by at least 10 percent. Studies and clinical experience indicates that about 25 percent of all dairy calves fail to get early and adequate amounts of quality colostrum.

Again, are you presenting this material for a particular purpose?

The baby calf should be hand fed 2 to 4 pounds (1 to 2 quarts) of colostrum within 2 hours of birth. Colostrum should continue to be fed for the first 3 days before switching the calf to milk or milk replacer.

Offer Calves Feed Starter

In addition to the importance of colostrum in the diet it is very important to include a nutritious palatable calf starter. A starter which contains 18 percent crude protein, 75 percent TDN (Total Digested Nutrients) and 10 percent fiber should be fed. Most ingredients should be ground to give a coarse, bulky texture with little dust.

and you're recommending this to Shover, then, by this statement?

Calf Savers recommends that calves be offered starter at 3 to 5 days of age. Also, clean, fresh water should be available at all times. The offering of starter and providing of water at this age has been shown to improve starter intake and growth rate in 92 percent of the herds Calf Savers services. The earlier the calf eats dry feed, the fewer the digestive upsets and other feeding problems you'll have, resulting in a healthier calf that is less susceptible to various diseases.

A check for point of view in this example reveals that the report was not presenting the information to Shover to analyze what caused his particular loss or to make specific recommendations concerning future preventative measures *in his case.* In other words, a check for point of view reveals that the presentation of the details was not unified around a well-defined purpose.

Revising for specificity

If the draft appears to pursue one main idea, then "How effective is my support?" is a good question to address next. Support can be evaluated by breaking down individual paragraphs or blocks of paragraphs for detail and by spotting untested assumptions.

Check Paragraph Breakdown.   Paragraph breakdown as a method
of evaluation is covered in detail in Chapter 1. (See pages 16–20.) Consider the annotation in Figure 9.2 as a review.

Freshman college students have a tremendous amount
of pressure as they make the switch to college life. New
and challenging responsibilities include being on your own
for the first time. Most college students welcome the feeling of independence. However, when you are independent, you must also be responsible for your own actions.
Another pressure is competition. Knowing you are competing with the top-notch students for your grades creates
stress. Freshmen also have to adjust to studying for tests
that cover more material and are probably more difficult
than high school tests. These mounting pressures are often
more than students can handle.

For these reasons, students must think about where they
want their lives to go. They must establish priorities in
order to accomplish what they want.

This paragraph tries to establish reasons for
having priorities.

• One reason is that having priorities might
help reduce stress.

I guess that's the only reason I give;
the bits about the switch from high
school to college and the competition
for grades are really showing the
causes for the stress in the first
place. Maybe I should go to a
problem (stress), effect (not being able
to cope), causes (new independence, tests),
solution (priorities) set up for
this paragraph.

FIGURE 9.2   *Evaluating through Paragraph Breakdown*

Through the breakdown shown in Figure 9.2, the writer has discovered that he was dealing with two sets of reasons: reasons to establish priorities and reasons for the pressure felt by freshmen students.

Check Untested Assumptions.   Sometimes evaluating support involves not only looking at what's there, but also determining what's not there. In other words, evaluating support entails spotting untested assumptions.

Because they form a part of the writer's world view, assumptions are not always easy to recognize for what they are. Assumptions are often mistaken for facts that do not need specific support.

In writing, the primary assumption to watch for is, "My reader has had the same experiences I've had and therefore will know what I'm talking about." In the following example, Robert Steffensmeier guards against this assumption by carefully defining terms necessary to understanding his paper on "How to Use Rate Tariffs to Calculate Transportation Charges."

How to Use Rate Tariffs to Calculate Transportation Charges

As a logistics manager, one of the most difficult and confusing areas of your responsibility will be the determination of prices of the various transportation services available for use as part of a logistics system. Transportation services are sold for a specific product or commodity between two specific points. There are trillions of different shipping routes alone. Add to that the number of possible products to be shipped, the number of modes to choose from, and the number of carriers within each mode and the results are staggering.

Some steps have been taken toward simplifying the process of rate determination. The railroads first developed a method for reducing the number of origins and destinations for pricing purposes. They divided the country into geographic squares; the most important shipping point in each square was designated as the *rate base point.* Distances between these rate base points were compiled into the National Rate Basis Tariff, which is on file with the Interstate Commerce Commission.

Next, the thousands of different products and commodities were rated and grouped together according to transportation characteristics so that one rating could be applied to a whole group. Items of high value were given a rating of 100, which means they cost 100% of the first class rate to ship, per hundred-weight (cwt.). Lower value products, such as coal, were given low ratings, such as twenty. A rating of twenty means that twenty per cent of the first class rate is charged to ship that particular good per cwt. This percentage number for the appropriate classification is called a *class rating.*

Now that you know some background about the tariff system in transportation, I will discuss how to find the lowest price for a particular product between two specific points, using the tariff tables. Throughout the instructions I will use the following hypothetical example. Your boss has just told you to find the lowest cost for shipping 40,000 pounds of wine in bulk in barrels, from Baltimore to Philadelphia.

NOTE The word tariff is commonly used to mean almost any publication put out by a carrier or a tariff publishing agency which concerns itself with the pricing or service performed by a carrier. All the information needed to determine the cost of a move is in one or more tariffs. In order to complete the process that follows, you will normally need a Rate Basis Table, a Freight Classification Table, a Class Tariff, an Exception Tariff, and a Commodity Tariff. Composite pages from each of these have been included in this manual for convenience.

Robert Steffensmeier

Two good ways to test for assumptions are to look for unsupported generalizations in your draft and to ask others to read the draft for beliefs presented as facts.

▶ EXERCISE 9.2

Spot the assumptions underlying the following partial draft of "Description of a Balance Sheet." What does the writer assume you know about business economics?

Description of a Balance Sheet

The balance sheet is one of the basic financial statements presenting the financial position of an enterprise at a specific point in time. The term "balance sheet" refers to the fact that the major areas of the balance sheet must balance: the top section of the balance sheet must always equal the bottom section. This concept is derived from the fundamental accounting equation: Assets = Liabilities + Owners' Equity. An example of a balance sheet, with amounts provided, is illustrated in Figure 1.

The balance sheet is important because it tells the different assets held, the liabilities by type and amount, and the sources and amounts of owners' equity. Each of these major areas and the more common account groups within each area will now be defined.

Assets

Assets can be defined as economic resources devoted to business purposes within a specific accounting entity. Assets include all items available to benefit business operations. Generally assets are grouped in decreasing order of liquidity (ease of ability to convert to cash).

Current Assets.   Current assets are always presented first. These assets are considered to be the most liquid. Current assets are cash and other non-cash assets which can quickly be converted to cash, sold, or consumed during the normal operating cycle of the entity.

The amount of current assets is important for the solvency of the firm. If there is an inadequate supply of current assets the business may have difficulty paying its debts.

Current assets, like assets, are normally presented in order of decreasing liquidity. Cash is listed first, followed by short-term investments, receivables, inventories, and prepaid expenses.

Fixed Assets.   Fixed assets appear below current assets. This group is the least liquid of physical assets. Fixed assets consist of long-lived assets acquired for use in the entity's operation and not intended for resale to customers.

The distinction between fixed assets and current assets is the required time and desirability of converting fixed assets into cash. Generally fixed assets are those assets used to produce income; therefore the funds are not available to meet short-term debt obligations. Common examples of items included in the fixed asset category include long-term investments in securities, land, buildings, equipment, and fixtures.

Intangible Assets.   Intangible assets are presented below the fixed asset category. This group of assets does not have a physical existence, but has value to the entity because of the special rights which ownership confers. The reason for including intangible assets on the balance sheet is because, like other tangible assets discussed above, they will benefit operations of the entity. Examples of intangible assets include goodwill and patents.◢

Revising for coherence

Sometimes a check for unity or a check for support reveals revisions needed to insure coherence. Take the Ford construction example (pages 285–86), for instance. In checking for unity by abstracting each paragraph's emphasis, the writer discovers that paragraph five (dealing with the general problem of updating schedules) is apparently out of place. Such displacement could interrupt the logical flow of the proposal and therefore cause problems with coherence.

Check Arrangement.   In most cases evaluating for coherence involves assessing the paper's arrangement. Such an assessment might reveal that your choice of arrangement actually inhibits reader understanding. In the Scarlett O'Hara draft (pages 13–15), for example, the choice of narrative rather than exemplification as a pattern of arrangement interferes with the writer's analysis of Scarlett as a character. Narrative encourages the writer to *retell* the events in Scarlett's life rather than to use the events as *examples* of Scarlett's personality traits. In other words, the writer ends up offering no coherent analysis, and the reader is left wondering about why the events are being presented at all.

Check Organization.   An assessment of arrangement can also reveal organizational flaws that hinder coherence. In the following example, flaws in the method of classification leave the reader wondering which items are coordinate and which are subordinate. (These flaws are pointed out by the marginal comments of a careful reader.)

Description of an Incandescent Filament Lamp

An incandescent filament lamp is an electric lamp in which a tungsten filament is heated to a glow by an electric current. This heating takes place in a gas-filled sealed glass envelope. A drawing of a lamp is shown in Figure 1.

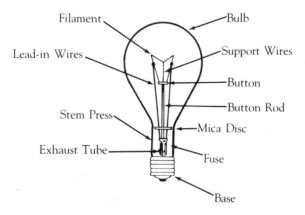

*FIG. 1   Typical incandescent lamp construction

Incandescent lamps are available in many bulb and base types and special designs for particular application.

Do as sub-parts below, for base.

The parts of an incandescent filament lamp *base, the bulb, and the main lighting device* are the bulb and the base. [The base itself consists of an exhaust tube, fuse, stem press, lead-in wires, filament, support wires, button, button rod, and in some cases a mica disc.]

DESCRIPTION AND FUNCTION OF PARTS

Your 3rd level heads should reflect your positioning sentence.

THE BULB

Exterior of the Lamp

1. Bulb: The bulb is a rounded projection made of thin, soft glass, The bulb is used to diffuse the light to the surroundings. The bulbs are either etched on the inside or are coated inside with white silica. This *PR* is done to increase the efficiency of the diffusion process. Inside the bulb is contained an inert gas used to retard evaporation of the filament. The glass bulb is fused to a metal base.

One-sentence definition.

2. Base: The base is *a .... (genus)* made of brass and is the means by which a connection is made to the socket and thereby to the source of electric current. Most lamps are made with screw bases of various sizes, the most common being the medium screw base as shown in Figure 1. The base is the [foundation for the *bulb and the* main lighting device.]

These are a separate part:

Within the Lamp   *Define first*

1. Exhaust Tube: [The exhaust tube is made of glass.] The tube, which projects out of the base,

the main lighting device. Subdivide it into its parts.

is the isolating medium for the travel of electric current. It also provides a means of pumping the inert gases into the bulb after manufacture. ~~Within this tube is contained a fuse.~~ *A fuse is contained* ...

2. Fuse: The fuse is a protection device used to prevent damage to the lamp from overload. *such as, ...* The fuse can be made of numerous materials.

attachment

3. Stem Press: ʌThe stem press is made of a combination of nickel-iron alloy and a copper sleeve. ~~The stem press is contained within the exhaust tube.~~ [It provides an airtight seal for the lead-in wires to assure that the wires have about the same expansion rate as the glass. This is to prevent breakage.] This *stem press also* ~~connection~~ seals the lead-in wires into the glass exhaust tube.

Define by giving function.

4. Lead-in Wires:ʌ The lead-in wires are made of copper and extend from the base to the stem and nickel from the stem press to the filament. [The purpose of the lead-in wires is *What? the filament?* to carry the current to and from, in a circular pattern the filament.]

Definition, then make up.

a ...

5. Filament: The filament is ʌmade of tungsten which is heated by the electric current until it glows. This is the process that provides the lighting source. The filament may be a coiled *a* coil as in Figure 1, ʌcoil, or a straight wire. This filament is basically flimsy so a support system is provided. The support system consists of support wires, button, and button rod.

Definition first, giving a purpose. You go up the parts above, then switch loses to go down here. Maintain parallelism.

Define first. You're getting sub-sub parts here.

A
6. Support Wires: ∧The support wires consist of two molybdenum wires. [These wires provide support for the filament.] The wires are molded into the button.

B
7. Button: ∧ The button is made of glass. During manufacture, the support wires are molded into this button, [The button which *which* provides support for the wires] is located on the tip of the button rod.

C
8. Button Rod: The button rod is also made of glass. The button rod extends for ? the exhaust tube. [It is the basis for the whole support system.] In some special cases, a mica disc is located at the base of the button rod.

D
9. Mica Disc: The mica disc is a thin ceramic plate used to reduce the circulation of hot gases into the neck of the bulb. The mica disc is used in higher wattage general service lamps.

CONCLUSION

you need to structure that very complex body further. Do base, bulb, lighting device. (bottom to top, outer to inner).

The means for operating the light is an electrical current. Current passing through the highly resistant filament heating it to incandescence which is (the emission of light by a hot object.) The light is ∧ *THEN* diffused throughout the surroundings by the treated bulb. Gradual evaporation of the filament causes the familiar blackening of the bulbs and the eventual filament rupture and lamp failure.

A quick check of your paper for transitional phrases and other reader cues, such as headings and subheadings, might also reveal where the draft needs to be more coherent, where it needs more connecting links.

Checking for unity, support, and coherence may not be appropriate to every draft or to every writer. If, for example, you have already ironed out problems with your support, you may concentrate on checking for coherence. In short, you can individualize your evaluation procedure.

You can even individualize your evaluation procedure when editing with others by following these steps.

1. Prepare a readable rough draft, preferably typed and double spaced, with numbered pages and paragraphs for easy referencing.
2. Contact two or three potential editors (volunteer to edit for them also), and xerox a clear copy of the draft for each.
3. Agree what the editors will be looking for, by specifying the editors' tasks on a one-page edit sheet; do not simply say, "Read this over and see if it's all right." (See Figure 9.3.)

(Please give me specific and constructive answers to the following questions concerning my draft. Thanks.)

PURPOSE: What is the primary question that I am dealing with? What are the main secondary questions?
   PQ:
   SQ:

SUPPORT: Do I leave any questions unanswered? Does my draft raise additional questions in your mind?

ORDER: Does my entire paper pursue my primary question? Do you ever get lost or become unsure as to what I'm doing?

STYLE: Comment on my word choice and method of presentation.

FIGURE 9.3   *Sample One-page Edit Sheet*

4. Deliver both the xeroxed draft and edit sheet to each editor, answer any initial questions, and arrange a time to reclaim the materials.

5. After reclaiming the materials, study the remarks and look for patterns in your editors' responses.

Figure 9.3 shows a sample one-page edit sheet. Edit sheets do not have to follow one particular design. You may construct your own.

Planning for Change

You plan for change when you evaluate and define the revisions needed in a draft. Once you have assessed the writing, you can determine how the revisions are to be carried out. The writer of the union example in Chapter 1 (pages 19–20) follows the evaluation-definition procedure-for-remedy sequence quite nicely, coming up with a five point plan for revision.

For another example, return to the Ford construction excerpt (pages 285–86). Abstracting the emphasis of each paragraph reveals that the proposal doesn't have a beginning section that establishes purpose; it also has a fifth paragraph that seems to be out of place. The revisions needed involve changes in organization. Given this analysis, the writer can plan how he is going to revise; he will (1) add an introductory section that states the proposal's purpose, and (2) move some of the material from paragraph five up to what is now the first paragraph where it can fit into the discussion of the *need* for a good method of scheduling. (Another option for this second part of the revision would be to eliminate the fifth paragraph altogether.)

▶ EXERCISE 9.3

The "Description of an Incandescent Filament Lamp" is also in need of organizational revision. With the help of the written comments, decide exactly what has to be done to revise the description and how you would proceed to do it. Present your plan for revision in list form. ◀

After completing Exercise 9.3, recall that the process of revision is not always this tidy. Reconceiving papers does not always proceed from a discrete list of planned changes. For example, right in the middle of rethinking your paper on "China's latest attempt at family planning" you might get an idea for writing a better paper on "The changing role of midwives in the United States." In other words, planning for revision involves remaining open to unexpected changes.

The next example, however, shows how others' evaluations can be used to define the problems in a draft and to suggest planned changes. In obtaining the evaluation of others, Jane Kilfoil uses the edit sheet on page 297. After collecting the edit sheets, she then looks for patterns in the evaluative comments by separately grouping the comments for each edit sheet category. The patterns help define the problems in the draft.

Included in the following sections are Jane's draft itself, the groupings of the comments on the draft, with Jane's responses to these comments also noted, and a "goal/means" chart that briefly defines the problems in terms of goals and gives the procedures she will use to address these problems in terms of means.

The draft

Animal House

Thousands of yrs. ago there was a man who offered the animals of the world a deal they couldn't refuse. Responding to his charisma they marched aboard the ark two by two and were saved from a certain death. By now they've probably figured out why Noah went to all that trouble for them. He did it so his descendants could strap apes into sleds and simulate car crashes to study injury. He did it so they could shave cats' faces to test the irritation of hand lotion. Animal experimentation in one form or another has been a part of our society for a very long time and scientists have been free to do pretty much whatever they chose to animals because, as Thurman Grafton of the National Society for Medical Research puts it, "God gave man dominion over animals. They are here to serve man." This Judeo-Christian attitude is shared by a large percentage of the public. Because the public so seldom protests animal experimentation, it has become a multimillion dollar industry. Each year in the U.S. over 60 million animals are used in one type of experiment or another. Perhaps the most alarming aspect of these experiments is that only a third of them are for medical research. The product of this experimentation is not a dusty set of observations and figures as many assume. Applications of these findings affect us from the medication we take to the cars we drive. I am not about to claim many good things haven't arisen from these experiments, such as polio vaccine. But because of animal experiments, thalidomide was thought to be free of side effects, and birth defects which need never have happened were induced. It is because of incidents such as these that we must conclude that animal experimentation, more often than not, is unnecessary; especially so when we realize there are more humane and efficient methods through which we can realize our goals. Whether you are more concerned with the ethical reasons or choose to approach it from a purely practical standpoint is not important. If you will examine with me both the ethics and practical questions of this situation, I feel you will be led with me straight back to that same conclusion: animal experimentation is unnecessary.

Many of us are most skeptical of and made most uncomfortable by the ethical arguments against animal experimentation. As Americans we like to believe that we are among the most humane people in the world. Yet, as Jeremy Stove of the Federation of American Scientists points out, animal rights is still a closet subject. We are usually more upset at experiments involving traditionally "pet" animals than those using rats or other less familiar animals. This "specie-ism" is compared to racism and sexism by Peter Singer, an Australian philosopher. He argues that the oppression of blacks and women was rationalized on the basis that they were inferior much the same as our defense of our treatment of animals. Certainly sentiment is not reason enough as an argument for humane treatment of animals. Michael Fox, veterinarian, psychologist, director of Humane Society's new Institute for Study of Animal Problems believes, "We can't use the argument that animal suffering is reason to be humane," because that is our own subjective judgment. He feels we must have consideration for animals not because they feel pain but simply because they exist. Because we have no sure methods of communicating with animals we are not able to see their existence as worthwhile. Yet scientists are discovering that animals feel, think, reason, and have sophisticated social systems that resemble our own. When we accept this we begin to realize that the differences between animals and humans, that is, lack of intelligence and sensitivity, which we have used to justify our actions are not as clear cut as they once were. It has now been shown that some animals have a more highly developed intelligence than some human beings—the retarded or senile for example. As psychologist and author Richard Ryder asks, "If we were to be discovered by some more intelligent creature in the universe, would they be justified in experimenting on us?"

The fact that animals do feel pain and that they are intelligent reasoning beings does not only make animal experimentation morally wrong but also impractical. Because animal society is so highly developed, disturbance of that society can affect an animal's health. For example, a Humane Society study showed that the dose at which half a population dies for rats kept in separate cages is different from that for animals kept in their own social groups. This doesn't mean animals need simply be kept in environments which resemble their native habitat. Because animals do feel pain and fear, and the treatment they receive often brings on that kind of stress, there is a large variation from lab to lab in results of the same tests performed on the same animals. Yet one of the prime reasons in favor of animal tests is that under controlled circumstances of the experimental lab they are likely to be objective and consistent. Even if the test results were completely reliable, they don't always show the true picture. Animal and human systems have many similarities but they don't always react the same. An example of this is the live animal testing of the heart drug Eraldin. Tests were run for ten years, yet when the drug was put to use, several hundred people were blinded and 20 died from peritonitis. The fact that much of this research is irrelevant to human welfare and there are more reliable and humane alternatives—for example, testing substances on tissue culture or using human volunteers—leads many to contend that much of this research is unnecessary. It can further be argued that there are long range gains to be made if we drastically reduce animal experimentation. The continuing concern for our eco-system has shown us how important it is that we maintain health and harmony with all living things. It is increasingly apparent then that there is a problem. Animals are being deliberately and needlessly hurt while no one gains anything of real value. It's true this problem isn't being totally ignored. However, if we are to solve it before it's too late, we must move faster than we have in the past. Many researchers proudly point to the Animal Welfare Act of 1970 as the answer to many a poor lab rat's prayer. That pride is not totally misplaced but a close examination shows how terribly inadequate the law is. First it covers only about 7% of the animals used in laboratories. The act specifically excludes rats and mice which make up over 75% of all animals used in experimentation. In the act some standards are set for the housing of animals but places no restriction on the types of experiment to which they might be subjected. It even goes so far as to indicate pain-relieving drugs should be used and then gives scientists the option to claim the pain as a necessary part of the experiment so that analgesics or anesthetics may be withheld. Something is obviously lacking. Perhaps the most promising of the advancements to date is the growing concern of researchers themselves. A few of these scientists have become worried enough to abandon their experiments. One researcher stopped aggression studies on pairs of mice which he gave electric shocks to provoke fights because, "I ended up doing things to animals that really made me sick." But for each of these steps forward there are two or three back. A good deal of this backward motion is made by the National Society for Medical Research. Harry Rowsell, Director of Canadian Council of Animal Care, describes the NSMR as a "reactionary group of scientists . . . who fear being interfered with." Realistically, however, when there is so much at stake, one group should not have sole control of the situation. In fact, the newly formed Scientists' Center for Animal Welfare is working to balance the influence of the NSMR. However its scope is limited because it is simply a non-profit educational organization. Even other countries are waking up to animal needs. The export of monkeys has finally been banned by the Indian government.

Yet the U.S. has stubbornly continued on its destructive path by finding other countries to supply its needs.

While each of these advances is encouraging, only the scientist center for animal welfare even begins to solve the true problem, that is, unnecessary experiments. The solution I'm about to propose to this problem is fairly simple yet has not been implemented because of lack of awareness and understanding. The solution has four parts which in conjunction with the SCAW should bring about an almost total resolution of the problem. The first step being an immediate ban on needless replication of experiments. Once the results of an experiment are widely accepted and put to their practical purpose there is nothing to be gained from repeating them; even for teaching purposes the relative value of gain is doubtful. It is argued that there is a world of difference between reading about a procedure and actually doing it. While this may be true, it is not ample justification for wasting life. Secondly, we need a ban on experiments for which a more humane alternative exists. As I explained earlier, many experiments on animals can offer no conclusive proof of human reaction. Therefore it is only logical to use the new techniques in tissue culture, which not only yield more of the information we are looking for but also prevent suffering in sentient life. Third it is necessary to ban experiments on live animals which aren't relevant to the treatment or prevention of disease. Many forms of experimentation can be defended but there is no possible justification for using animals to develop a longer lasting mascara. Finally, the government should set up a board whose purpose would be to determine whether the value of an experiment would be great enough to justify the use of animals and monitor the care the animals receive.

These regulations will not completely obliterate animal experimentation. However, they will serve to make us aware of the fact that animals are capable of feeling pain and that their needs aren't so greatly different from our own. And those that refuse to stop believing "animals are here to serve man" surely must conclude that animal experimentation is not always helpful and often even dangerous to man. Earlier I suggested Noah saved the animals so his descendants could use them in whatever manner they chose. Well, none of us will ever be certain of his motives but who would you be more likely to blame: a man who built a big boat with which to save animals or men who build big laboratories in which to kill them?

Jane Kilfoil

Sample notes for revision

The editor's comments on the draft are grouped on the right, with the author's comments or conceptualizing on the left. (See pages 303–4.)

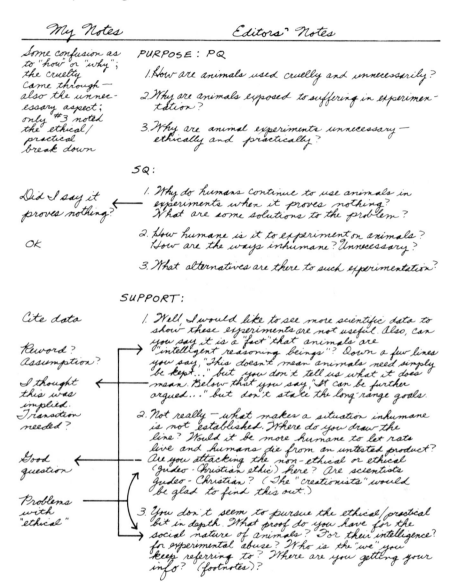

FIGURE 9.4 *Notes Collected for Revision*

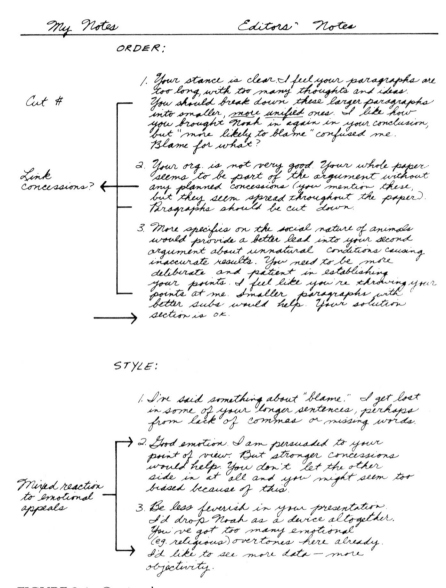

FIGURE 9.4 Continued

The "goal/means" chart

Goal	Means
1. Clarify primary question.	1. Revise thesis—perhaps eliminate double emphasis on ethical and practical.
2. Beef up support.	2. Cite data (footnote); statements about animals' nature need expert back-up.
3. Reorganize.	3. Cut paragraphs; label concessions and think about grouping them in one place.
4. *Worry about shortening sentences later.*	

The chart then guides initial changes in the draft.

Executing Your Revision Plan

Although your revision plan will not always be as specific as the goals/means chart of the preceding example, it is a good idea to have something in mind before you begin revising. Having a revision plan is like having a tentative controlling generalization; each serves as an initial guide to your composing. Each is subject to change and neither prevents the discovery of new tasks or ideas.

Let's say, for example, that the "animal draft" writer is pursuing her reorganization goal. She might begin by listing her concession statements:

1. Paragraph one: I am not about to claim many good things haven't arisen from these experiments, such as polio vaccine.
2. Paragraph two: Certainly sentiment is not reason enough as an argument for humane treatment of animals.
3. Paragraph three: It's true this problem isn't being totally ignored.
4. Paragraph four: While this may be true . . .

After doing so, she might decide that to concede all these points might weaken her argument. So she might content herself to conceding the first point, especially if she would want to revise her controlling generalization to read:

Animal experimentation *except in cases where vital medical research is involved* is unnecessary.

She then would have to define what "vital medical research" was; presumably, she would not include testing of commercial products as "vital medical research." Of course, she might run into problems making distinctions between vital and non-vital research, but she might end up with a more convincing argument in the process. She also might have to revise her controlling generalization a number of times to reach a defensible premise.

Having a revision plan gives you a starting point, then. It also helps you avoid being too localized in your revision efforts. An example of being too localized would be when a writer looks at the rough draft and simply goes through and corrects the spelling errors. Correcting spelling errors has to be done eventually, but it counts as proofreading, not revision.

▶ EXERCISE 9.4

For practice in executing a revision plan, take the plan you designed for Exercise 9.3 involving the Filament Lamp and execute that plan. While revising, note any additional tasks or ideas that "come up." ◢

▶ EXERCISE 9.5

For further practice in dealing with revision plans, examine the two memos that follow in Figures 9.5 and 9.6. Make a list of the changes made between drafts. Then write a paragraph in which you explain the author's apparent revision plan. In so doing, you should consider not only how the changes were made but also why. ◢

Freeland Contracting Company
Box 287
Blairstown, Iowa 52209

DATE: July 14, 1981

TO: Joe Blackburn

FROM: James R. Fry   *James R. Fry*

SUBJECT: NEW COMPANY PETTY CASH POLICY

wordy?

The petty cash vouchers on hand to account for the withdrawals from the petty cash fund are $20.80 short of what they should be for the month to date, and I now find it necessary to institute a new system for the disbursement of petty cash funds.

1. From now on we will need to sign a voucher for any given amount needed from the petty cash fund. It will then be necessary to return to the petty cash clerk a reciept for the item purchased as well as the difference in cash between the reciepted amount and the amount originally signed for. In this
2. way there will always be cash or signed reciepts for the total amount of petty cash in the fund.

list steps?

too negative?

I hope this new policy doesn't create too many problems for you or the business, but it is essential that it be adhered to in order to facilitate the auditing of the business records for income tax purposes.

If you have any suggestions you feel might help improve this system, stop by my office and we can talk it over. This will also give you a chance to see the coffee maker I've installed. Now we won't have to look for change for the vending machine anymore.

this is really off the subject, isnt it? I can do better.

Do I really want suggestions? I've decided on a new system already.

FIGURE 9.5 *First Draft*

Freeland Contracting Company
Box 287
Blairstown, Iowa 52209

DATE: July 14, 1981

TO: Joe Blackburn

FROM: James R. Fry   𝒥.ℛ.ℱ.

SUBJECT: NEW COMPANY PETTY CASH POLICY

Because the petty cash vouchers on hand are $20.80 short of what they should be for the month to date, I now find it necessary to institute a new system for the disbursement of petty cash funds.

From now on it will be necessary to follow these steps in order to obtain petty cash funds:

1. Sign a voucher for any given amount needed from the petty cash fund.
2. Return a receipt for the item purchased, as well as the difference in cash between the receipted amount and the amount originally signed for.

In this way there will always be cash or signed receipts for the total amount of petty cash in the fund.

Although this new policy may create some problems for you as well as the business, it is essential that it be followed to facilitate the auditing of the business records for income tax purposes.

If you have any suggestions you feel might help in revision of the system, stop by my office between 9:00 A.M. and 10:00 A.M. any weekday and we can talk it over.

FIGURE 9.6   *Revised Draft*

After a draft has gone through a number of revisions, it might be ready for the type of fine tuning represented in the following example by student Wesley Griffitts.

Here, the general revision plan seems to be "add specifics to increase understanding and interest." (The annotations for the revised draft highlight the changes that were made.)

First draft

Catch-21

Youth, that time period in life before you celebrate your twenty-first birthday, can greatly hamper your success in obtaining a job, as it did me, when I applied for the job of custodian at the F. W. Harper Corporation. After receiving my diploma from Valley Falls High School, I felt ready to tackle the world with both hands. First, I would locate myself a high-paying union custodian job, and then I would move into my own apartment in Kansas City where I could live alone and do whatever I pleased. Since I had submitted an employment application two months prior to my graduation, I was not surprised when F. W. Harper, Inc. requested an interview for Tuesday, June fourth, only one week after my graduation. I was confident that I could fill the job of custodian, because I had hired-out cleaning houses, garages and bird cages ever since I was ten years old; so, I entered that office on Main Street Tuesday morning with all the confidence of a man who knows his job. The interview lasted a full two hours and twenty-seven minutes, for I was taken on a tour of the eight-story office building and treated to lunch by Mr. Dosler, the corporation's head custodian. Mr. Dosler felt that I could handle washing stools, mopping floors, and vacuuming carpets; so, he instructed me to report to work on the third floor of the building at 7 a.m. Monday, June 10th.

Well, on Friday I received a phone call from Mr. Dosler. Although he was very apologetic for his mistake of not noticing my age on my application, he informed me that the corporation could not under any circumstances consider a person under twenty-one years of age for employment.

Just three days earlier I felt as though I was on top of the world; now, my future as an employee of F. W. Harper, Inc. was at an end, and there was nothing to blame except my youth.

Wesley Griffitts

Revised draft

Catch-21

1	*Increase specificity of lead*
2	*Tantalize reader with incomplete revelation*
3	*Give details in a flashback*
4	*Use adverbial conjunction for variety*
5	*Increase specificity of sentence elements*
6	*Add transition*
7	*Use possessive instead of preposition*
8	*Eliminate unnecessary ever*
9	*Use repetition of opening to show return to present*
10	*Add adjectives*
11	*Add dialogue*
12	*Add interior monologue*
13	*Add comment to show desirability of job*
14	*Add to specificity of sentence elements*
15	*Add details to show reliance on job*

As I entered the office at 1018 Main Street that Tuesday morning, I never expected the undeserved disappointment that was in store for me.

After receiving my diploma from Valley Falls High School, I felt ready to tackle the world. First I would land a high-paying custodian job; then I would move into my own apartment where I could live a bachelor's life and hang my tennis shoes from the ceiling if I wanted. I was not surprised when F. W. Harper, Inc. requested an interview for June 4th, only one week after my graduation. Instead, I was confident that I could do a custodian's job, because I had hired out cleaning houses, garages, and bird cages since I was ten.

As I entered, Mr. Dosler, a thin man with deeply marked dimples, greeted me warmly. "Hello, Wes. As the Head Custodian, I'm here to show you the ropes." "That means," I thought, "I've got the job already!" I smiled as Mr. Dosler added, "I'm sure you can handle washing stools, mopping floors and vacuuming carpets." I nodded. ". . . You can report to work this Monday, 7 a.m. sharp. Welcome aboard!"

The interview lasted two hours and twenty-seven minutes, for I was taken on a tour of the sparkling eight-story office building and was treated to steak and fries afterwards. The next day I found a terrific efficiency apartment for only $165 per

15	*"Reliance" details*	month; Thursday I bought an overstuffed[15] couch and some groceries; Friday I returned to my Mom's for my "last"[15] weekend home. It was there that I received the phone call.
16	*Add dialogue*	"Wes. I'm afraid I have[16] some bad news for you," Mr. Dosler said gently. "The personnel people overlooked the fact that you're only eighteen. I'm sorry, but we can't use you until you're twenty-one."
17	*Add to specificity of reaction*	
18	*Convert trite phase to an original one*	Although Mr. Dosler had hung up, I stood[17] paralyzed with the receiver still pressed to my ear. Just three days earlier I had felt as though I held a Royal[18] Flush.
19	*Continue card analogy*	
20	*Complete thesis idea*	Now I was[19] "busted," and there was nothing[20] to blame except my youth.

By thus adding clarity through dialogue and detail, Wes has improved the specificity of his paper and created an interesting description for his readers.

The following Process Sheet highlights the concerns of this chapter. Use it to guide your initial post-product revisions.

NOTES

1. Thanks to Susan Helgeson of Ohio State University for this apt phrasing.
2. Linda Flower and John R. Hayes, "A Cognitive Process Theory of Writing," *College Composition and Communication,* XXXII (December 1981), 365–87.

POST-PRODUCT REVISION

Preliminaries

Have I tried to decenter my perspective of my draft?

Can I detect the assumptions I have projected on my subject and my audience through my draft? Are these valid assumptions?

Evaluation

Is this draft unified? Do the controlling generalization, the introductory and concluding frame, the emphasis of each paragraph, and the point of view all relate to the same subject and purpose?

How effective is the support? Is it relevant? Sufficient?

Is the draft coherent? Is the arrangement well conceived? Are there enough transitional links?

Planning

What exactly are the problems in the draft? In correcting these problems, what are my goals?

How can I go about solving the problems? What will be my revising procedure?

Executing

Am I remembering my purpose and my audience as I'm making my changes? Do my changes suggest further tasks or ideas that I should pursue?

INDEX

NOTES

NOTES

NOTES

NOTES

NOTES

NOTES

NOTES

NOTES

NOTES

NOTES